THE LUCKY GENERATION
Growing Up in Depression and War

A MEMOIR

ROOSEVELT AND GARNER
TOWNSEND PLAN
LANDON KNOX

THE LUCKY GENERATION

Growing Up in Depression and War

A MEMOIR

Allen F. Davis

GREEN WRITERS PRESS *Brattleboro, Vermont*

Printed in the United States

10 9 8 7 6 5 4 3 2 1

Green Writers Press is a Vermont-based publisher whose mission is to spread a message of hope and renewal through the words and images we publish. Throughout we will adhere to our commitment to preserving and protecting the natural resources of the earth. To that end, a percentage of our proceeds will be donated to environmental activist groups. Green Writers Press gratefully acknowledges support from individual donors, friends, and readers to help support the environment and our publishing initiative.

green writers press

Giving Voice to Writers & Artists Who Will Make the World a Better Place
Green Writers Press | Brattleboro, Vermont
www.greenwriterspress.com

ISBN: 979-8-9923988-0-9

All photos courtesy of the author and The Hardwick Historical Society.

PRINTED AT KASE PRINTERS, ON FSC-CERTIFIED PAPER AND PRINTED WITH SOY-BASED INK, DEDICATED TO SOUND ENVIRONMENTAL PRACTICES AND MAKING ONGOING EFFORTS TO REDUCE OUR CARBON FOOTPRINT. WITH PAPER AS A CORE PART OF OUR BUSINESS, KASE IS COMMITTED TO IMPLEMENTING POLICIES THAT FACILITATE CONSERVATION AND SUSTAINABLE PRACTICES. KASE SOURCES PRINTING PAPERS FROM RESPONSIBLE MILLS AND DISTRIBUTORS THAT ARE CERTIFIED WITH AT LEAST ONE CERTIFICATION FROM AN INDEPENDENT THIRD PARTY VERIFICATION, SOURCED DIRECTLY FROM RESPONSIBLY MANAGED FORESTS. WE ALSO MAKE ONGOING EFFORTS TO REDUCE OUR CARBON FOOTPRINT, REUSE ENERGY AND RESOURCES, MINIMIZE WASTE DURING THE MANUFACTURING PROCESS, AND RECYCLE 100% OF SCRAPS, TRASH, CARTRIDGES, EQUIPMENT, AND SOLVENTS WHENEVER POSSIBLE. WE ARE A FAMILY-RUN BUSINESS, LOCATED IN HUDSON, NEW HAMPSHIRE.

For Courtney, Skyler, Nelson, Emily, and Madison:
The Next Generation

CONTENTS

THE LUCKY GENERATION
Growing Up in Depression and War

A MEMOIR

INTRODUCTION

I WAS BORN IN 1931 in the midst of the Great Depression. My parents must have thought that it was an inauspicious time to come into the world, but it proved a good year to be born. It was a low-birth year so there was less competition later for college, for graduate school, and for jobs in the late 1940s, the 1950s and the 1960s. I was influenced only vicariously, through my parents' stories, by the Depression. I was too young for World War II, too old for Vietnam, and, because of draft deferments for college students, I missed the fighting in Korea. I was not alone. Those of us born between about 1928 and 1936 might be called "the lucky generation," or perhaps "the lucky cohort." Some people have called us "The Silent Generation," or "The Other-Directed Generation," but I prefer to call us lucky. Calvin Trillin, born in 1935, calls us "demographically blessed."

Our generation was stuck between "The Greatest Generation," and "The Baby Boomers." When we were children there was no television, no transistor radios, and no ballpoint pens. We grew up in an era before the Civil Rights Movement, before the Women's Movement, and before the counter culture. Still, we were young enough to benefit from those transformations. When we were adolescents we listened to Frank Sinatra and Doris Day, to Vaughn Monroe and Patti Page, not to Elvis or the Beatles.

The late 1920s and early 1930s were good years to be born, at least if you were white, male, middle class, and, I might add, American. I once stayed up most of the night drinking and talking to a German scholar in 1975 after we discovered that we shared the same birthday. He was old enough at fourteen to be drafted into a Hitler Youth Brigade. In the last, hectic days of the war his unit was called up and sent to the front where most of them were slaughtered. He was saved only because his father, a prominent businessman, refused to let him go, and in the chaos at the end of the war he stayed behind. He was lucky, he maintained, because when he went to the university and to graduate school he had an advantage; there were almost no men older than he in the universities. There was little competition for prizes, for fellowships, and for women. I also have a Japanese friend, who might have died at Hiroshima, except that his Navy youth corps was out of town on the day that the atomic bomb destroyed the city. And I have a Dutch acquaintance, a Jew, who spent time in a Nazi concentration camp and was rescued at the age of fifteen by the advancing American Army.

Those born outside of the United States may not be part of the "lucky generation," but the luck certainly extended to those who survived. Yet those years were not very kind to Americans who were female, Black, and poor. Very few women in my generation went to law school, medical school, or graduate school, and the few who did had a difficult time competing in a male world. There were a number of bright women in my graduate history seminars at the University of Wisconsin in the late 1950s, but many were quietly discouraged by their professors, and they eventually dropped out. Others fell in love and married fellow graduate students, but the women usually deferred to their husbands' careers. There are a few exceptions, but women are largely missing from my generation of historians.

There were only four African-Americans in my Dartmouth College class of over 700. In the days before the Civil Rights Movement only a handful of Blacks (who had usually gone to elite private schools) found their way into Ivy League colleges, and there were no African-Americans in my graduate school seminars. Many of the men in my high school class, whose parents were too poor to send them to college, joined the Armed Forces. A year later they found themselves in the front lines in Korea. Some used the G. I. Bill to go to college when they got out of the service, but others took low-paying jobs.

Still, American upward mobility did work. One of the women in my high school class taught elementary school and then married a local businessman. She recalls how poor she felt during the Depression, but then remarked: "who would have predicted that now we have enough money to live in Florida during the winter?"

Those of us in the "lucky generation" who went to college were certainly favored by the odds. I once told my Dartmouth classmates (class of 1953) that they were successful (and most have been very successful), not because they were brilliant and hardworking, but because they were born in 1931. At first they rejected the "luck" factor as a key to their success, but after I sketched the demographic statistics they began to admit that their year of birth had helped the trajectory of their careers in business, law, and medicine.

Studying my own family history I see clearly that the accident of birth didn't always serve my ancestors well. My great-grandfather was born in 1834. He served in the Union Army during the Civil War and was discharged because of illness. His brother-in-law, a few years younger, was not as lucky. He joined the Union Army, was captured, and died at Andersonville Prison in 1864. My grandfather was born in 1864 and escaped all wars, although his life was strongly impacted by the depression of the 1890s and the Great Depression of the 1930s. My father was born in 1894. He served during World War I but saw no action. Several of his friends, however, died in the war or in the great influenza epidemic of 1918. If I had continued the thirty-year pattern and been born in 1924, I would have graduated from high school in 1942 and quickly joined the Army. But I was born seven years later, and that made the difference.

Not all the difference, for place of birth was a factor as well. I was born and grew up in a small town of 2500 in northern Vermont. I have often remarked that I was born in the nineteenth century because the twentieth century did not arrive in my part of Vermont until after World War II. That is an exaggeration, of course, but the old ways persisted longer in my little town than in the cities and suburbs. I was privileged to observe a world that was fast disappearing. My mother cooked on a wood-burning, iron range. We used an icebox, not a refrigerator, and wash day was always on Monday. To make a phone call we rang the operator, who asked pleasantly: "Number please?" When I visited my uncle's farm, ten miles away, I was thrust back into an even earlier era, an age without electricity or indoor plumbing. More importantly, I grew up with a strong sense of community and a pride in place.

I was fascinated by history from an early age, but it was many years before I made a connection between my memory of growing up in the 1930s in a small town in Vermont and history as it is written. The history I read, perhaps because I came of age during World War II, was often the story of wars, of generals, statesmen, and adventurers. I was intrigued by the story of the American Revolution and the history of Vermont, the romantic tales of Ethan Allen and the Green Mountain Boys, who fought for independence from both Great Britain and New York. Some people find a personal connection to history by visiting a Civil War battlefield or an historic house museum; for me it was a family visit to the Bennington Battle Monument and to Fort Ticonderoga the summer I was ten. But it is the reconstructed fort that I especially remember, though I did not realize at the time that it was a replica.

I had read Daniel Pierce Thompson's *The Green Mountain Boys*, a story about Rogers' Rangers, and *Northwest Passage* by Kenneth Roberts. It suddenly struck me, especially at Fort Ticonderoga, that the wars and adventures I had been reading about had actually happened. I went on to read most of the writings of Francis Parkman from a set given to me by a great aunt. It was years before I learned as a graduate student that Parkman was a great historian, and even more years, while teaching graduate and undergraduate students, that I learned that there were many flaws in his interpretation. It was the narrative, the adventure stories of men struggling in the wilderness against the forces of evil, that attracted me. I read all the books I could find on Vermont history, the French and Indian War, and the Revolution in the Jeudevine Memorial Library in Hardwick, Vermont.

My interest in Vermont history and the history of early America began to fade as I studied history in college and graduate school. At the University of Wisconsin in the late 1950s we still read Frederick Jackson Turner and Charles R. Beard. We approved Beard's dictum that "objective history is history without object." Yet our mentors told us to try to be objective and unbiased, and to document our writing with citations from manuscript collections. Our professors warned us that we should never use the first person, except perhaps in the preface. At Wisconsin I became fascinated with urban history and the Progressive movement, history that had no connection to my remembered past. The rise of the new social history in the 1960s, with its emphasis on ordinary people and everyday life, occasionally helped me link my memory and history. However, it was using family history as a teaching strategy that forced me to examine my childhood memories.

In the early 1970s, while teaching at Temple University in Philadelphia, I searched for ways to engage disinterested undergraduates in the study of history, and to convince them that their own experiences, their memories, were part of history too. I experimented with sending them home to study their own families. I discovered that my friend and former teaching assistant, Jim Watts, was having success using a similar scheme at City College in New York. We talked on several occasions at my camp in Vermont and at a bar on the Upper West Side of New York, and soon we were working on a book together. The result was *Generations: Your Family and Modern American History* (Alfred A. Knopf, 1974, 1978, 1983.) The thesis of the book, we argued, was that "your own grandfather is more important than Grover Cleveland." We helped students discover several events in the history of their family and to relate those events to the history they were studying. We asked them to recover a migration or immigration experience, the Great Depression, and World War II. In a chapter we called "The World We Have Lost," we urged the students to imagine a world without autos, radios, television, and McDonald's hamburgers. We challenged the students to ask their parents and grandparents about the food they ate, the places they lived, the schools they attended, and to try to imagine what it felt like to live in another era. Many of our students became fascinated with their family heritage, and the papers they wrote were much more interesting to read than those on new interpretations of Jacksonian Democracy, or the importance of the Compromise of 1850.

While teaching my students how to recover their family history I felt compelled to learn more about my own past. I had never been very interested in genealogy. I thought of it as an upper-class and elitist hobby. Inspired, however, by my students, I began to take the bare facts of genealogy and construct a family history that explored what it meant to be a farmer, a craftsman, or a housewife in 1830 or 1890. Because so many of my ancestors were buried within a radius of twenty-five miles of Greensboro, Vermont, where I spend time in the summer at the family camp, I started to explore the old cemeteries. I was surprised that my sons (teenagers in the early 1970s) were enthusiastic about searching out the old family gravestones. As I pored over the manuscript census, studied probate records and land transactions, I began to connect the stories I had heard from my parents and grandparents with the records I discovered. Gradually I began to realize that the old ways of cooking and preserving food, my grandfather's general store, and my memories of my uncle's farm were also history, a more vital history than I had been reading and writing.

Most of my students and many of my friends and colleagues, I discovered, had a grandparent who had actually emigrated from Italy, Ireland or Eastern Europe. I could not recover that immigration experience, the arrival story, because my ancestors had emigrated from Great Britain (from England, northern Ireland or Wales) in the seventeenth or early eighteenth centuries. Geographical mobility is one of the main themes of American history—the trip to America, the movement west, the migration from small towns to cities. Yet my family story, I discovered, was mostly one of stability, not mobility. I lived in the same house from the time I was an infant until I went to college, and my parents were born within a few miles of that house. Their ancestors, back through several generations, were buried in cemeteries nearby. In each generation one or more children moved west or to the city, but I am descended from those who stayed behind. I broke the chain by moving away.

I had great fun exploring family documents and family stories. I discovered that most of the stories had an element of truth, but many were also exaggerated, or at least the facts were rearranged. Memories are much like that. We tell ourselves stories in order to make sense of our lives. We edit those stories, leaving things out, rearranging the facts. When we tell those stories to others we edit them once again.

I can't promise that the stories I tell here will be useful to students of history. I have attempted in these pages to recall a lost past rather than to construct an argument or point of view. My memories, like most memories, are scattered and jumbled, often out of focus, and they lack a coherent narrative. I have tried to use history to extend, and find a context for, my memories, but in the end I hope my stories will add meaning and a personal connection to history.

This book is my attempt to make sense of my memories of growing up as a member of the Lucky Generation in a little town in northern Vermont. It is a dialogue between the boy that I once was and the person I have become. It is also a collaboration between history and memory.

Chapter 1

MY FATHER'S HOUSE

THE SPRING after my father died, my sister, Florence, and I spent a week cleaning out his house, a rambling Victorian structure on South Main Street in Hardwick, Vermont. It is a sad task to empty closets, sort through papers, books, and clothes, to decide what to throw away, what to keep, and which objects to sell at auction. The house had been built about 1880 before Hardwick became a granite boom town. It sits on a lot of more than an acre across from the town cemetery and down the street from the general store that my grandfather, Charles F. Davis, purchased in 1901, and that my father, Harold F. Davis, took over in the 1920s and finally sold in 1968. My parents purchased the house in 1931 in the depths of the Depression, a few weeks after I was born. My arrival apparently made the family apartment over the store too crowded.

It is my father's house, but it is also my house. In a real sense it is the only home I have ever had. I have lived in many places: dormitories, army barracks, apartments, and other houses, including three that I owned. I married and had two sons, traveled to many parts of the world, but when I think of home it is this house. In many ways it ceased to be home when I went away to college, and especially in 1954, when my mother died. I returned from time to time, including a sad trip in 1965 for my younger sister Marjorie's memorial service. I watched my father grow older and the house change in minor ways. The wrap-around porch, which we always called a veranda, was removed in 1946, and the house was altered by the addition of white asbestos shingles that replaced the more traditional clapboards. These were unfortunate changes that destroyed the proportion and the color of the Victorian house. The alterations were understandable, in light of the postwar urge to modernize and the tendency of the porch to rot and need constant repair. The large elm and several maple trees that once provided shade have fallen prey to disease and to the salt applied to the icy road in winter, leaving the house standing naked and forlorn.

The kitchen was remodeled in the early 1950s. The piano that occupied a corner of the living room while I was growing up has been replaced by a television set, and I look in vain for the large upright Philco radio that was my constant companion in the late 1930s and 1940s. But my father's Morris chair is still there, and essentially the house has not changed. My room, over the kitchen, is just as I left it when I went away to college. The Eastlake-style bed, where I slept since I was ten, remains, as does the oak desk with the attached bookcase. High school pictures, letters from girlfriends long forgotten, certificates from a boys' camp from 1943, my high school letters for basketball and football, even the jackets and neckties I wore in high school, are still in the closet. I also find my college notes and my army uniforms that I had dumped there on my discharge in 1956.

My bedroom is connected to another room that we called "the store room." It had once been part of a separate apartment constructed in the house sometime before my parents bought it, perhaps to house granite workers. While I was growing up I used this room as a place for my projects, to build model airplanes, organize my stamp collection, set up my electric train, but I was often driven out of the room during the winter because very little heat reached it. Here on the wall are photographs of World War II planes and maps of Europe and Asia on which I followed the progress of the war. My stamp albums, along with jigsaw puzzles and board games, are stacked in the corner, and underneath a pile of blankets I discover my Mace Brown baseball glove. I find boxes filled with Tinker Toys, Erector Sets, and Lincoln Logs that were once Christmas gifts, and the basis of my projects that never quite lived up to my hope for them. As I walk around the house, every object, every sound, triggers memories, and the process is made more difficult because my own marriage is breaking up; in a sense I am dismantling two houses at once. Every object reminds me of people, events, incidents, but the memories are jumbled together with no timeline, and the remembering is complicated by the realization that it was this house and this town that I had struggled so hard to leave. Now I am back for one last time.

It is difficult dismantling my father's house, and strange to discover my own things long abandoned, but it is not so much these things that made me sad as the utter familiarity of the house. Coming in through the hall from the carriage house (which we always called "the barn") I know just how to walk, even in the dark, to avoid the large jelly cabinet on the right and the chair piled with newspapers on the left. My hand automatically finds the light switch even though it is covered with a jacket. There is a familiar rhythm and pace as I move about the house, based on long practice. I go through the living room to the front hall by the "what-not" in the corner, its shelves filled with small dishes and mementos. I run up the stairs, two steps at a time, my hand placed on the banister to help me vault around the corner. I pause to look out of the little window a third of the way up the stairs where I used to stand, waiting for my mother as she returned from down town, or later for a high school friend arriving by car. In the bathroom I can still smell the combination of odors—bay rum, shaving cream, hair tonic—that remind me of my father. I glance in the mirror and think, that is not me, that is my father's face. As I get older I seem to resemble my father more and more, and I catch myself repeating some of his habits and mannerisms that I have unconsciously acquired.

I walk down the hall, through my parents' bedroom and into my room with my eyes closed because I have done it so many times in the dark—right hand on the side wall, left hand reaches for the edge of the bureau, right hand finds the door knob. I take several steps, feel the bed with my knees, then I reach up to find the cord that turns on the light. After dark the light from the street lamp shines into my room, casting the same shadows I remember from my youth. The cars and trucks going by on South Main Street make more noise than I recall, but the sound of the back door slamming, the toilet flushing in the bathroom, are utterly familiar. I wind the eight-day clock that still sits on top of the cabinet in the dining room, and it strikes the hour and the quarter hour with the same tone I remember. Unlike most of their generation, my parents did not move while I was growing up. I lived in the same house from the time I was an infant until I went to college and then, even after my mother died, my father stayed in the same house until he died. Many families today move several times, and finally the old folks end up in a nursing home or a retirement center, and in the process they sort through, give away and throw out many possessions.

My sister and I are quite unusual at the end of the twentieth century. We are examining several lifetimes of paper and possessions and the house we are cleaning out is our home. We are engaged in what a friend of mine calls "above ground archeology." And like archaeologists we are searching out objects and then trying to piece them together into a narrative, to make sense of our lives and the lives of our parents and grandparents. We are sorting through the artifacts of memory.

I feel a mixture of sadness and exhilaration. Sad that my father is gone and that we will have to sell the house, excited because the old jelly cabinet, a blanket chest from the early nineteenth century, four thumb-back Windsor chairs, and other objects that I had long coveted, will now be mine. The same kind of mixed feelings must have disturbed children throughout all time as they inherited their parents' property. For the sons of New England farmers it was especially true because they often had to wait until their father died before they could own the land.

Along with the anticipation of inheritance there is grief. I am more affected and saddened by my father's death than I anticipated. He lived a long life, dying after a short illness at the age of eighty-three. The obituary in the local newspaper mentioned his "serene charm and natural affability," but I was not especially close to him; my mother was a more dominant influence on my life. And, unlike my mother, who died at fifty-eight before I had a chance to tell her how much I loved her, I had time to ask my father many questions about his youth and about the family. Still, as I wander around the house, I feel the impulse to ask him another question, and then I realize that I now have no one to ask. My father's only brother (my Uncle Herman) died just two weeks before he did. My grief is compounded by the realization that my sister and I are now part of the oldest surviving generation.

It is painful to empty drawers and boxes. There, hanging in the closet, are my father's suits and jackets, along with Christmas presents unopened and unused after many years. I found it difficult to buy presents for him. "I have everything I need," he would say. I feel like an intruder as I look through files, as I empty cabinets and explore closets. The worst moment comes when I discover his old, brown sweater that he wore constantly. I handle it carefully and throw it in the trash can. I wipe a tear from my eye and get back to work. I half expect my father to walk in and confront me. He was a very private man who rarely shared his feelings. A few years before he died, when he went to the hospital in St. Johnsbury for a minor operation, and he showed me a lock box where he kept his important papers. "If I don't come back," he suddenly announced, "I want you to open this, but if I recover I don't want you to touch it." Now that he is gone I open the box, but I feel a little guilty. There, carefully organized, are insurance policies, Army discharge papers, a social security card, car title, deeds, and other documents. I also find accounts detailing the money paid for college expenses for me and my sisters, as well as a note detailing the money I borrowed from him when I first bought a house in Columbia, Missouri. I paid him back in full including interest. When I told my friends that I was paying my father interest on a loan they were horrified, but I liked the idea of a business transaction. It made me feel less guilty.

I feel mixed emotions as I sort through things accumulated over the years. Old decorations remind me of how excited I used to be as a youngster as we prepared for Christmas. My eyes wander over old family bibles and photo albums stored in the closet in the front hall. I find a Monopoly game and several packs of playing cards, reminding me of the many times our family sat around the table and played games in the evening. I smile as I discover a family medical encyclopedia, and recall that when I was about twelve I studied that volume, hoping that it would help me unravel the mysteries of sex.

My sister and I empty the drawers of the sideboard and the glass-front cabinet in the dining room and place their contents on the dining room table, the same table where we had Sunday dinner and holiday meals, and the place where I studied and wrote papers while in high school. I had an oak desk in my room but I usually chose to be in the middle of things. Perhaps that is how I learned to concentrate despite many distractions. I still like to read while listening to the radio or watching television. We sort silverware (mostly silver plate), napkins, table clothes, sets of dishes. There is no library in the house, no room with floor-to-ceiling bookcases, but there are books in every room; many belonged to my mother—Chaucer, Shakespeare, Milton, Wordsworth, Keats, Byron, Emerson's Essays, novels by Henry James and George Eliot. My mother's presence is everywhere even though she died nearly twenty-five years ago. As I thumb through some of the volumes I am reminded of how much I like the smell of old books. There are books in the living room, a twenty-volume set of *The Book of Knowledge* near the telephone in the dining room, books in the upstairs hall way, some in a glass-front bookcase, and books in all the bedrooms. In my room I discover *Treasure Island*, *Kidnapped*, *The Swiss Family Robinson*, *Citizen Tom Paine* by Howard Fast, and *Strong and Steady* by Horatio Alger. There are also books I read during the war: *Guadalcanal Diary*, *God Is My Co-Pilot,* an illustrated book on World War II aircraft with a publication date of 1943. I wonder what happened to my collection of Big Little Books?

After a day of sorting and discovery, we return to Greensboro where we are staying at camp. Camp is a summer cottage built on Caspian Lake by my grandfather in 1923, on land purchased by my grandmother, Florence Haines Davis, my grandfather's first wife, in 1913. But no one ever called it a cottage; it was camp. Caspian Lake is clear and cold and deep; it has attracted fishermen and campers since the late nineteenth century. We always spent most of June and July there, and in many ways it is more important to me than this house. My father recognized that and ten years before he died he put my name on the deed, so now it is mine. Greensboro is about seven miles north of Hardwick and 800 feet higher. We drive through the main street of Hardwick, cross the Lamoille River, go past the Jeudevine Library, a Romanesque revival building, where I spent a great deal of time reading when I was growing up. We cross the railroad tracks and drive up Slapp Hill. We pass the new suburban-style houses on the edge of the village, but soon we are in the open country. We are driving along the hill road, which some call the center road. There are still several working farms. Some of the fields have been newly plowed, but others have been turned yellow by the dandelions now in full bloom. It is a beautiful spring day, blue sky with a few fluffy, white clouds. The leaves on the maple trees are the size of the tip of my finger and those on the birches even smaller, while there are no leaves at all on the ash trees. There are several shades of green on the hill sides, punctuated by occasional red buds and the white of apple blossoms. The rolling hills with mountains in the distance, and the checkerboard look of forest and cleared land, makes the landscape in Vermont look very different from New Hampshire. Wallace Stegner writes somewhere that you have a sense of how the landscape should look based on the land where you grew up. I realize as I look at the beautiful scene that even though I worked hard to leave this part of the country, it is this landscape that makes me feel that I am home.

The next day we return to Hardwick, and to the task of sorting and unpacking. My sister, Florence, and I have few disagreements over what we want to keep; her tastes are different from mine, and she agrees that I should be the family archivist and take care of the family bibles and photo albums. But as we talk about the family we do disagree about our memories. "You used to sit on this side of the table," I say. "No, I always sat over there," she replies. I recall how the two of us used to have a picnic lunch in the backyard and how we sat on an old tree stump. She has no memory of that. We can't even agree on who slept in which bedroom when we were young and our grandmother lived with us. "You were always the favorite," she announces at one point. "I had to do the dishes, help with the housework, and make the beds, you never did anything." I disagree. I didn't do dishes, that was women's work in our household, but I mowed the lawn, shoveled the walks and driveway in winter, and brought in the wood for the kitchen stove before I went to school. I secretly agree that perhaps I was the favorite. It may have been because I was often sick as a child that our mother paid more attention to me, or perhaps it was because we shared many interests, or simply because I was the only boy.

Our conflicting memories are caused, in part, by age and gender. She is four and a half years older and has a different angle of vision on our past. My other sister, Marjorie, three years younger, died tragically of a brain tumor when she was only thirty. It is painful to sort through her books and papers. She had a master's degree in religious education and had come within one course of another master's in social work. In one of her classes she had apparently been asked to write about herself and her family. I found a "biographical sketch" in her papers. "I was the youngest of three children," she wrote, "and I was raised in a family which I consider now to have been a very stable one, though one in which feelings were not expressed openly." She was right; we didn't talk about feelings. We didn't cry at funerals or laugh and sing at weddings (perhaps because there was no drinking). We didn't hug or kiss. We did shake hands a lot. I have always thought of my family as a story of success, not flashy, but solid, but looking at my sister's things and thinking of my mother, it suddenly occurs to me that our family history is filled with tragedy, sadness, and unfulfilled dreams.

To get away from the confusion, and to clear my head, I decide to take a walk. I go along South Main Street toward "the store." We always called it "the store" even though it was officially the H.F. Davis Store, and before that, the C. F. Davis Department Store. We always went "up to the store" even though it was south of the house, but we went "down town" when we walked to the business section of town (some people called it "down street"). I have forgotten how sharply South Main Street curves between our house and the store. I pass the Racette house next door, the smaller house where my friends Bill and Harry Pilbin lived, and then an abandoned garage. Next came my grandparents' house, after that another house, whose owner I have forgotten, and then the store, now converted into apartments. Nothing on the street is quite the way it exists in my memory. None of the people I remember, or their children, live in these houses. This section of town seems a little run down and shabby. It never was the best part of town, but it has declined further as Hardwick's economy has stagnated.

Before returning to the house I cross the street and enter the cemetery. This was a familiar backdrop to my house while I was growing up, and I suppose that is why I never acquired a fear of cemeteries. I played here, skied around the stones in the winter time, and accepted it as part of the scenery. I locate my grandparents' and my parents' gravestones and then, as I approach the newer part of the burial ground, I see the markers for a great many of the people I knew growing up, including several from my generation. In fact, looking at the gravestones, I feel a little like an actor in Thornton Wilder's *Our Town*. I walk back through the cemetery, toward home, admiring the way Buffalo Mountain towers over the town. While I was growing up the mountain was my playground, the place where my friends and I built huts and hideouts, played cowboys and Indians and war, but I never really appreciated the mountains and the hills of Vermont until I spent several years in the flat expanses of the Midwest, studying and teaching. I came back on one occasion to visit my father. I looked out of our dining room window and exclaimed in wonder, "There is a mountain in our backyard."

My house has several entrances, four to be exact, if you count the entrance through the barn. The door we used most frequently opens directly from the porch into the kitchen. There is also an entrance from the back hall to the backyard, the garden, and the clothes line. I preferred this back door as a youngster in the summer as I rushed out to play with my friends. Then there is the front door. This is the formal entrance to the Victorian house where visitors, salesmen, and friends would call and be greeted by a servant. We rarely used this entrance—in fact, we never shoveled the walk to this door in winter. Occasionally a stranger or salesman came to this door, thus revealing that they were from out of town. But the door remains as a reminder of a past age. Coming through the door, one entered the front hall with the stairs on the right. The hall led to a room that we used as a guest bedroom, but which may originally have been an office or a downstairs parlor. The caller could enter this room without going into the living room.

In the hall there was a Victorian hall stand. It is no longer there. I wonder when it was sold or given away? The hall stand had a mirror, hooks for hats and coats, and a seat. In the proper Victorian house the servant would greet visitors, hang their hats and coats, and then the visitors would sit on the rather uncomfortable seat while waiting for the master or mistress of the house. There also was a place for calling cards where the visitor could leave a card if the family was not home. Next to it was an umbrella stand. None of these things were used in our house, at least in my memory. We had no servant. The nearest we came to a maid was a woman who helped my mother with spring cleaning.

No one I knew used calling cards in Hardwick, and only women used umbrellas. Perhaps this custom was the association of the umbrella with Neville Chamberlain and appeasement at Munich in 1938, or perhaps it was just considered too British and effete. The only man in town who carried an umbrella was J. C. Spaulding, the photographer. He even dressed like an Englishman. Everyone wore hats of various kinds to protect them from rain and snow. In winter I wore a "tuque," a formless knit hat that could be pulled over the ears, but I disliked hats and never felt comfortable with the male Stetson. I was happy when President John Kennedy made going without a hat fashionable. I remember buying my first umbrella in 1961 when I spent the summer at Harvard University. It was very black and very British. A colleague at the University of Missouri, where I was teaching at the time, remarked: "If you can carry an umbrella, I guess I can, too."

I have one memory that relates to the hall stand, but I have no way to tie it down to a specific date, though as I replay the event on the movie camera in my head I seem to be quite small. It was Christmas, and Christmas was an exciting time. I had many plans and projects. Somewhere I had discovered a bell and I planned to ring it when it was time for dinner. I placed it on the seat part of the hall stand so I could retrieve it at the proper moment, but when I went to look for it, my grandparents, uncles, aunts, and the other guests had piled their coats on the stand, and I was too small to move them and recover my bell in time. My elaborate plan failed. Why do I remember this very small disappointment?

The front door was always locked, but all the other doors were open. Even if we were away, the kitchen door was only latched with a flimsy hook that could have been easily pushed in. Everyone came to the kitchen door, and in Hardwick most people dropped in unannounced. There were no numbers on the houses in Hardwick because there was no mail delivery, but everyone knew where we lived. My mother would entertain informally by serving coffee or tea, together with freshly baked cookies, at the kitchen table. When relatives or friends visited on Sunday they might be ushered into the living room, but even the minister sat at the kitchen table when he came to call, or to talk my mother into doing something for the church. It was the same kitchen table, always covered with an oil cloth, where we ate almost all of our meals when I was growing up. The dining room was only for Sunday dinners and for holidays, or if we had guests from out of town.

I sit at the kitchen table and look around the room. The floor, once covered with linoleum, is now tiled, but except for the living room, which has a room-size imitation Oriental rug and a runner on the front stairs, all the floors in the house are still covered with linoleum, with small rugs placed here and there. Linoleum, originally introduced in the 1870s as a luxury floor covering, was very popular in the 1880s when this house was built. The linoleum in the kitchen, if my memory is correct, was dark green, but it turned a lighter shade when it was mopped.

I look around the room. There have been some changes since my early childhood. An electric stove has replaced the wood-burning Glenwood Range of my childhood. There is no longer an oil cloth on the kitchen table. The iron sink has given way to a stainless steel version, and a washing machine and dryer have been installed in the pantry. Like most Victorian houses, this house had a large pantry with open shelves for dishes and supplies. Our pantry also had a "Hoosier cabinet" to store flour and sugar and other staples, as well as places for rolling pins, pots and pans, and other cooking equipment. The lower portion of the cabinet formed a shelf with a porcelain top designed for rolling dough and mixing ingredients. The "Hoosier cabinet," first produced in Indiana in 1897, was very popular in the 1920s. It was a "work-saving, comfort-giving kitchen convenience," according to one advertisement. At some point my father sold or dismantled the cabinet, but I can still see my mother standing in front of that cabinet in the pantry as she rolled out dough to make a pie crust.

I take the stairs that descend from the kitchen to the basement (which we called the cellar). I was always a little afraid of the cellar when I was a child. There were dark corners, a huge furnace that roared in the winter time, a mysterious root cellar, and shelves filled with jars of home-canned vegetables, fruits, jams, and pickles. The cellar seemed like a different and dangerous world. The coal furnace has been converted to oil, but I find a few pieces of coal on the floor and remember how I liked to watch the coal truck back up to a cellar window and send the coal down a chute into the coal bins with a great roar. My father was proud of his ability to build a coal fire that would last for twenty-four hours even in the coldest weather. Before he went to bed on a winter night, he went 'down cellar' to bank the fire, and the first thing he did in the morning was return to the furnace to shake the grate with a special tool to allow the ashes to fall to the ash pit. Then he shoveled enough coal to last the day. It was a hot-water system and every room in the house had a radiator, but some rooms were always warmer than others. A coal-fired hot-water system was the preferred way to heat houses in Hardwick during the long, frigid winter months, but many people used hot-air furnaces: that depended on registers to distribute the hot air, while the less fortunate depended entirely on wood-burning stoves. My grandfather, who built a house in 1913, installed two furnaces, a coal, hot-water system for the cold months and a wood-burning hot air furnace for spring and fall. One problem with burning wood or coal is that both produce ashes. My job, as I got to be ten or twelve, was to haul the coal ashes from the basement up the stairs and out to the backyard, where the ash pile betrayed the way we kept warm during the long winter. Before the ashes were discarded they had to be sifted to recover any unburned coal. It was that sifting that I disliked the most, partly because of the dust and the smell, but mostly because it was tedious work.

I climb up the stairs from the cellar and wind my way: through the back hall, up the back stairs, to the second floor hall, and up another set of stairs to the attic. One advantage of growing up in a Victorian house was that there were many places to hide and so many different routes to take in maneuvering about the house. The back hall and back stairs, which disappeared from American houses about 1910, were originally designed so that servants could move from the kitchen to a small bedroom without going through the main part of the house. As a child I delighted in moving about the house and hiding from my sisters and my parents.

My mother loved the house, but she often complained that there was too much wasted space. To me the extra space meant opportunity and places to hide. One of my favorite places to read was in the attic. There was a trap door that had to be pushed up, but I managed to do it even when I was quite small. As I climb up the steep stairs and open the trap door the smell of the attic is at once strange and familiar—a combination of old cloth, mice droppings, and moth balls.

Two rooms at one end of the attic had been finished, plastered, and papered at some point in the past, but we never used these rooms except as storerooms. One had to negotiate a long stretch of unfinished attic to get to those two rooms, and I remember as a boy being a little nervous while walking across that section to get to the storage rooms. Once there, I loved to sit and look out the window from what was really the third floor. I got a completely different angle of vision on the world below, a different perspective, almost as if I were hiding and spying on people who could not see me.

The attic is a storehouse, a place where old, unwanted, or outdated things are deposited. There are broken lamps, dismantled beds, a wicker baby carriage, boxes, trunks, and books. I recall sitting for hours browsing through books, many of them left over from my mother's college years, and from the time she taught English and Latin in high school. There are also a number of family portraits, oil paintings, and enlarged photographs. There is one large portrait, three feet by four feet, of a formidable, grim-looking woman. I look at that painting and laugh because when I visited my father a few years before he died I discovered the portrait while poking around in the attic. I rushed downstairs and asked my father, "Who is that large, tough woman in the attic?" "Oh," my father responded. "She doesn't belong to our family; she was in the house when I bought it." As I look at the woman in the elaborate frame I am glad I had that conversation because without it I would feel compelled to preserve her as an ancestor. Now I could let the painting go in the auction and someone else could acquire an anonymous ancestor.

Scattered around the attic are other objects from the past; a certificate issued by the state of Vermont to the parents of Charles Freeman testifies that he died at Andersonville Prison during the Civil War. He was my grandfather's uncle and it is from him that I acquired my middle name. There is also a sword, slightly damaged, from early in the nineteenth century, and a canteen from World War I. There are a couple of dozen metal sap buckets with covers given to me by my Uncle Lovell when I was perhaps twelve to help me in my ambitious plan to tap maple trees on Buffalo Mountain and make maple syrup. I spot a bird house that I made at a boys' camp sometime during World War II, and a trunk in army tan with "Lt. Harold F. Davis" stenciled on it, a souvenir from my father's World War I adventures. There are several other "steamer trunks," for in the Victorian era, even in the 1920s, everyone had to have a trunk. I recall looking in my grandmother's trunk, my mother's trunk, and one that belonged originally to an aunt and being fascinated by all the mysterious objects that I imagined were located there. I never found the valuable postage stamp or the forgotten gold coin I searched for, but I discovered other treasures from the past. I would linger for hours with a book looking out of the window at people and cars, satisfied that no one could see me.

Next to one of the trunks there is an old-fashioned electric toaster, the kind that required you to toast one side of the bread, and then flip it over to toast the other side. It led to many burned pieces of toast. This toaster must have been retired when my family got a more efficient model. There is also a pressure cooker, probably purchased after World War II. I remember my mother's excitement as she tried out this new invention that was supposed to reduce cooking time and to create all kinds of magical meals. But I also remember the time when my mother was canning beets, and somehow the pressure got too high and the machine blew its top, depositing the beets all over the kitchen, including the ceiling. I suspect the pressure cooker got assigned to the attic after that event. In one corner I spot an old Singer sewing machine, the one my mother used to make and repair clothes. It was powered by a foot pedal and used to sit in a corner of the dining room. At some point it, too, was assigned to the attic, a relic from a past age.

Another reminder of my youth turns up near the trunks. It looks like a small suitcase, but I recognize it as a laundry box that I used in summers starting in 1947 when I worked first at a boys' camp and then at summer hotels in New England and New York State. The container consists of two boxes, one slightly larger than the other. The larger box telescopes over the smaller one, forming an expandable case. Made of hard plastic or fiberboard, the laundry case is secured by two straps and has a place for an address card that can be turned over when it is returned to the sender. For several summers and then during my freshman year at Dartmouth, about every two weeks I put my dirty laundry, including sheets and towels, in the case and mailed it home to my mother. She washed and ironed the clothes, replaced a button or mended a sock where needed, and mailed it back to me usually including some homemade cookies and a copy of the *Hardwick Gazette*. My two college roommates laughed at my laundry box, but they always looked forward to the cookies.

As I look around the attic I discover objects from a more distant past, including a candle mold, a collection of kerosene lamps—including one with elaborately painted shades—flat irons, or sad irons, which were once heated on a stove before being used to iron clothes. There is also a toilet set including pitcher, basin, chamber pot, soap dish, and mug, used in bedrooms before houses had running water. These things probably came from my uncle's farm in Craftsbury, originally built by my Grandmother Wylie's ancestors in the 1820s, and sold in 1944. They came from an age before electricity and indoor plumbing, an age not that long ago in rural Vermont, not part of my memory, but remnants of the world of my parents and grandparents.

My sister and I take a break to walk "down town" to have lunch at the Village Diner. I don't recognize most of the people on the street. At one time I used to know everyone in town. Many of the landmarks of our childhood are gone. Hardwick, which I locate for my friends as about thirty miles north of Montpelier, the state capital, and about thirty miles from the Canadian border, has suffered over the years from many fires. None of the four churches remain in original form. The "new gym," built in 1940, burned, and the Academy building, where I spent twelve years, has been torn down. The Idle Hour Theater, where I spent many hours watching movies, is now a vacant lot, the victim of television I suppose. And the pool hall and bowling alley are no more. But there is enough that remains to trigger memories. Hardwick, viewed from the top of Slapp Hill, as it nestles under Buffalo Mountain, looks like a typical Vermont pastoral village with a church spire and the tops of houses peeking out from the tree-shaded streets. But as one gets closer the town's history as a granite center becomes obvious. The main street is jammed between the river and a hill and looks a little like a Western mining town. The construction of the Hardwick and Woodbury Railroad in 1898, connecting Hardwick to the granite quarries in the neighboring town of Woodbury, set off a boom that made Hardwick the leading producer of building granite in the nation. The Woodbury Granite Company in Hardwick employed six to eight hundred men in its sheds and, over a fifteen-year period, cut and polished the stone for the Pennsylvania State Capitol, the Wisconsin State Capitol, city halls in Cleveland and Chicago, and hundreds of commercial buildings in many cities around the country. The peak of the granite boom lasted from about 1900 to 1915. In a sense, Hardwick has been in a process of slow decline ever since.

Returning to the house from downtown, I notice that, out of habit, I walk down on one side of the street and back on the other. I ponder the survival of old childhood rituals and habits. I enter the barn, or carriage house, which is connected to the house. It has stalls for two horses, and space for a least two carriages or buggies. The floor boards are still scarred by the hooves of the horses that once lived here. There is also a loft for the storage of hay and a basement where I once raised chickens in an attempt to increase my monthly income. My father used the barn as a garage. There are old Vermont license plates tacked to the wall and bumper stickers advertising "Ausable Chasm" and "Old Orchard Beach, Maine," souvenirs of family trips. The loft and the old stalls provided plenty of additional space for storage. My father was neat and well-organized (traits I did not inherit), so everything from nuts and bolts and screws to bigger items that had not been used in decades were perfectly arranged and preserved. The barn, like the attic, is a museum of material culture from another age, except there were no labels or interpretation. A faint smell lingers: a combination of gasoline, carbon monoxide, and oil, a smell that reminds me of returning from a trip or a Sunday drive. My father would announce: "We're home at last,"and it always did seem good to be home.

I poke around the barn and find an old croquet set with wire wickets, several striped wooden balls, two chipped mallets and one end post. We often played on the side lawn, but we had to invent special rules because the lawn was not level.

Several sets of snowshoes emerge from the clutter. They were used by my parents and grandparents before skis became popular winter transportation. In the corner is my prized Flexible Flyer, a sled with runners that I laboriously kept polished so that I could compete in winter sliding contests. During the winter, the village of Hardwick prohibited cars from using Lower Cherry Street (the steep hill next to the United Church) and reserved it for the young and not-so-young who wanted to go sliding (not sledding). No salt or sand was used on the road, so at various times during the winter, between snow storms, the hill became icy and fast. Large crowds gathered in the late afternoon and often in the evening. Young children and girls usually rode sitting on the sled steering with their feet, but adolescent boys rode head-first, stretched out on the sled, and they got a running start to increase their speed. "Belly bunt," we called going head-first. I recently found that word in a book on Vermont folklore, so we must have somehow acquired an authentic language for our sliding. On a good day you could coast as far as Granite Street or beyond on "glare ice." One of the objectives was to let a girl or a group of girls go first, then catch up with them and push them into a snow bank. I now understand it was an early form of preadolescent courting, but it was fun at the time and part of the joy of winter in Vermont. Sliding could be dangerous, and the ice was hard. One Sunday, Muriel Clark, the little girl who lived across the street and up the hill from my house, slid down the hill and into the path of a car. She was killed instantly. She was my younger sister's best friend. We were allowed to leave school to go to the funeral. It was the first funeral of a young person I ever attended.

Hidden against one wall in the barn loft, and covered with boards and other material, is a traverse (accent on the first syllable), a kind of bobsled. It had belonged to my father and uncle, but I remember inviting a gang of friends to slide down Lower Cherry Street on a winter afternoon or to go on a longer expedition. Once, a group of us dragged the traverse more than a mile to the hamlet of Mackville, and then we careened all the way to the foot of Plank Hill. It took several people to move it around so usually it stayed in the barn. Next to the traverse was what we called a "scooter," a homemade winter toy consisting of a single runner and a seat. I remember racing other boys on their own scooters over crusted snow, over jumps, and around corners. But I never really mastered the art of balancing and controlling the scooter. It was more popular during my father's youth. I spent my time skiing, and there, leaning against the wall, are a half dozen pairs of wooden skis, some of them more than seven feet in length and now clearly antique.

On the first floor of the barn, I discover my little red wagon (with a plate on the front that reads "1935") and the heavy and elaborately decorated bicycle with balloon tires that I bought with my own money, saved from Christmas gifts and odd jobs, when I was about ten. That bicycle enabled me to expand the territory that I could easily cover around town, and it helped me become independent. With the bike I could travel to West Church Street to play baseball, or to various trout streams within a ten-mile radius of Hardwick. I think about those bike trips as I climb the back stairs to my room and continue the dismantling process. I start to unload a wooden box in the corner of my room, which had probably been used in the 1920s to ship tea, but we used it to store blankets. At the bottom of the box I find my favorite stuffed animal, a rabbit. It has been repaired many times by my mother or grandmother. It helped me through many childhood traumas and illnesses, but as I look at it I recall my mother's little speech to me on my fifth birthday. She told me that now that I was five years old and a big boy it was time I abandoned my "bunny," and I did. But to this day, when I sleep, I cradle an imaginary bunny. My "bunny" lives on, and my mother's speech about how a five-year-old should act remains one of the earliest memories I can clearly date.

Two months after my sister and I dismantle my father's house and select the items we want to keep, there is a public auction to sell the many remaining objects. I vow that I will not go to the auction because it will be too painful to watch familiar objects sold to the highest bidder, but in the end I can't stay away. I stand across the street in the cemetery and watch. Even though I went through the content of the house many times and made sure that I rescued all the family records, photographs, and other materials, I still feel pangs of regret as I watch my high chair, my little red wagon, and my Flexible Flyer sold. Once the auction is over and the house completely empty, I wander through the house while I wait for the auctioneers to settle their accounts. The empty rooms seem sad and forlorn. I watch one of the men go from room to room, placing his hand over the frame of each door. I ask what he is doing and he says: "Sometimes people place gold coins in odd places." I reply, "If there were gold coins in this house I would have found them long ago."

Two years later I return to the house to negotiate with the family who rented it and are now interested in buying. I enter through the kitchen door, as was my habit. I am immediately shocked to discover a strange table, a modern stove, even a different smell. Later we sit in the living room on a couch that is the wrong color and is even in the wrong place. Nothing seems familiar. It is no longer my father's house.

Chapter 2

MEMORY AND PHOTOGRAPHS

IN MY EARLIEST MEMORY I am sitting in a little bathtub outdoors. I am using a cup to dip water from the tub into a pail and then from the pail back into the tub. This memory is like a faded snapshot, but if I concentrate I can recapture the moment, I can even hear the water and feel a sense of accomplishment for the work that I am doing. In the family photo album there is a picture of me as a little boy of a year and a half sitting in a bathtub on the lawn 'dipping water.' Does the photograph authenticate my memory or is my memory triggered by the photograph? Or is it some combination of the two? There is another photograph of me smelling a rose bush, but I have no memory of that. I do recall vividly lying on the grass and looking up at soft, puffy, white clouds moving rapidly across the sky and thinking that I could see the whole world. But there is no photograph to document my imagining. As I study family albums I come across photographs that help me recall an event, or illustrate the stories my parents told, but there are others that I cannot locate at a particular time and place. William Styron writes somewhere that his memories of his childhood are not framed as from a boy's eyes, but rather they seem to be viewed through a movie camera. He imagines that camera on a boom crane, angling down from above, recording the events he remembers. My memories, by contrast, seem to be a series of snapshots, often random, with no chronology, all blurring together. Perhaps this is because I have studied so many family photos that memory and photographs have become mixed and confused in my mind.

Family photos are fascinating even if they record the faces and activities of an unknown family; they preserve a moment in time and capture the look of the landscape, the vernacular architecture, and a variety of objects that accidentally surround the subject of the photograph. The professional photographer carefully frames a picture, and the subjects often pose stiffly, or at least formally. Snapshots are usually taken by a family member or friend, and the result is more candid and casual. Family photos are often out of focus, poorly framed with heads cut off or the image distorted, but the defects make them more interesting. They freeze a moment in time. Virginia Woolf writes that we often see more in a photograph than we do in real life. Perhaps that is because the photo stops action and allows us to examine every detail. Some snapshots become icons, carefully preserved in an album, even enlarged and framed. They come to represent or to symbolize a person or an event.

My fascination with studying old photographs is perhaps related to my need to return to places where I once lived, or even to cities that I visited years ago. There is something about going back and touching the past that forces you to contemplate what has changed and what remains the same. I have a similar feeling when I study old family photos. Is that really me, the little boy in the sailor suit smiling at the camera? Is that the porch in the background of the snapshot, the one torn down in 1946? Can that possibly be the same tree that now towers over the dock at camp? But I recognize the old boathouse; it looks almost the same seventy years later.

When studying family photos from my youth, there is at least the possibility of recognition and the convergence of memory with the images, but it is quite another thing to examine my parents' photograph albums and to try to imagine what they were like before I was born, before I have a memory of them. But in a sense these albums represent a twilight between what I remember and the stories my parents told. All children, I suppose, become detectives as they try to figure out what their parents were like before they were born. There are no diaries or letters so I must depend on the photographs to bolster my memory. My grandparents and great-grandparents had formal albums filled with cabinet and *carte de visite* portraits. I do not know what my earliest ancestors looked like, for they died before the camera was invented. Both my father and mother owned cameras and created more informal scrapbook albums.

My mother's album begins when she was in high school at Craftsbury Academy, in a town ten miles from Hardwick. There are ten in her class of 1913, seven men and three women. Her nickname is "Sukey." I wonder where that came from? Later in college she would be called "Bunny," but when I knew her she had no nickname. There are photos of the basketball team, the Indian Club (an exercise group), a class play, and candid shots of friends. My mother, Bernice Allen, is slender, attractive, but not beautiful. In most of the pictures she looks serious and she always wears glasses, because she had myopia, a condition I inherited. The photo album with black pages is artistically arranged, with photographs clipped to different sizes, some mounted at an angle. My mother has selected the photos to tell a story, but it is a narrative that would have been familiar to most of those who looked at the album. Now it is an artifact and there is no one alive who remembers: there is a photo with a young man, perhaps a "date," taken on July 4, 1913. My mother, who was sixteen, has on a fashionable white dress with a white hat. I can recognize her as my mother, but it is hard to imagine her being sixteen. There is a photo of a young man in a car labeled "At Uries, 1914." Photos of cars, especially in the second decade of the twentieth century, are common, but, in this album there are frequent pictures of horses—work horses, horses hitched to buggies, horses with names—for my mother grew up on a farm.

My mother created the album some years after most of the photos were taken, and she was most often the photographer, although occasionally a friend or family member took a picture. In one snapshot she is holding a kitten; it seems to be the only one where she is smiling. On one page there is a photo of the farmhouse and barn, a shot of "the old pine tree," and then, significantly, a photo of her brother Lovell, constructing a packing crate. The caption reads: "Packing for Burlington, 1913." Bernice moved to Burlington in the late summer of 1913, where her mother rented a house and took in boarders so that her daughter could go to the University of Vermont. This was part of my mother's narrative about her past, part of the story she told me. Her father had died when she was only five, and her mother had managed the farm with the help of hired men. Looking at the photos taken more than ninety years ago, I marvel at the courage shown by my mother, and even more at the commitment of my grandmother to help her daughter get a college education, not just a teaching certificate from a normal school.

The next pages of my mother's album are taken up with college activities and summers spent back on the farm. There are groups of young women, photographs of soldiers (the United States entered the Great War in the spring of 1917, my mother's senior year). There are no photographs that document the great influenza epidemic of 1918 that killed a number of her classmates. There are graduation photos, June 16, 1917, and a group shot of four women and five men (with the fifth woman taking the photo). All, including my mother, are smiling or laughing. The caption is "The Bunch 1916" and was taken at a party, men in suits, women with shirtwaists and long skirts. There is a chafing dish on the table and family portraits on the wall that identify the location as my grandmother's boarding house, at 132 Colchester Avenue in Burlington. My mother once told me that she was embarrassed to bring her friends back to the boarding house, but in this photo it looks quite respectable. My mother is the only one in the photo wearing glasses. I wonder if she ever felt embarrassed by her poor eyesight and her need to wear glasses?

My mother, Bernice Allen, was one of thirty-three women in the class of 1917 at the University of Vermont, out of a total of 127 graduating students. The semi-humorous sketch in her yearbook begins, "We wish we could find a flaw in Bernice's character," but then continues, "You have to keep an eye on her. She'll come in and borrow a book from you and say that she is going to study all afternoon. Five minutes later she will come bouncing back and tell you to keep it, she's going out in a car with a man from home." As I study her picture in her yearbook and read the sketch I wonder who that man from home was. Years later, when I was applying to graduate schools, my mother remarked that her professors wanted her to apply for a fellowship for graduate study in German literature or Latin, but she felt an obligation to teach high school in order to care for her mother. "I wonder how my life would have been different," she mused, but then announced that it could not have possibly been better than the way it turned out.

The photo album continues with a year, 1917-1918, teaching in Underhill, near Burlington—the only year she was able to use her college major to teach German, before the war. The anti-German hysteria eliminated German from most high school curricula. Then there are photos of Hardwick where she and her mother moved in the fall of 1918, perhaps because it was closer to their farm in Craftsbury. There are shots of faculty and students, of various outings including a trip to Colorado (probably the most adventurous travel my mother undertook), and then in 1921, Harold F. Davis, my father, begins to appear. There is a casual photo of him in an auto, hand on the steering wheel, and a page called "Trip to Barton," in which my mother and father appear together for the first time. It was an auto trip taken with another couple, and in one photo my future parents stand side by side (but not touching), my mother is dressed with a fashionable hat, an oversize coat, and long skirt, while my father has a suit and vest with shirt and tie and a cap. My mother is smiling slightly, my father is serious. My mother was twenty-five, my father twenty-seven, and it would be three years before they were married. Here in this portrait, ten years before I was born, they appear like a fashionable couple from the roaring twenties. They are almost the exact age of Zelda and Scott Fitzgerald, though their lives were dramatically different. Harold lived with his parents and worked for his father at the store, while Bernice taught Latin and English at Hardwick Academy and lived with her mother in rented rooms. What were they like at this age? What was their courtship like?

There is another set of photos taken at a camp on Caspian Lake in Greensboro. There are a number of young couples clowning around doing silly things. In one of these photos my mother is laughing. I rarely remember her laughing—she smiled, she chuckled, but she didn't roar with laughter. I do recall one time when I was probably under five. I had been sentenced to a nap at our camp in Greensboro, and I looked down on the adults trying to play ping pong. My mother laughed so hard that I thought she was crying and I ran down stairs to see what was troubling her, only to be told to go back to my bedroom. It is difficult to look at snapshots, photo albums and formal portraits, and to try to piece together a narrative about their lives. The camera records accidental moments. I never asked my parents about their courtship when they were alive, so I can only study the photographs and imagine.

My father's photo album is not as well organized as my mother's but his also starts with high school. Two years older than my mother, he graduated from high school a year after she did. He always explained his late start by saying his family moved around a lot when he was young. He did not begin school until he was seven. There is a carefully posed photo of Harold as a senior at Hardwick Academy in 1914. He looks handsome and confident. There are also group photos of various baseball teams with my father and his brother, Herman, as members. The next year he went to Lowell Commercial College (LCC) in Lowell, Massachusetts, where he spent one year learning bookkeeping, accounting, and penmanship, an important business skill in 1915. I remember his impressive handwriting and how he moved his hand in an imaginary circle before signing his name in the best Palmer-method fashion. Lowell was a thriving textile center in 1914, filled with a multicultural mix of workers and managers from dozens of different countries. It must have seemed a sharp contrast to Hardwick, Vermont, which had a lot of foreign-born workers and their families, but not nearly as wide a range of countries of origin. But I don't remember talking in any detail about that year. Only one photo survives from that year, a studio portrait of the LCC Basketball team with Harold Davis as the manager. Did he have girlfriends? Did he date the Irish and French-Canadian girls who worked in the mills? After Lowell he spent one year in Watertown, Massachusetts, near Boston, working in a store as a clerk, but then he returned home. There are photos of family and friends, several with women, one a jaunty photograph of Harold on a motorcycle with an attractive woman on the back. There is another one with him driving his father's car with his parents and grandmother as passengers. He once told me that he did not have to take a test to get a driver's license; he simply wrote to the state motor vehicle department which mailed him a license.

Most of the photos in my father's album relate to World War I. Harold entered the Army in late 1917, and a few months later he was commissioned a Second Lieutenant. He was stationed in Newport News, Virginia, Washington, D.C., and New Orleans, and the photos show him in and out of uniform. His wartime service in the Army was the most memorable experience of his life. He never saw action, never even went overseas, but as he got older he told his World War I adventure stories over and over again.

The adventure ended, and he came home in 1919 and, before long, the sign on the store read C. F. Davis and Son. There are a few photographs from these years, including one of the extended Davis family sitting in front of my grandparents' house on chairs brought from the dining room and the parlor. The caption reads: "At C. F. Davis July 4, 1921, 97 in the shade." Perhaps it was weather like this (unusual for northern Vermont) that prompted my grandfather to build the camp in Greensboro. Eventually Harold Davis met Bernice Allen, a teacher at the high school, who became his wife and my mother. As a child I assumed that my parents' marriage was inevitable, but as I look through their photo albums I see evidence that they both had other possibilities. Their marriage was not inevitable at all.

My parents were married on July 30, 1924, and they took a honeymoon trip of four weeks, a more extended trip than most middle class couples could afford in the 1920s. They drove a 1922 Buick (probably belonging to my grandfather) into the Adirondacks, down the Hudson River Valley to New York City, back through Connecticut, to the Maine coast, New Hampshire, and home. They stayed in hotels or tourist homes, ate in restaurants, visited occasionally with relatives, and I suppose they had a wonderful time. Wallace Stegner has the narrator in his novel, *Angle of Repose*, try to imagine his grandparents having sex. He has a difficult time thinking of them making love and I have similar difficulty imagining my parents on their honeymoon. The photos in the little album are not personal, but record places, hotels, and occasionally the Buick. There is one shot of my father holding a ruined tire, but his head is cut off in the picture. The caption reads: "The End of a Perfect Tire." A few of the photos are actually postcards sent home to Harold's father and Bernice's mother and added to the album when they returned home. My mother always wrote the cards, but again there was nothing personal in the messages. The only photo of the two of them is on the sand at Hampton Beach, New Hampshire. They are fully clothed and appear to be having a picnic lunch with a friend. They seem to be comfortable with each other. That is the way I remember them. I don't recall angry fights or voices raised in disagreement. I do recall overhearing calm discussions and my mother negotiating to get her way or to make her point. They always seemed to enjoy living together, but perhaps a child is not the best person to judge parents' relationships.

My mother seems to be the author of most of the photo captions, but my father kept an account book recording the cost of meals, hotels, gasoline, and other expenses. They paid twenty-two to twenty-four cents a gallon for gas, seventy-five cents for a tire repair, two dollars to replace a spring. They paid two dollars for dinner at a hotel in Norwalk, Connecticut. "Best food and service for the money so far," my father remarked. In New York they stopped at the Hotel Pennsylvania and paid $10.80. The only comment about New York was that it was "Hotter than H . . ." On Wallingford, Connecticut my father remarked: "Very old hotel built by N.Y. man who hired Italian carpenters. Very good rooms. Town of about 9000. Good movie house, but punk pictures." My father kept a list of about thirty different state license plates spotted on their trip, an indication of the popularity of auto touring during the 1920s. At one point he wrote: "Saw first Vermont car since leaving Saratoga Springs."

The account book reminds me of the father I knew. His subtle sense of humor, and his habit of writing down every expense, are completely in character. After he died and my sister and I cleaned out the house, I found a stack of account books recording the cost of trips, even down to a postage stamp or a tube of toothpaste. It was a habit that made him a good business man, but a habit that became something of a problem as he grew older.

My parents returned to Hardwick August 26, 1924 and began their married life in the apartment over the store. Years later, Leone Cobb, my mother's best friend, told me that my grandfather tried to get them to move into his house, but my mother would not consider it. My grandmother (my mother's mother) did move in with them at some point, so their lives were not entirely private. My father became a partner with my grandfather in the store, and he purchased it within a few years. My mother became a homemaker. In another age she probably would have continued teaching, but in Hardwick, and in a great many other communities in 1924, it was unthinkable, and against the law, for a married woman to teach. Eventually my mother served on the school board for more than thirty continuous years, and in that capacity she defended and represented the teachers. Leone Cobb once told me that on one occasion, in addressing a new group of women teachers, my mother announced that one advantage of teaching in Hardwick was that they might emulate her example and marry a local businessman. Willa Cather remarks somewhere that "The world broke in two in 1922 or thereabouts." She meant that on one side of the divide was the Victorian World and on the other the world of modernism. My parents remained mostly on the Victorian side of the divide.

In August 1926 my sister Florence was born, and my mother started another photo album. I was born in 1931 and my younger sister, Marjorie, in 1934. I look at a photo of my father and mother, my great aunt and grandmother along with my sister when she was about one year old in 1927. It occurs to me that they were a happy family, getting along fine without me. I make my first appearance in the album in March 1931. I am two and a half months old and I lie placidly on a bed, the picture of health. But I was often sick as a child. I had eczema and a hernia and I had my tonsils and adenoids removed all before I was a year old. Then I had measles, mumps, chicken pox, and whooping cough. More devastating, I was allergic to cats and horses among other things. Often I found it difficult to breathe, and I was diagnosed with asthma. There is no photographic record of my illness, but the smell of Vicks VaboRub reminds me of agonizing nights. Eventually I outgrew most of my childhood troubles. I recall them now, not through a photograph, but because of a chance aroma.

The photos in this album provide a record of my sisters and me as we grew up. The last pictures are about 1940. After that, my mother gave up on the albums, and the occasional snapshots were stored in the desk drawer. They became an unprocessed archive rather than a narrative. Still, they help me recall and reconstruct, and some photos cause a flood of memories. There is a snapshot of me helping my father wash the car, a 1928 Willys-Knight. I remember that car well—its running boards, its spare tire on the back, the prominent fenders—because my father did not trade it in for a new car until 1940, but I have no memory of helping my father wash the car. In the photo, taken by my mother, the car is in the driveway . It is a warm day, perhaps early summer, and in the left background, recorded by accident, is sawmill housed in an old bobbin factory. I loved to sneak down there to watch the logs move toward the screaming saw. The lumber was stored on a portion of the lot behind our house, and the lumber stacks were wonderful places to play. A few years before my father died, when I visited him, I suddenly had a flashbulb of memory of watching a blacksmith at work, of being fascinated by the bellows, the hot coals, and the sound of the metal being struck on the anvil. I asked my father if there was ever a blacksmith shop nearby. "There was a blacksmith in the corner of the mill," he replied. For once my memory and what was real seemed to agree.

Another photograph catches my eye. Taken about 1936, it shows me at the age of perhaps five and a half. I am holding a lake trout that almost equals my size. I am standing in front of the house in Hardwick between my father and grandfather. My grandfather is wearing a suit with shirt and tie and a hat. My father has on a shirt and tie but no hat. I am dressed in shorts and a light shirt. I suspect that my father and grandfather have returned from an early morning fishing trip to Greensboro. On their successful return my mother probably got out the camera to document the big trout, and she included me in the photo. But it is possible that I have invented a story to go with the picture. The photo is over-exposed and we are all looking into the sun, but as I examine it carefully it takes on new significance. It is the only photo I have of three generations of Davis men. We all have "Freeman" as a middle name. My grandfather, Charles Freeman Davis, was born in 1864 a few months after his uncle, Charles Freeman, died at Andersonville, the notorious Confederate prison in Georgia. I heard that story many times as I was growing up, and I learned the significance of my middle name. We have now extended the tradition to five generations, for I gave the name to one of my sons, and one of my grandsons uses Freeman as a middle name. This blurred photograph is the only one I have of Charles Freeman, Harold Freeman, and Allen Freeman all standing together.

Some of the most interesting photographs in the album and the archives are those that are blurred, out of focus, or flawed in other ways. Each fall, my mother tried to take a photograph of me and my sisters to send to friends at Christmas time. Perhaps she succeeded in creating a group portrait, but it was often difficult to get us all to smile at the same time. In one failed picture, my older sister Florence is apparently berating me for fooling around, just as older sisters often do. In another, my friend Bill Pilbin sneaks into the photo, ruining it as a Christmas gift, but making it, many years later, one of the most compelling snapshots in the collection.

One formal family portrait survives from about 1943. It may have been commissioned because my older sister was about to leave for college, and this was a last attempt to record the family while it was still together. My parents are in their late 40s. I am about twelve and my sisters nine and seventeen. My mother and father are seated with my younger sister, Marjorie, standing between them. Florence and I are standing in the back. My parents are quite serious, but all the children have a slight smile, prompted, I am sure, by the local photographer, J.C. Spaulding.

I remember walking up two flights of stairs in the Hardwick Trust Building to his studio. My memory suggests that I did this frequently, but this is the only formal portrait that survives. Spaulding, tall and dressed impeccably would dash from his camera to adjust a curtain on his window or sky light, then dash back to hide under his hooded camera, only to dash to adjust the position of one of his subjects. The process seemed to take forever, but he managed to document my family during wartime. My hair is carefully combed and I am wearing a suit with a necktie carefully knotted. My father also has on a suit with shirt and tie while my mother has on a rather formal dress. It is not the stylized portrait of the upper class family, but we look solidly middle class. As I study the photograph of the Davis family, it occurs to me that one reason that I was not especially close to either of my sisters when I was growing up was that I was separated by nearly five years from Florence and more than three from Marjorie. Sometimes I felt like an only child.

About 1945, somebody gave me a Kodak Brownie camera, and I proceeded to document my adventures. Unfortunately I never got around to editing those photos to create an album. But my younger sister, Marjorie, told the story of her life in two carefully organized books. She knew she was dying and she set out, I suppose, to tell the story of her life while she had a chance. She starts with a section that she calls: "Undated Beginning." Here she borrows from the family albums to tell the story of her childhood and then she goes on to document her high school and graduate school years. It could be a sad story, but it is not, because my sister had a sense of humor and a penchant for detail. Her captions are informative, her photos carefully organized to tell her story. She created a legacy for all those who came after.

Photographs are an imperfect record of the past. Our photo albums contain few indoor shots and none of people working. My generation had their growing-up years recorded with black and white images. Color prints did not emerge until the 1950s. Now those images are faded. They seem less real than the earlier black and white shots. I have no photograph of my mother in the kitchen or my father at the store. I have many snapshots taken outdoors on perfect summer days, but few that record winter scenes. Yet many of my memories of growing up in Vermont are of winter, which was cold and unrelenting. Snow lay on the ground, sometimes several feet deep, from Thanksgiving to Easter. The average annual snowfall was nearly 140 inches, and the temperature dropped to 40 degrees below zero for at least a few days each year. One February, perhaps in 1943, it was so cold, with highs of 20 below, that school was closed because it was impossible to heat the building. When I think of winter I recall the particular sound made when walking on snow with the thermometer below zero and how the extreme cold sucks your breath away and makes your ears tingle. I also recall that on very cold days the smoke from the chimneys went straight up. Years later, when I experienced intense cold in Alaska, Finland or Minnesota, I was reminded of my childhood in Vermont.

I survived winter in part because I learned to ski. At first I used three-foot skis held on by rubber bands cut from inner tubes, and I tried to negotiate the slight incline on the back lot behind our house. How old was I? Perhaps five or six. I recall the sense of frustration as I went a few feet and then fell into the snow. However I persisted and eventually graduated to seven-foot, ridge-top hickory skis made by Lund in Norway. We skied on Cannon Hill behind the Academy Building. The hill had no ski tow. We had to climb up using the side-step or the herring-bone before we could get one quick run down. Our square-toed boots and bindings left the heel free to move, so we used the same skis for downhill and cross-country. We tried to master the Arlberg style, knees slightly bent, a low crouch, then lift and swing into the turn. But any style was difficult on the narrow trails we packed through the woods. It was exhilarating to go straight down a steep hill and just as much fun to travel across the frozen landscape. I learned to appreciate the stark beauty of Vermont, and I often went skiing alone after school. One photograph survives of me when I was twelve, taken as I returned from one of those adventures. My wooden skis tower over my head and my woolen jacket is covered with snow, the result of a fall, I am sure. Other winter memories come flooding back—snowball fights and snow forts, endless shoveling to keep the sidewalks and the driveway clear, overshoes that were difficult to buckle with cold fingers, snow plows, including the horse-drawn sidewalk plow, the way men and women who wore glasses had those glasses steam up when they came into the warm kitchen on a sub-zero day. It is that intense cold that I recall most vividly. And there are no photographs to document that feeling.

My earliest memory that I can document has nothing to do with a photograph; instead it concerns the birth of my sister Marjorie when I was a little over three. Marjorie was born on March 25, 1934. I recall vividly being lifted up (perhaps by my father) to get my first look at my new baby sister. However, that's not why I remember the incident. A woman took care of my sister Florence (who was seven and a half) and me, or perhaps she was a nurse. Was her name Mrs. Underwood? I had a "Buck Rogers" pistol which someone had given me and, at least in my memory, it could fire little sticks if I forced them into the muzzle. My mother had warned me not to put sticks into the gun because I might hurt someone. While my mother was "confined" in the bedroom downstairs I got a stick stuck in the gun. After trying to get it out myself, I finally went to seek help from Mrs. Underwood, but she couldn't get it out either. "When your mother is better," she announced, "she will get it out." That didn't solve my problem. What I remember is my guilt for doing something that my mother warned me against and my determination to solve the problem so she wouldn't find out about it. My memory, however, does not include the resolution to my dilemma.

Most of my childhood memories float free of time and are like mental snapshots that come back to me from time to time, called up by a smell, a taste, a place, or some unconscious and mysterious mechanism. One other memory that I can date is the Hurricane of 1938 that devastated New England in September. There was massive destruction along the east coast, especially in Massachusetts, Connecticut, Rhode Island, and Long Island. Over six hundred people lost their lives. Instead of going out to sea, the storm moved up the Connecticut River Valley, and across Vermont. There had been several days of heavy rain before the storm hit, saturating the ground and making the trees vulnerable to the storm. Most of the trees were uprooted rather than broken off.

The storm hit Hardwick in the early evening on Friday. I was seven and a half and in the second grade. I remember going to the movies that night at the Idle Hour Theater, paying my ten cents and sitting in the hard seats in the first five rows reserved for children. I went, as I usually did, with my best friends Harry and Bill Pilbin, who were two and three years older than I. We had just gotten seated when the lights went off. After a few minutes the owner of the theater (Mr. Carr?) announced that there would be no movie and that we should all go home as quickly as possible. I don't remember whether or not we got our money back. As we walked home the wind and the rain increased and we had difficulty walking. As we backed our way into the teeth of the wind, already approaching hurricane force, we watched a large elm tree, only a hundred feet away, come crashing down into the street. It didn't seem dangerous, only exciting.

My mother was happy when I arrived home, a little wet and windblown. I joined my sisters as we looked out of the small window halfway up the stairs and watched other trees come down. The electricity was off, so we lit several kerosene lamps that had been stored in one of the cabinets for just such an occasion. My father went to the store to make sure that nothing was left outside that could be destroyed. While he was there the wind rolled up the tin roof and sent it sailing several hundred yards away. We got through the night, and the next day we wandered around inspecting the damage. Men were already out with saws and axes attacking the fallen trees. In 1938 there were very few gasoline-powered chain saws, so it was a slow and laborious process to remove the debris. On Sunday we drove to Greensboro to inspect the camp. We discovered that a fallen tree had narrowly missed the camp and the garage. A great many trees were down and a number of camps were badly damaged. On Monday morning it was exciting to go to school, picking our way around the fallen trees.

This is the way I remember the Hurricane of 1938, and it is the story I have been telling for many years. Three or four years ago while researching my book on Vermont postcards I did a little research on the famous hurricane, and I discovered to my surprise that the storm hit on September 21, 1938, a Wednesday, not a Friday. As I thought about my story of going to the movies with my friends, I realized that it was highly unlikely that my mother would have permitted me to go to the movies on a stormy night in the middle of the week when I was only in the second grade. In constructing my narrative I had probably taken an incident from some years later (because I did frequently go to the movies with my friends on Friday night when I was ten or twelve) and added it to my story. Schools were probably closed Thursday and Friday, thus confusing my memory.

Only five people died in Vermont in the Great Hurricane of 1938, but the damage was widespread. My Uncle Lovell tapped 3,500 trees in his big sugar place in Craftsbury in the spring of 1938, but only a few scattered trees were left standing after the storm. He never tapped that sugar orchard again. There was great damage in Greensboro and many large trees fell in Hardwick. There are no photographs of the hurricane in the family albums, but there are many snapshots of the flood of 1927. Perhaps floods seemed more newsworthy than hurricanes. I have read the newspaper accounts of the storm, but that does not help much. The other narratives that I have constructed to explain my life are probably also flawed, but that is the nature of memory, and history.

Chapter 3

GRANDMOTHERS

When I was growing up in Hardwick during the 1930s, most of my friends had a grandmother living with them at home. Some of these grandmothers spoke with an Italian or French accent, or with a Scotch brogue that made them difficult to understand. In my memory, they all had white hair, and they were constantly present. Some were strict and quarrelsome, others were calm and pleasant, but a grandmother seemed always to be in the house when I visited my friends. There were a few elderly couples, but in a town where granite workers often died tragically young of silicosis, there were many widows. In the days before retirement centers, nursing homes, and monthly social security checks, a widow usually lived with her daughter. There were many three-generation families in Hardwick. I remember several families consisting of a grandmother, a mother, and children. There were whispers around town suggesting that it wasn't quite natural for a boy to grow up with only women in the home. He might easily become a sissy or effeminate. More natural, it seemed, was for two older women to live together. No one I knew called these arrangements "Boston marriages," or the women "lesbians"—a word I never heard when I was growing up. But everyone accepted the presence of a grandmother in the house. A family legend reports that on one occasion, when I was three, we visited relatives in a neighboring town on a Sunday afternoon. I was confused by the two old ladies in the house and I asked in a loud voice:" Why do they have two grandmothers?" I apparently had a sense, based on my own household, about how the world should be organized, and it did not include two grandmothers in one house. I have no memory of this incident, though I do remember visiting elderly relatives, even one house in Craftsbury where there were three grandmothers, or rather two great aunts and a distant cousin. I did not like their powdered cheeks, which I was forced to kiss.

I had two grandmothers. My mother's mother, Lola Wylie Allen (1858–1940), lived with us from my earliest memory. I called her "Gramma." My other grandmother was really a step-grandmother, my grandfather, Charles F. Davis' second wife. His first wife had died in 1923, and in 1926 he married a widow, Sara Clark Holton Davis (1867–1957). She lived with my grandfather in a large house between my father's store and my house. I called her "Gramma Davis."

I liked both of my grandmothers, but I was closest to the Gramma who lived in my house. She died in October 1940 when I was a few months short of ten years old, so my memories are filtered through my childhood impressions and are difficult to date. Very few photographs survive, and I seem to recall that she did not like to have her picture taken. There is a formal portrait in an oval frame taken by a professional photographer when she was perhaps forty. Her brown hair is done in braids and then turned into a bun. It is a serious picture, and she has a serene and peaceful look. That is the way I remember her—quiet and self composed. She used to sit in a rocking chair by the window in the kitchen knitting, crocheting, basting a hem, braiding a rug, mending clothes, or repairing socks by placing a wooden, darning egg inside the sock so that even a large hole in a heel or toe could be mended. She had a large tin filled with buttons. When a button disappeared from a shirt or a dress she would look in the tin until she found a match. Nothing was discarded in my family in the 1930s until it had been mended several times; even sheets that had worn thin were cut down the middle and then sewn back together with the worn spots on the outside. When clothes or sheets were too worn to use, they were assigned to a rag bag and reused for cleaning and for making rugs and quilts. I still have a braided rug that my grandmother was working on when she died. It was completed by Mrs. Jackson, the grandmother next door. It is easy to tell my grandmother's work (which is woven much tighter), from the looser style of the woman next door.

My family's habit of mending, repairing, reusing and recycling in the 1930s owed something to the Depression, but it was also the continuation of the old "waste not, want not" ways of the nineteenth century that my grandmother brought to the household. She criticized the way my sisters and I wasted paper; she told us that when she was a girl, paper was valuable and had to be used carefully and reused over and over again. She made soap using scraps of beef fat, wood ashes and lye. The soap was a gray liquid and never replaced the more modern soap powders, but I am sure she did it out of a habit acquired when she was growing up on a farm. She also saved slivers of soap, put them in a metal cage with a handle, and then used that to create soap suds for doing dishes. She showed me how to make candles in a mold and how to dip candles using melted paraffin. She had a quart of butter milk delivered to the house every week. I suppose it reminded her of her youth when butter milk was a by-product of making butter, the main cash crop of late nineteenth century Vermont dairy farms. My mother used butter milk for cooking, but my grandmother thought it was good to drink. I never liked plain milk, and I liked buttermilk, with its little lumps, even less.

In my memory, my grandmother was always surrounded by old objects—books, a family bible, photographs of ancestors, jewelry, and lace doilies. I would often sit in her room and listen to her tell stories. She was also famous for her old "sayings" that were often a combination of folklore and rural wisdom. She was a weather forecaster: "Red sky at night, sailor's delight. Red sky in the morning, sailor take warning." When I planned a fishing trip and woke up disappointed because it was raining, she would say simply: "rain before seven, clear before eleven." I discovered later that the weather didn't always work that way, but at the time it was comforting, and I have always remembered it. When I was impatient or impulsive she would say: "a watched pot never boils," or "don't count your chickens before they hatch," or "don't bite off more than you can chew." Many of her sayings I discovered later came from Benjamin Franklin or from other sources, but as a child I thought they were original. If something was worthless or cheap she said it was "not worth a hill of beans." I knew what she meant because we had a garden, but we planted beans in rows and corn in hills. She called "pants," "trousers," and she called trash "rubbish." She referred to her bureau, as a "chiffonier," her room as a "chamber," and she called all frying pans "spiders." She taught me many useful things such as:" a pint's a pound the world around." And she showed me that there were two cups to a pint and two pints to a quart, eight quarts to a peck and four pecks to a bushel. She taught me how to peel an apple and not break the peel—the trick was to move the apple, not the knife. And she showed me how to thread a needle—it was easier to put the needle into the thread and not the other way around. When I was quiet and lost in my own thoughts she would ask: "Cat got your tongue?" When I was sick she would say I looked "a little peaked," but she would bring me water, read me stories, and rub my back. She fixed lemon and honey to cure my sore throat, and she taught me to swallow ten times without breathing to cure the hiccups. When I skinned a knee I went to her for sympathy and a hug. Yet she thought I read too much when I should be out playing, so occasionally she would criticize me: "You have your head in the clouds" or "Your nose is always in a book."

My grandmother helped around the house, set the table, swept the floor, prepared vegetables, but I don't recall her cooking or using the sewing machine. She was always there to greet me when I came home from school and she always supported my projects. She favored me over my two sisters, perhaps because I was a boy. She told me one day that when she was young she wished that she had been born a boy. When I asked her why, she said that boys had more opportunities, could do more things. Once when I tried to build a snow fort on a mild winter day, she supplied me with dry mittens all afternoon. She kept an extra pair drying in the warming oven over the stove so that I could swap my wet mittens for a dry pair. I don't remember whether or not I ever completed the fort, but she told my mother that I had "gumption," and that, from her was high praise.

I always looked forward to the first of May when I was a youngster. It was the opening of the trout season and the Pilbin boys and I got up about five o'clock to attempt to catch brook trout in one of the local streams. She would get up before my parents to prepare my breakfast. I remember once she said: "I bet you didn't sleep much last night." When I asked how she knew that, she told me how she would lay awake as a girl anticipating an exciting event. I marveled at her wisdom and I usually believed her stories. One night I walked in my sleep (a habit I had when young) and embarrassed myself by walking into the bedroom of a guest who was staying with us. She consoled me by describing how she walked around her house one night with no clothes on when she was a girl. One of my favorite snacks as a youngster was dried apricots. I remember she told me not to eat too many because they would swell in my stomach. To this day the taste and smell of dried apricots reminds me of my grandmother.

I spent many hours in her room listening to her stories. She recalled hearing that Lincoln had been shot when she was seven. She also remembered her own grandmother was born in 1792, the year after Vermont became a state. It occurred to me many years later that with two leaps of memory I could recover the entire history of the country. Lola Wylie was born on a farm in Craftsbury in 1858. She was Scots-Irish, or Ulster Scot, in background, though she would have denied any ethnic alliance. Her family came originally from northern Ireland to Marblehead, Massachusetts in 1729. They moved to Voluntown, Connecticut because as Presbyterians, they were not appreciated in Congregationalist Massachusetts. Her great-grandfather served in the Revolution, making her eligible to become a member of the Daughters of the American Revolution, but she was not interested. She was proud of her family and the farm that her grandfather first settled in 1829. She once told me (or was it my mother?) that her great-grandfather had been an aide to General Washington. I discovered many years later that he was a private in General Washington's Army. He served for three months, took part in the Battle of Brooklyn Heights, and retreated with Washington's Army to Manhattan Island. Such is the nature of family legends.

In my memory I see my grandmother as a slightly stooped little woman with gray hair. How to reconcile that image with the stereograph view taken about 1880 when she was twenty-two and recently married? She is a trim, attractive, well-dressed young woman who stands with her husband of one year and her parents in front of a Greek Revival farm house. She looks confident, young, and happy. As a farmer's daughter, and then a farmer's wife in a small town in northern Vermont, she lived a rather simple and restricted life. Yet a diary kept by her husband (my grandfather) the year before they were married revealed a life with many activities, including croquet parties and oyster suppers, lectures and music. Much of the social life seemed to center around the Methodist Church, for the family had switched denominations somewhere along the way. She appears in Henry Allen's diary as one of several young women he was courting by meeting them at church and offering to drive them home. Her little town of Craftsbury was ten miles from the nearest railroad, but she traveled to Burlington and St. Johnsbury, and her family took one major trip. They went to Chicago in 1893 to attend the World Columbian Exposition, and to visit Wylie relatives who had migrated to Illinois. I have a plate and a map they brought back as souvenirs. Her son (my uncle), who was four at the time, once told me that all he remembered from the fair was a log cabin made of butter.

My grandmother had many tragedies in her life. She lost her older brother, who was fifteen, when she was twelve, and her older sister died at twenty when she was fourteen. She told me how much she admired her brother. Perhaps she treated me as a replacement for the brother she lost, or for the son who always seemed to disappoint her. Most devastating of all, her husband died suddenly at the age of forty-five when she was forty-three, leaving her with a son twelve and a daughter (my mother) only five. My uncle once told me that one of the hired men came to him and said: "If you want to see your father alive you better come quick." My grandmother was stunned by the loss. Still, she managed to run the big farm with the help of hired men. When my mother graduated from high school in 1913 she rented the farm and moved to Burlington where she ran a boarding house to enable my mother to attend the University of Vermont. My grandmother was part of an unsung generation of widows who worked hard and sacrificed much to give their daughters the opportunities they never had.

My grandmother Allen lived with my family for as long as I can remember, but she did not move to the camp in

Greensboro as we always did in mid-June. She said she didn't like the water, but I expect she also wanted to give the family a vacation without her, so she and the cat moved to the farm in Craftsbury for most of the summer. I thought the farm belonged to my Uncle Lovell, but my grandmother still owned it. I now realize that the reason my uncle often dropped by for dinner at our house was that he needed my grandmother to sign a note for a loan from the bank. My grandmother worried about my uncle. He was wild, tended to drink too much, and when he was young he frequently got into trouble. A few years ago I was doing some research in the town clerk's office in Craftsbury when the clerk, who knew my family, came over with one of the old vital record books and said, "I think you will be amused by this." He showed me the birth record of a baby girl in 1910. There was listed the mother's name but under "father" the doctor had written: "Said to be Lovell Allen." He was reporting the rumors that were circulating around town. I heard other rumors about him when I was a boy, but he still was my favorite uncle.

My grandmother always said that if she lived through October and November she would live for another year. Later I discovered that her brother and sister, her mother, her husband, and many other relatives, had died in the fall. She died on October 19, 1940. Her death was a traumatic experience for me because she died very early in the morning in the room next to mine. I heard her struggle, her cries of pain and, even though I was only nine, I knew what was happening. Finally I got up to go to the bathroom and my mother put her arm around me (something she rarely did) and said: "You don't have a grandmother anymore." I was devastated by her death. I sat in a daze through the funeral, held in the family farmhouse in Craftsbury, but I refused to go to the cemetery because I did not want to see her casket lowered into the ground. My grandmother died when I was nine, yet she lives on in my memory.

My other grandmother, "Gramma Davis," lived a few

doors away from my house. Although she was nine years younger than my grandmother Allen, she also had gray hair and seemed old to me. She had two passions—flowers and music. When she was staying at camp in Greensboro with my grandfather, she often played the little foot-pump Estey organ in the living room while everyone gathered around to sing. She had fresh flowers in every corner of the camp, not just on the dining room table. At her home in Hardwick, she had the best flower garden in town, and she grew poinsettias in the winter. They always bloomed just in time to decorate the United Church for Christmas. And this was long before florist shops, let alone the grocery stores, sold greenhouse-forced poinsettias, and made them commonplace rather than exotic.

I went with my grandparents on expeditions to collect wildflowers in the spring. She looked for many different kinds and knew the Latin names for every variety. Painted trillium and trailing arbutus were her favorites. I collected pine branches and various kinds of vines for her in the late fall for the Christmas wreathes she gave many of her friends. I recall the smell of her kitchen and the taste of her bran muffins and filled cookies. The entire family gathered at her house for Thanksgiving. Most of all, I remember long conversations with her about the books I was reading or about an article in the latest *National Geographic* magazine. I don't recall similar conversations with my grandfather, Charles F. Davis. In fact, I got along better with my grandmother. My grandfather was stubborn, a little gruff, and we had a guarded relationship. He did tell me stories about the Davis family, but they were not really discussions. Gramma Davis and I usually sat in her living room, especially in the afternoon. It was furnished with Arts and Crafts furniture and had a library table stacked high with books and magazines. There was also a parlor, but that was used only when she played the piano. We never talked on Saturday afternoon because that was the day she listened to the radio broadcast of operas.

My grandparents' house on South Main Street in Hardwick was built in 1913. Before it was completed, the family lived in an apartment over the store. The house was large and solid, built in a style sometimes called "Foursquare." It had a large porch that wrapped around half the front and the entire left side. There was a front entrance on one side of the porch and a door into the kitchen on the other. It was painted in two tones, a light cream on the first floor and a dark brown on the second. The house was probably based on a standard pattern, but altered by my grandfather. He always claimed that it was the world's best house. No one else, that I know, agreed, but it was an attractive house with hardwood floors, five or six bedrooms upstairs and all the modern features for the time. It was one of the most impressive houses built in Hardwick during the granite boom years. It had a walk-out basement with laundry tubs and a washing machine located well away from the kitchen. Unlike my house it had no carriage house attached and no backstairs to a maid's room. Even though he owned several other lots, my grandfather chose a small lot within easy walking distance to his store rather than a larger lot in another part of town. Built at the beginning of the automobile age, the house was constructed close to the South Main Street (which was also the main highway to Barre and Montpelier), and within a few years the road was widened and began to encroach on the front yard. Even though he was one of the first in town to buy an auto, my grandfather built a house without a garage—instead he constructed a separate garage some distance away. Still, I liked the house, and at some point I was given the task of watering my grandmother's many house plants while she was staying at camp in August and September. It was a job I enjoyed. I liked the coolness and the smell of the basement on a hot day, and I loved being in the house alone. I often visited the bedroom on the second floor that my grandparents used as a storeroom. I would spend hours poring over old *National Geographic* magazines, copies of *The Atlantic Monthly* and other magazines. Sometimes my mother came looking for me wondering why it had taken so long to water the plants.

I remember my grandmother as an old woman in her seventies and eighties. It is difficult for a child, even for an adult, to comprehend what grandparents were like before we were born, before our memory. I can recover some of my Grandmother Davis' early life, because she was so angry when her son put her in a nursing home when she was eighty-nine that she wrote her autobiography. She wrote it in longhand, but in a typed version it comes to about thirty-five pages.

Sara Clark was born in New Hampshire only two years after the end of the Civil War, but she grew up in Vineland, New Jersey. She recounts in her autobiography how she made a trip as a little girl with her father to the New Jersey Shore to cut salt hay for the horses. She also remembers going to the Centennial Exposition in Philadelphia when she was nine. And she writes of taking the overnight ferry from Fall River, Massachusetts to New York City, a trip made more exciting because the ferry caught fire. She described herself as a tomboy. "I climbed to the tops of the tallest trees and swayed back and forth and thought nothing of going up to the ridge pole of the barn," she writes. It is hard for me to imagine the elegant, gray-haired old lady that I knew as a tomboy, even hard for me to picture her as young. At some point the family returned to New Hampshire, but after graduating from high school, Sara taught school for a year and then spent a year in Washington, D.C., where her uncle taught Latin and Greek at Howard University. She was enthralled by the concerts, the museums, and the social whirl in the nation's capital. She also recalls visiting Asheville, North Carolina, where another brother, a self-taught botanist, worked for the Vanderbilts before Richard Morris Hunt designed "Biltmore," the huge mansion modeled after a French chateau. She traveled most of the way by train, but the last few miles were in a horse-drawn taxi. She was so excited by all the flowers along the road that she had never seen before that she kept asking the driver to stop to allow her to pick specimens. She arrived at the estate with a huge bouquet.

In another era, Sara Clark might have become a botanist herself. However, a Washington friend recognized her musical talent (she had learned to play the organ when she was nine) and encouraged her to enroll at the New England Conservatory of Music in Boston. She studied voice as well as organ and piano, but her career plans were interrupted and her life course changed when she fell in love with Russell Holton, a farmer from Hardwick, Vermont. He was the brother of one of her Boston friends. In her autobiography there is only a hint of regret, only a moment of wonder, at the age of eighty-nine, about what her life might have been if marriage had not altered her career plans. The young couple was married in Boston by Minot Savage, the liberal and controversial clergyman, who was one of the first Protestant ministers to adapt Charles Darwin's theories of evolution to his theology and his preaching.

Sara and Russell Holton moved in the early 1890s to a farm on Holton Hill overlooking Hardwick, a village that was just beginning to grow and prosper as a granite center. The life of a farmer's wife in a provincial town in northern Vermont must have seemed dull after the excitement and cultural stimulation of Boston and Washington, but she made the best of it. "I loved the farm, the pasture hills, the sugar wood, and the meadow land," she recalled. "I knew them all from wandering in search of wild flowers." Despite the duties of a farm wife, she still found time for music. She played the organ at church on Sunday, and she taught piano and voice to the young students in Hardwick and neighboring towns. Even after her two children were born, she drove her horse and carriage once a week to Greensboro (seven miles) and another day to Wolcott (six miles) where she spent the entire day giving individual music lessons. She hired a young woman to care for her children while she was gone, but her husband objected to her being away, so eventually she gave up her weekly trips. She does not spell out the exact nature of his objections, yet he probably felt it was not an appropriate role for a lady, and he wanted her home to get his supper.

When Sara Holton gave up most of her private music pupils, she poured her energy into directing the choir at the Baptist Church. She also organized a discussion group and a women's quartet, and for twenty years she played the organ and directed the choir at the Congregational Church, where she was a member. "I loved the different combinations and stops and spent hours, *just listening*," she remembered.

Russell Holton died in 1918. Sara supported her family by giving music lessons and by her other musical activities until 1926, when she married Charles F. Davis. Sara Holton also married Greensboro and Caspian Lake, for Charles had built a cottage on the lake in 1923 on land his first wife, Florence Haines Davis, had purchased in 1913. "Caspian Lake is a beautiful spot and all our relatives on both sides of the house loved to visit," she wrote. According to the camp register, kept sporadically by various family members, she also enjoyed entertaining the Good Hearted Club from the Congregational (and then the United) Church in Hardwick and many times the large dining room table was expanded with extra leaves to accommodate a dozen or more friends and relatives. Through the years, Sara Holton Davis tried to transform the camp into a Victorian cottage, while my grandfather wanted to keep it a camp. Eventually she bought the first electric refrigerator with her own money.

I have several photographs taken at the Davis camp in the 1930s when the Holton clan gathered for family reunions in August. Three generations are arranged carefully by an unknown family photographer. Some are seated in chairs brought outside from the camp. Others stand in back while children are grouped in front or sit on the laps of the adults. The older men wear shirts and ties, and the women wear dresses. It may have been Sunday, but in the 1930s one dressed even when at camp. In all of the photographs, Sara Clark Holton Davis is in front, surrounded by her grandchildren.

This last part of her autobiography, which only takes up a few pages, intersects with my memory. She describes an auto trip to Florida in 1935. I have some of the postcards she sent to my sister and me during that adventure. At the camp, Sara Holton Davis' grandchildren's names are still recorded on the kitchen wall, marked off year after year as they grew older in the 1930s and 1940s. The Estey organ is no longer there, but her flower vases are put to good use every summer, and many things around the camp remind me of her. If she had not taken the trouble to write down her memories I would have no knowledge of her early life. I use her as an example when I urge others to write down their memories, and one shouldn't wait until age 89.

Margaret Mead writes about the importance of grandmothers to pass on traditions and folkways to the younger generation. I certainly learned a great deal from my two grandmothers, but as I think about all the grandmothers I knew in Hardwick, I realize there were advantages and disadvantages to those three-generation families. They introduced the reality of old age, sickness, even death into our young lives. The grandmothers were readily available babysitters, and they could start dinner when the mother was away. Yet the presence of a grandmother often crowded the small houses in Hardwick, many of them originally built to rent to granite workers. My friends Harry and Bill Pilbin shared the same bed, in part because their grandmother needed a room of her own. Even in my large house, the presence of my grandmother caused the juggling of sleeping arrangements. I loved my grandmother and she taught me much of value. Yet she did not get along well with my older sister, who used to complain that she could do nothing right in our grandmother's opinion. I witnessed the tension between generations in other households as the old ways clashed with the new. Without a mother to care for, my mother might have gone to graduate school, but without a grandmother living in the house. I would have missed a special education. The grandmothers in Hardwick passed on a rural tradition of old ways and small towns. Some of them told stories of the old country. My grandmothers extended my memory to a time before I was born.

Chapter 4

ORANGE CRATES AND OTHER MATERIAL CULTURE

My small town in northern Vermont in the 1930s and early 1940s, was stuck in another era, and the old ways persisted longer than in the expanding cities and suburbs. I grew up with objects and artifacts already considered obsolete or old-fashioned in many parts of the country. Wooden boxes and barrels, wood-burning stoves, old-fashioned washing machines, and iceboxes came from an earlier era. My uncle's farm and my father's general store also recalled days gone by. I did not realize it at the time, but the material culture and the rituals of my childhood would soon disappear. After World War II even the small towns and farms of northern Vermont joined the modern age.

The Glenwood Range

Until sometime after World War II, when my parents finally bought an electric stove, the black, cast-iron, wood burning range dominated the kitchen. The gas stove had been adopted in the cities in the 1920s, often replacing coal stoves, and the electric stove grew in popularity in the 1930s. One study suggests that only five percent of middle-class families still used wood or coal stoves in 1935. Hardwick was different: before the war everyone used a wood stove. The fire box of the Glenwood Range was on the left and the oven in front. The left side contained a door through which the ashes could be removed, and a smaller door above it that served as a damper to regulate the heat. There was another door in front through which wood could be pushed into the fire box, and wood could also be added through the two round openings on top of the stove. There were two additional round openings to the right. These were all covered with round iron lids that could be removed with a special tool that fit into a slot in each cover. This tool is called a "stove lid lifter" in the 1897 *Sears Catalog*. I have several examples at my Greensboro camp, and they form part of my material-culture quiz for visitors of a generation too young to remember the old ways. This now antique tool always stumps them. They cannot imagine what it was used for, but it was absolutely necessary to lift the lid on a hot stove without getting burned. The left side of the stove was hotter than the right; pots could be moved to the right to cook more slowly. Although some wood stoves had a reservoir to heat water, our hot water came from a tank connected to the furnace in the basement. A tea kettle sat permanently on the back of the stove, always ready for a cup of tea. It served the additional function of adding humidity to the room on cold days. A warming oven extended above the stove top, and the heavy stove was supported by elaborate legs that sat on an asbestos mat designed to neutralize the occasional spark, or piece of burning wood, that inevitably escaped from the stove. Do I remember correctly that there was a thermometer on the oven door? To the right of the stove sat a large wood box. I think it was painted blue.

When I was a boy it was my task in the winter to fill it each morning before I went to school. During the winter my father would purchase several cords of hard wood. Perhaps he traded wood for groceries at the store. A farmer would come with a horse and wagon and throw the wood into the snow bank to the left of the driveway. The wood (maple, ash, or yellow birch) was cut into blocks about twelve to fifteen inches thick. When spring came and the wood began to emerge from the snow bank, it was my job to chop the wood into stove-size pieces and then stack them in the basement under the barn, where they would season for at least a year. I had to carry in two armloads of wood in the winter before I went to school; it was dusty and somewhat unpleasant work. I tolerated that chore, but I loved splitting and stacking the wood in the spring. Most of the wood split easily, though I had to use a wedge for the tougher pieces. There was something satisfying about the sound of the ax hitting the wood, especially the maple and the ash, and something triumphant about watching the two pieces fall apart after one blow. It was even fun to pick up several pieces of the green wood and to hear the "ping" as they hit together, and especially rewarding to watch the stacked wood in the basement of the barn gradually extend from one side to the other. Some Vermonters still judge their neighbors by the quality of their stacked wood pile.

I still enjoy splitting wood in the summer time, stacking it to dry before burning it in my fireplace in my camp in Greensboro. "Each stick I deal with has a history," Henry David Thoreau wrote in his journal on October 20, 1855, "and I read it as I am handling it, and, last of all, I remember my adventures in getting it, while it is burning on a winter evening. That is the most interesting part of its history." Like Thoreau's wood, the wood I carried in each morning while I was growing up had a history. When I now select a piece of wood for my fireplace at my camp in Greensboro I often think, "Oh, I remember that piece, it came from the old maple tree up near the road that came down three years ago."

My father started a fire in the stove when he got up in the morning, but in the winter there were often enough coals left over that all he had to do was open the damper and add wood. If the coals had gone out, a little kerosene and a quick strike with one of the wooden matches kept near the stove did the trick. About once a week I had to remove the ashes from the stove. A box with a handle pulled out from under the fire box. It was a little awkward to carry, but the wood ashes were much lighter than the coal ashes, and I usually threw them on the snow where the garden would emerge in the spring. Unlike coal ashes, which accumulated in piles, wood ashes added nutrients to the soil.

During the day my mother was in charge of the stove. She baked pies, cookies, cakes, bread, muffins, and other things in the oven while at the same time frying, boiling, steaming and poaching, and making donuts on top of the stove. I remember how she would open one of the lids to singe a chicken to burn off the unwanted hair. In my memory I can still smell the peculiar odor of the burning chicken. My mother regulated the stove's temperature by opening or closing the damper, adding a piece of wood or poking the wood in the firebox into flame. The stove required constant attention. The iron kitchen range, which used coal rather than wood in some models, seemed like a primitive cooking instrument. In fact, it was a great modern innovation adopted in the mid-nineteenth century to replace cooking in an open fireplace.

The kitchen stove was also a source of heat. My sisters and I raced downstairs on cold winter mornings to get dressed in front of the stove. The stove had a comforting warmth when I came in from outside on sub-zero days. I would rush toward the stove, take off my mittens, and warm my hands over the stove top. As a child I delighted in picking small pieces of snow off my woolen pants and jacket, dropping them on the hot stove top and watching and listening to them sizzle and skid around the lid before disappearing. The oven was also useful on cold days to dry mittens, although one had to be careful that the woolen mittens were not left in too long. Wet wool, when heated, gives off a distinctive smell, and that smell, when I encounter it today, always reminds me of my childhood, and the kitchen stove. One downside of burning wood was that creosote built up in the pipes and chimney, creating the potential for chimney fires. I remember being awakened very early one morning by firemen walking through my bedroom on their way to the attic to make sure a chimney fire did not spread to the roof.

My mother often tutored my older sister in Latin before she went off to school, and they both sat close to the open oven door, absorbing warmth and knowledge at the same time. During the summer, the heat given off by the kitchen range became a problem when "slaving over the hot stove" became an uncomfortable reality. We abandoned the Glenwood Range for the summer months. My father set up a kerosene stove which had two burners and an oven. I remember this temporary stove well because one summer, I burned my arm badly when I touched the boiling tea kettle. Most of that summer I went around covered with an ugly purple salve, which seemed to do little to heal the infected burn. During the winter my father set up an additional wood stove in the corner of the dining room, perhaps to save on coal, perhaps because the furnace did not heat every corner. This tall, black stove burned large chunks of wood with too many knots to split easily. Yet it is the kitchen range that was more important—the friendly warmth, the smell of the food cooking, together with my mother's greeting, are very much a part of my memory of my childhood.

Orange Crates

I grew up in a place and time when cardboard had not yet completely replaced the wooden box. An earlier age depended more on the wooden barrel, which could be both stacked and rolled. A few barrels survived, but wooden boxes were everywhere. At my father's store in the 1930s, many food items still arrived in wooden boxes of various sizes and shapes. Dried salt cod, prunes, raisins, apples, and bananas all had their special containers, and Vermont cheddar cheese came packed in round boxes. Even shoes, boots, rubbers, and other items were shipped in wooden standard railroad containers. Tea came in special boxes made in China and lined with tin, while cigar boxes were very useful for preserving little treasures. I kept extra stamps from my collection in a King Edward cigar box and my most valuable coins in another. We also found a use for discarded cans. Small tobacco cans were perfect for carrying earth worms on fishing expeditions, and lard pails were perfect for berry picking.

Wooden boxes could be used in a variety of ways. My father had several boxes nailed to the wall in the barn, which he used as a garage. Small boxes held nails, larger boxes became convenient storage for spare parts, paint cans, and countless other things. By far the most useful and interesting boxes were orange crates. They were about three feet long and eighteen inches deep, with the ends and a middle board made of half-inch pine, or some other soft wood, and thin boards nailed along the sides. There were spaces left so that air could circulate around the oranges. Unlike the bottle boxes, orange crates were discarded by the stores and anyone could easily acquire them. They still smelled of the oranges and occasionally had the remains of a rotten orange attached. Gaudy, colorful paper stickers, advertising the various brands from Florida and California, were attached to both ends. They represented exotic faraway lands, yet they were incredibly useful in many practical ways. One could add wheels to an orange crate and make a cart, add barrel staves and have a sled, turn them on end and use the crate as a night stand or a book case. My sister even turned two orange crates and a couple of boards into a dressing table. The end pieces of orange crates could also be sawed into various shapes to make guns for shooting rubber bands, although a notched stick made a better slingshot. Orange crates were great for furnishing the club houses and mountain huts and hideaways that my friends Harry and Bill Pilbin and I built, destroyed, and rebuilt many times. The Pilbin brothers, who were two and three years older than I, lived up the street with their mother and grandmother. We used scrap lumber from the Beede sawmill near the Cooper Brook, in the valley a half mile from my house, to build our huts. We also collected used dry-cell batteries from the telephone company and hooked them up so we could have an electric light. Our most successful and elaborate clubhouse was built on the back lot behind my house. Admittedly, I could not have built it alone. The Pilbin boys were skilled at working with wood and repairing electrical and mechanical equipment. Harry was especially talented. I read his obituary a few years ago, and I was not surprised to learn that he had dropped out of school and, after the Army, had spent most of his life working as an auto mechanic.

Orange crates were the most useful and exotic boxes, but soft drinks such as Coca-Cola and Moxie came in wooden boxes divided to allow twenty-four bottles to fit snugly without breaking. The empty bottles were placed back in the boxes and then picked up by the wholesaler and the bottles washed and refilled. In Hardwick our favorite soft drinks or sodas, sometimes called "pop," but never "tonic," were made by Barr's Better Beverages, a local softdrink manufacturer, located just down Plank Hill from my father's store. In our vernacular we called soda "belly wash," and Barr's Better Belly Wash had a nice ring to it. The bottling works were owned by the Barrs, an Italian-American family that had shortened their name at some point. But we did not think of them as Italian. Acquinaldo, whom we call "Pop" for the soda he produced, was a large, jovial man who always had an unlit cigar in his mouth. He called me "Skip Jr." because, for some reason, my father was called "Skip." Barrs produced wonderful flavors—fruit bowl, cream soda, lemon, ginger ale, orange, and other common varieties. We searched the dumps and roadsides for Barr's bottles. The small bottles could be turned in for two cents and the large bottles were worth five cents. In the 1930s even two cents bought several pieces of candy at my father's store.

Wash Day

Wash day in our house was always on Monday, as it was in most of the other houses in Hardwick. A few people sent their laundry to the commercial steam laundry, and there were a few women, mostly widows, who could be hired to come into the house to do the family laundry. My mother, as a matter of pride, did her own laundry. Before my father went to work at the store on Monday morning, which was always before 7 A.M., he rolled the washing machine (perhaps a 1930 model) from the back hall into the kitchen. The washing machine was hooked up to the faucets in the sink, and an outlet hose was also placed in the sink. Although it was hardly automatic it certainly was an improvement over the scrub board or the copper kettle, placed on top of the stove to boil clothes—methods still used for stubborn stains. My mother used soap powder (Rinso or Duz I think), not introduced until the 1920s, but she also had a yellow cake of Fels-Naptha for use with the scrub board. The washing machine had an up-and-down and side-to-side motion, but the wet clothes had to be removed by hand and put through the electric wringer and then dropped into a rinse tub. The wet clothes were removed from the rinse tub and put through the wringer again. Putting large items, like sheets, through the wringer could be tricky, and in my memory I see my mother stopping the wringer several times to make sure the clothes didn't get tangled or torn. By washing the white clothes first, and then the less soiled items, and finally the dirtiest clothes, my mother managed to avoid filling the machine more than once. Bluing was added to the rinse water for white clothes, and sometimes the clothes were rinsed twice before they were deposited in a large basket. My mother then carried the basket to the clotheslines in the backyard. Usually she did all these operations by herself, and everything had to be finished by noon because the whole family expected dinner even on wash day.

Occasionally, if there was no school on a Monday, my sisters and I were pressed into service to help with the various tasks, but washing clothes in our house was considered a woman's job. Washing machines were constantly being improved. Just before the war stopped production of household appliances, Lila Racette, who lived next door, purchased a new Bendix. All the children in the neighborhood gathered in her house to see the clothes go around through the little window in front. It was almost as exciting as the first television would be for the next generation.

During the winter I was assigned the chore of shoveling a path to the clothesline in the backyard. There was a basket filled with clothespins that hung on one of the lines. I can see my mother hanging sheets with several clothespins in her mouth as she held a corner of the sheet with one hand while using the other hand to attach the other corner.

On very cold winter days the sheets and other items sometimes froze solid. Long John underwear, or BVDs, would stand up unsupported and appear like some cartoon character. On those days I helped to bring the frozen clothes indoors and placed them on a clothes rack, set up near the kitchen stove. Automatic washers and dryers have ended the drudgery of wash day, but when I lived in the Netherlands for a year in the mid-1980s, I discovered that the Dutch, although they had automatic washing machines, rarely used dryers. Even the washing machines were much smaller than the American models. Because the machine heated its own water, it took a long time to spring into action once it was turned on. The Dutch, even in a wet country, still hung their clothes to dry on outside lines or on racks in their houses. In some third-world countries women still scrub their clothes in streams and rivers. How people do their laundry, just as how they prepare food, is influenced by time, place, and culture. When I was growing up in Hardwick, washday had changed from the scrub board and the boiling kettle, but it had not yet been transformed by the automatic washer and dryer. Wash day in my memory, especially in winter, meant a hot kitchen filled with steam, windows covered with condensed water, the smell of soap, and the rhythmic *chug-chug* of the washing machine.

Tuesday was ironing day, and my mother once admitted to me that of all the tasks she performed in housekeeping she liked to iron clothes best of all. Unlike washing, ironing was a quiet task. It allowed her time to think and to plan. She appreciated the electric iron, because she had grown up on a farm in Craftsbury without electricity. She remembered a time when flat irons, sometimes called "sad irons," had to be heated on top of the stove. It was easy to pick up a speck of dirt on the iron, causing a black mark on the shirt or blouse, meaning that it had to be washed all over again. My mother, having ironed clothes one way as a girl, appreciated the electric iron. I can see her standing at the ironing board, which had been brought into the kitchen from its storage spot in the back hall. She took shirts and other items to be ironed from the laundry basket; sometimes she sprinkled the clothes with water from a bottle to remove wrinkles and to avoid scorching.

I can still smell the clothes on ironing day, the hot iron on damp cloth, the slight hint of starch, the smell of clothes that had hung all day in the fresh air. Electric or gas dryers and modern fabrics have reduced the amount of ironing done in most households, but when I was a child, ironing on Tuesday was just as sacrosanct as washing on Monday.

Icebox

My boyhood occurred at the very end of the culture of ice. The electric refrigerator became popular in the 1930s. Sears, Roebuck and Company introduced the streamlined Coldspot, created by industrial designer Raymond Loewy, in 1935, and there were over three and a half million electric refrigerators in use in the United States in 1941, but not in Hardwick. We had an icebox in the back hall that could take a piece of ice weighing as much as thirty or forty pounds. Near the icebox was a collection of ice tongs and ice picks. The ice was placed in the top right-hand compartment of the icebox. On the left was a full section for food, milk, and other perishable items, and under the ice compartment was a smaller section for food. The food was cooled by the melting ice. The resulting water was carried outside by a lead pipe through a hole in the floor, but many people with iceboxes in their kitchens had to remember to empty the pan under the icebox or risk a flood in the kitchen. The iceman in Hardwick was Harlan "Bub" Rowell, a large, gregarious man who delivered ice twice a week from his truck. Before my time he had a horse-drawn ice wagon. In the summer all the children in the neighborhood followed the ice truck hoping to get a sliver of ice to suck. The iceman used an ice pick to cut the right size for each icebox, then used ice tongs to carry the ice to the icebox. At our house he could go in through the barn to the back hall and never enter the house, but often the iceman came directly into the kitchen. There are a whole series of ice man jokes, many of them with a sexual subtext, which are now irrelevant because few remember icemen or iceboxes. Bub Rowell used to cut ice on Mackville Pond, and I have memories of watching the operation on a Saturday. Horses dragged a scraper to remove the snow from the ice, and they pulled a saw to make the initial cut. Men then made the final cut with handsaws, and then maneuvered the big blocks of ice through the open water with poles and finally onto a conveyor belt that moved the blocks into the ice house, where they were packed with sawdust. It was difficult and dangerous work. I also watched ice-cutting on Caspian Lake in Greensboro and the slow, dangerous process of moving the blocks of ice from the lake to the icehouse close to our camp. The icehouse is still there, now remodeled into a substantial camp.

After World War II the electric refrigerator replaced the icebox even in Hardwick. Still, when I worked as a bellhop at a hotel in the Adirondacks in the summers of 1950 and 1951, the first task we had to do in the morning was to back the truck up to the ice house and cut and wash a dozen hundred-pound blocks of ice. We then distributed them to the kitchen, the cocktail bar, and the coffee shop.

My father had a large commercial refrigerator at the store and a freezing unit for ice cream and a few frozen foods, including the new Birds Eye frosted peas, beans, and corn. I learned one day (when I was perhaps five or six) the difference between a freezer and an icebox. One of my favorite summer snacks was an orange Popsicle. These came in pairs, so after eating one I decided to save the other. I placed it in the icebox only to return a few hours later and find only a stick and a little orange liquid. I learned a valuable lesson that lasted until iceboxes, ice trucks, ice tongs and icepicks became antiques.

Bathroom

The American bathroom, with white enameled bathtub, shower, toilet, and washbasin, tiled walls and floor, is still the envy of the world, though gradually the world is catching up. Especially impressive to foreign visitors in the postwar years, was the unlimited supply of hot water and the privacy found in the American bathroom. In 1976, as part of the bicentennial celebration, I helped to organize an international conference at the Smithsonian Institution in Washington, D.C. on the large topic: "The Influence of the

United States on the World." One afternoon a distinguished group of scholars, artists, filmmakers, and businessmen from many parts of the world (most of them born in the 1920s) concluded that the most important American contribution to world civilization was the modern bathroom. They considered American art, literature, film, jazz, and the assembly line, but they waxed poetic when they described the American bathroom with its white enameled fixtures, a lock on the door, and unlimited hot water. It, more than anything else, was the symbol of American affluence for their generation in Asia, Europe, and Africa.

The standard American bathroom really dates from the 1920s. In much of the nineteenth century, the three functions we now associate with the bathroom were widely separated, and they still are in many parts of the world. Bathtubs made of tin were portable and usually placed temporarily in the kitchen near the source of hot water, while privies were outside the house, and a pitcher and bowl in the bedroom served for washing up, while a chamber pot took care of night time necessities when the privy was too far away. The bathroom changed slowly over time, and the house where I grew up showed some of that transition. The floor was covered with linoleum, and wainscoting went halfway up the wall. There was an enameled toilet, a marble-top washbasin, and a huge bathtub, without shower, which sat on impressive claw feet. According to my father, Mr. French, who owned the house before he bought it, was a very large man.

Taking a page from the hefty William Howard Taft, who had a custom-made bathtub installed in the White House, French purchased a tub that measured six- and-a-half-feet in length (the standard length was five feet). It was fun to stretch out in this tub, but when I was growing up we did not have unlimited hot water, so I had to be content with a filling the tub only up to six or possibly eight inches. Occasionally after a tough football game, I infuriated my sisters by filling the huge tub almost to the top, using the entire contents of the small water heater and forcing them to wait for the water to heat again.

There was a toilet in a small room off the kitchen, but the whole family had to share the one bathroom. With two sisters that was sometimes difficult. The bathroom was large and may have been a small bedroom or library when the house was built. It had no white tile and, because the small radiator didn't heat very well in the winter, a portable kerosene space heater made it barely comfortable. My memory of the bathroom includes the smell of kerosene burning combined with the smell of soap and water and the slight odor of the bay rum my father used after shaving. My father was a conservative man who did not change his habits easily. While most of his generation adopted the safety razor, especially after it was issued to all American soldiers during World War I, he continued to use a straight razor. I can see him now, standing in front of the washbasin in his undershirt, sharpening his razor with a rhythmic motion, on a leather strop.

Telephone

Dial telephones were common in the cities by the 1920s, but in Hardwick through the 1930s and 1940s we had to call the operator who would then connect us to the desired party. For the rare long-distance call, the local operator would make a connection to an operator in New York or another city. Even when I was in college I remember returning to my dormitory to find a message that read: "Please call Operator 53 in Boston." Like most people in town, we had a black Bakelite candlestick phone with a mouthpiece at the top and a receiver that hung on a short cord. Our phone, and nobody had more than one, was in the dining room, and that offered little privacy. The long cord that enabled the user to move the phone perhaps six feet didn't get me far enough away from my sister's ears.

When I called my high school girlfriend I sometimes went to the telephone central office on Main Street where there was a payphone. My girlfriend's telephone number was easy to remember: it was 100. Our number was 117-2 (pronounced *one-one-seven-ring-two*). We were on a two-party line with the store where the number was 117-1-2. The ring for the house was two shorts; for the store, a long and two shorts, so my father could answer a business call at the house. The two-party line was convenient (and some people had as many as six or seven on the same line), but it meant that if someone at the house was on the phone, customers could not get through to the store. My father finally made a rule that my mother could only make brief calls to her best friends in the morning, when customers often called in their orders.

The main telephone operator was Elva Archer, a short, bustling, and efficient woman who could manage the whole exchange during peak hours, constantly plugging and unplugging the lines and never missing a beat. I found it fascinating to visit the telephone office, especially because several high school girls filled in on a part-time basis. One of my high school classmates recently told me that when she worked in the telephone office after we graduated, she had to know where the policeman on duty was at all times. That meant that one officer had to give her the number of the woman with whom he was having an affair in case there was an emergency in the middle of the night. The telephone operators knew everything that went on in town. There was no need for a 911 call—if there was a fire or a medical emergency, everyone in town called Central and Elva called the doctor, the police, or the fire department.

When I was home for Christmas vacation during my freshman year at Dartmouth, a classmate from Boston called me and got the operator who said, "He is not at home; he's at the basketball game." My friend laughed at the backward ways of my hometown, but he had to concede that the system worked.

The Farm

My uncle's farm was about ten miles from Hardwick and a mile from the village of Craftsbury, near a branch of the Black River. With more than 150 acres of meadowland, pasture, and forest, it was one of the most prosperous farms in town. It had been settled in 1829 by my great-great-grandfather. Sometime before the Civil War, the original house was converted into a blacksmith shop and replaced by a white Greek revival house with two large dormer windows overlooking the valley. About 1900, a large barn was constructed and attached to the house by an extension to the ell, creating the continuous architecture quite common in this part of Vermont. The barn, painted red, was a high-drive barn that enabled the wagons to deposit hay directly into the loft, where it could be distributed to the cows almost four stories below.

The farm had no telephone and no electricity until about 1941 when, like much of rural America, the Rural Electrification Administration (REA), a New Deal agency, plugged the farm into the twentieth century. When my grandmother died in October 1940, my mother called the general store in Craftsbury, and they sent a messenger to tell my uncle. With no electricity and no indoor plumbing the farm seemed old-fashioned, and a throwback to another age. There was a water pump in the kitchen sink that I loved to work as a child, and there was a privy, with three seats, located in the extended ell that connected the house to the barn. The privy came complete with a stack of old magazines, a few Sears, Roebuck catalogues, and some ancient calendars on the walls. The wood-burning stove and the icebox were familiar to me, as were the kerosene lamps, but on the farm these lamps were actually used when the sun went down. No electricity meant there was no washing machine, no electric iron (the flat irons were heated on the stove), no electric toaster (toast was made on top of the stove), no electric mixers, heaters, or record players. There was a battery powered radio, but it was used sparingly. Most important, there were no milking machines; all the cows had to be milked by hand. The farm was run by horse power. My uncle had an old pickup truck, but there were no tractors until after World War II. The farm was old-fashioned and primitive, and that was the reason I loved to go there. Most of my ancestors, back through many generations, were farmers, and by visiting that farm I was connecting to my family history, although I did not realize it at the time. A few years ago in the summer I stopped at the farm. Unlike many Vermont farms, which have been abandoned or turned to another use, my uncle's farm (sold to the Ryans in 1944) is now owned by Pete's Greens, which grows produce near the Black River for sale in the Boston area. The house needs a coat of paint, the kitchen has been remodeled, but the three-seat privy is still there, although now it is a storage room.

We visited the farm frequently when I was growing up. I especially looked forward to three family trips to the farm. On the Sunday after Thanksgiving, as soon as the dishes were cleared from the dining room table, we piled into the 1928 Willys-Knight and drove along the Gulf Road (now Vermont Route 14) past Hardwick Lake and Elligo Pond to the farm in Craftsbury, where we spent the afternoon tramping around the snow covered pastures looking for a Christmas tree. It took us all afternoon because my uncle always searched for the perfect spruce tree, an impossible task in the days before Christmas tree farms. Despite our careful search, our tree often had a slight flaw, but we could hide that easily by turning the good side to the front when we set it up in the window at the house in Hardwick. The annual ritual of cutting a Christmas tree became much more important in the end than finding a perfect tree.

Even more exciting was the spring trip to the farm during sugaring season. Like many Vermonters I was captivated by the romance of sugaring. Before the 1938 Hurricane, my uncle tapped 3,500 trees and had a sugar house large enough to contain a dormitory that housed the extra men he hired for the season. Sugaring for me meant riding on the horse-drawn gathering sled, checking the buckets and the storage tanks. It also meant the wonderful smell that came from the giant evaporator as the sap moved through the various compartments until it was drawn off at the other end as syrup. I especially looked forward to "sugaring off," when my uncle would pour hot sugar on a clean snow bank. We all dug in with our forks to eat the maple taffy.

In mid-July, while we were staying in Greensboro, we visited the farm to celebrate my uncle's birthday. Usually the whole family, including my two sisters, made a trip to Long Pond the day before, so we arrived in Craftsbury with nearly 100 perch for a giant fish fry. Summer on the farm meant taking part in the ritual of haying, riding on top of a load of hay as the horses pulled the wagon up the long ramp to the top floor of the barn. One year, while I walked behind the horse-drawn mowing machine, smelling the grass and picking an occasional flower out of the newly mown hay, the mowing machine hit a hornet's nest, and the hornets expressed their anger on my legs. I was stung six times on one leg and eight on the other before I out distanced them. I had never run so fast. My uncle treated the bites with mud, and within an hour I was back, trying to help, chasing a lost calf, mending a fence, searching for the eggs that the hens had laid in hidden nooks in the barn, even trying to milk a cow without much success.

The spring when I was nine, my parents, or rather my mother, allowed me to go to Craftsbury alone. It was spring vacation and sugaring season. I packed my little suitcase and walked down to the post office in Hardwick late one afternoon at the end of March. There were gray snowbanks still three feet high; it was one of those Vermont days when the weather had not caught up with the calendar. I paid my fare and boarded the "stage" to Craftsbury. The name was left over from the days when a horse-drawn stage connected the two towns (there was also a "stage" to Barre and Montpelier). The vehicle I boarded was powered by a gasoline engine, though it was more car than bus. There were two other passengers, a sack of mail, and a few packages. After several stops we arrived at the general store in Craftsbury Village. I set out to walk to the farm, about a mile and a half across the flat. The road was mostly frozen mud, the sun had set, and it was getting cold. Passing two gray and apparently abandoned barns I crossed a bridge and turned left on the road to the farm. I could see welcoming lights in the farmhouse window. The next morning I went with the men to the sugar place. I spent the day gathering sap, but because I was allergic to horses I had to pause frequently to blow my nose. I must have made a pathetic sight as I wheezed and coughed and struggled through the snow with a pail much too heavy for my young arms. Neither my uncle nor the hired men laughed; they even pretended that I was a big help. At night I slept in an unheated bedroom in a feather bed piled high with quilts, but I slept little, for even indoors, I could not escape the horse dander that made it almost impossible to breathe.

The farm was dominated by horses; at least it seemed that way to me. There were cows, pigs, chickens, assorted cats and dogs, but the horses were king, and indispensable. There were two pair of work horses (called by their names), a couple of other horses that could be used to pull a plow, a rake, or hitched to a buggy. My Aunt Myrtie raised racehorses (trotters and pacers), and every summer and fall she followed the racing circuit at fairs in Vermont, New Hampshire, and Maine. The barn and the house on the farm were filled with harnesses, saddles, blankets, bits, and bridles. The blacksmith shop produced horseshoes, repaired wagon wheels, and created all the other items needed in the age of the horse. My uncle, a skilled blacksmith, was in great demand to shoe racehorses. Even if I had not been allergic to horses (an ailment called "horse fever" in the nineteenth century) I would not have been attracted to the life of the farmer. As much as I admired my uncle, I appreciated, even as a youngster, that the farmer's life was restricted and narrow. Cows had to be milked twice a day every day. My uncle had to leave our home early on Christmas to get back to the farm to "do chores." Farmers, when they came to town, dressed different, even smelled different, than the village folk. I loved to visit the farm, and I appreciated the lifestyle that was disappearing, but my hopes and dreams were with the village, the town, the city, not the farm.

The Store

We always called it simply "the store;" others called it the Davis Store. It was located on South Main Street just at the top of Plank Hill, perhaps two hundred yards from our house. The store was actually several connected buildings, two stories tall with a flat roof. There were two entrances in front, one for customers, and another with a platform where delivery trucks could unload goods. The store was built about 1890 and purchased in 1901 by my grandfather, Charles F. Davis, who apparently decided that there was more promise in running a store in a granite boom town than in tending a hill farm in West Woodbury. He had worked as a clerk in stores in several towns before buying the farm, so he was not completely innocent. The store quickly became a success. My father joined the business after World War I and took it over in 1925. He finally sold it in 1968. Over the years, the store made some compromises toward self-service and modern marketing techniques, but throughout its history it remained an old-fashioned general store.

The store, as I remember it from the 1930s and 1940s, had hardwood counters that went nearly halfway around the interior. A customer who climbed the granite steps and entered the store would have noticed the dry goods section to the right. Here were bolts of cloth, lace, thread, yarn, pins, needles, and a great many odds and ends. The store also sold some clothes, especially men's work clothes. The counters were used not only to display goods, but also to separate the customer from the clerks. The customer asked for an item and the clerk retrieved it from a shelf or from one of the storage rooms. String came down at several points from large rolls near the ceiling and was used to tie up the packages. In the days before the Scotch tape revolution almost everything had to be tied in string. One of the reasons I never liked working in the store as a boy was that I never mastered the art of tying the string efficiently. My packages often came undone. But with everything from cookies, to sugar and flour, potatoes, dried beans, salt cod, hot dogs, chipped beef, prunes, and raisins coming in bulk, there were a great many bags and packages to tie up. There were some goods in packages and cans with brand names like Heinz, Campbell, Nabisco, and Kellogg, but the store hadn't yet been transformed by the pre-packaged and plastic revolution. A barrel of salt pork in brine and a barrel of vinegar with a wooden spigot recalled a time when many goods came in barrels. Almost everything in the store was cut and measured to order. Each banana was cut from the large bunch with a special knife. Each pork chop was carefully sliced and each piece of cheese was cut from a huge round of cheddar. My father was proud that he could get within a half-ounce of the amount ordered.

On the left side of the store was the meat counter, really a giant butcher block that was hollow in the middle from many years of use. There was a hand grinder used to make hamburger from chucks of beef, or to grind beef and pork together for meat loaf.

Cold cuts and boiled ham were hand-sliced for each customer. There was a collection of knives, saws, and cleavers that were used to cut pork chops, steak, or a beef roast to order. In fact almost everything was cut to order, with the exception of hamburger, which might be ground in anticipation and displayed in the refrigerated glass case along with the various cuts of beef and pork, tripe and liver.

The store carried a great many items besides food; in fact it sold a little of everything. In addition to the dry goods section there were drug shelves stocked with Sloan's Liniment, cod liver oil, and a variety of cough syrups and patent medicines. A special room housed the shoe department, and the store was famous for the quality of its work shoes and boots. An old friend still recalls how his father took the whole family (and there were thirteen children) to the store in the fall to outfit them with shoes that he expected would last for the year. Everyone in our family got shoes at the store, one advantage or disadvantage of having a father in the business. My younger sister remembered that she did not wear shoes that fit until she went to college. There was a hardware section that sold nuts, bolts, rakes, hoes, and even baseball bats and fishing tackle. Near the back door was a tank of kerosene with a hand pump. Customers came in with their own containers to obtain fuel for their kerosene heaters and stoves, and, in some cases, their lamps, because the rural area around Hardwick had no electricity until just before World War II. My grandfather refused to sell tobacco (perhaps a result of his Methodist upbringing) but my father added a complete line. I remember my confusion one day when a customer ordered "Copenhagen." I had never heard of snuff. The store never carried beer and wine because both my father and grandfather were opposed to selling alcoholic beverages. Customers were directed down the hill to Barr's Bottling Works for their beer. Yet the store sold a wide variety of patent medicines and "tonics" heavily laced with alcohol. Neither the owners nor the customers appreciated the irony.

The store was never a "Mom and Pop" operation. My mother gave advice from time to time, but she never worked in the store. Still, the store was intertwined with our family life. We ate food from the store, wore shoes from the store, and shopped elsewhere only when absolutely necessary. We ate fruit that was bruised, lettuce that had started to turn brown, and meat that was a little stale. The store was closed on Sunday, so especially on Saturday night my father brought meat and produce to the house that he feared would not survive until Monday morning. Sometimes my mother would smell the meat and reject it as too far gone. We also acquired boxes that were damaged and cans that were dented. Most exciting to me were the cans that had lost their labels. They might contain pumpkin pie filling, beef stew, or canned peaches. It was fun to guess what was in the unlabeled cans, although not so easy to decide what to do with the contents once the cans were opened.

The store operated from 7 A.M. to 6 P.M., and to 9 P.M. on Saturday. There was activity all day long. Men going to work stopped in to buy something for their dinner pail or simply to get warm. Women stopped in to buy coffee, bacon, eggs, or cereal to take home for breakfast. Later in the morning the more serious shoppers arrived. Trucks pulled up to deliver groceries, milk, and bread. At noon children stopped on their way home from school. Many children who grew up on the south side of town remember their first shopping experience when they were given a note by their mother to buy a few items, and often the note said, "And Johnny can have two cents for candy." Near the main entrance there was a large glass-front candy case filled with jelly beans, gumdrops, orange slices (my favorite), Tootsie rolls, bubble gum, red and black licorice, Cracker Jacks, as well as candy bars: Baby Ruth, Sky Bar, Payday, and many others. Christmas candy and Halloween candy appeared in season. Sometimes the children lingered for several minutes spending their two cents. Occasionally, my father would remark that, in terms of money earned in time and space, the candy case was a failure. Still, he never gave it up. He always enjoyed waiting on the children. When the whistle blew at 4:00 P.M. signaling the end of the work day for those who worked in the granite sheds, there was another flurry of activity at the store.

The store had no potbellied stove, but people from the neighborhood gathered to gossip, in any case. In the winter they hovered over the hotair register as they shook off the snow from their clothes. In the summer the old radio, near the rolltop desk, was always tuned to the Red Sox game, and many customers lingered to listen and to discuss the fate of the Boston team (usually bad). There were other things to talk about as well—the high school basketball team, a big trout caught at Caspian Lake, a successful deer hunter, and of course, the weather, and all the other triumphs and tragedies of a small town. Often the local philosophers were joined by traveling salesmen. Early in the century they came by rail and rented a horse and wagon at the local livery stable; by the 1930s they traveled by auto with their samples in the trunk. They still brought their off-color jokes, as well as news and gossip from neighboring towns.

My father was a small man, five-feet-five inches and perhaps 135 pounds, but he was strong and wiry. He could lift heavy boxes and sacks and stay on his feet for twelve hours without complaining. He presided over the store, waiting on customers, talking pleasantly to neighbors and strangers, at the same time managing the business and keeping close account of the numbers. He was a private man who was almost an introvert at home or in a large group. Yet at the store he was friendly and outgoing. It was his natural element. As the town declined and general stores everywhere went out of business he talked of moving to a larger town and buying a business. Still, he stayed in Hardwick and at the store until he finally sold it when he was seventy-four.

Groceries, hardware, and other items were delivered to the store by truck, although as late as the 1920s, wholesalers shipped goods in boxes and barrels by train to the Hardwick Depot, where a clerk with a horse and wagon would pick them up. By the 1940s the general store was no longer the broker or middleman where farmers could sell their meat, butter, and produce. Only eggs were still negotiable and were often traded for shoes or meat. During the summer and fall my father often bought local produce for resale, and occasionally he traded groceries for firewood. During the granite boom in Hardwick the store hired as many as six clerks, but in my memory there was one, and sometimes two, full-time clerks, plus a high school or college student in the summer. I was employed quite young to restock shelves on Saturdays, a task that I disliked. As I got older my father found more and more for me to do around the store, and I began to make excuses for not working. As much as I admired my father, I never wanted the sign on the store to read "H.F. Davis and Son."

The store changed its name over the years. At first it was the "C. F. Davis Department Store," then it was "C. F. Davis and Son," then "H. F. Davis Store." There was a large, silver-plated cash register with four drawers that continued to be used until the store was finally sold. During my father's time the store was affiliated with "Nationwide," and then "Red and White," both organizations that represented and supported independent merchants. They were not to be confused with "A and P," "First National," and "Sears and Roebuck," all swear words in our family, and subsumed under the name "chain store," in my father's mind. He argued that the chain stores could unfairly reduce prices on certain items because of the large volume of sales. On one occasion my mother ordered something from the Sears, Roebuck catalogue, and because she knew my father would be upset, she had the item delivered to the neighbor's house, and I don't think my father ever found out.

The Davis store remained in business for nearly seven decades, in part because it did two things that no other grocery store in town did. Both my grandfather and father gave credit, and delivered groceries, to all parts of town. Until after World War II, the deliveries were made by horse and wagon. About 8:30 in the morning, Monday through Friday, one of the clerks set off to take orders on one of five routes that covered the entire village. He repeated his route in the afternoon with bags filled with groceries and other items.

For some elderly couples and widows, the delivery service not only supplied needed groceries when it was difficult for them to get to a store, but it also provided a link to the outside world. It was not "Meals on Wheels," yet it may have been more effective. The wagons were stored under the store and the horse was housed in a small barn behind the store. A truck replaced the horse and wagon after the war, but the granite hitching posts in front of the store survived for many years. The age of the horse lasted longer in Hardwick than in most places.

My father was a careful business man. He managed the store from an old rolltop desk near the back door and next to the kerosene pump. Here he kept his records, a large checkbook, a telephone, and an ancient typewriter. Every January he took inventory, counting every item in the store so he could tell what departments and what items had been profitable in the past year. In an age before computers and scanners, it was an arduous task, but necessary. Those store owners who lost track of the numbers quickly went out of business. My father spent little money on advertising, although occasionally he ran sales on dry goods. On large items, shoes, clothing, and hardware he recorded the wholesale cost in code on the item, as well as the retail price. Somehow I remember one of the codes:

1 2 3 4 5 6 7 8 9 0
h a r d w i c k v t

A wholesale price of $1.34 would be written "hrd." If at some point he wanted to discount the price of a pair of shoes that had not sold, he could instantly see what he had paid for them.

When a customer came into the store and purchased several items and paid with cash, my father would write the cost of each item on a bag. He could add a column of numbers and check the figure by adding it the other way faster than I could add the items one way. Many families had a credit account at the store. Each time they made a purchase the items and the prices were carefully written out on a pad that created a duplicate using carbon paper. One copy would then be filed under the family name and placed in a special fire-proof cabinet near the safe. During hard times my father often extended credit to families in trouble; still, most people paid on a regular basis. It was difficult to hide bad credit in a small town, and a stranger was easily spotted and asked who in town he might be related to. The store cashed paychecks, took telephone messages, for not everyone had a phone, and in other ways served as a community center. Occasionally there was a bad check or a shoplifting attempt, but dishonestly was usually discovered quickly. My grandfather told of one man who would frequently pick up a pair of shoes or a shirt as he left the store. The clerk who observed him would simply add the item to his account. Each week he paid his bill without questioning the extra charge. The game went on for years. My grandfather once remarked that a year spent working in a store was worth four years of college. At the time I disagreed with him, but in retrospect he may have been right, at least when it came to learning about human nature.

Although I did not realize it while I was growing up, the orange crates and other items of material culture, even the general store that shaped my youth would soon be archaic, replaced by more modern techniques and inventions. I now feel fortunate that, more than most of my generation, I can still remember a small part of the world we have lost.

Chapter 5

BAKED BEANS FOR SATURDAY NIGHT SUPPER

EVERY SATURDAY NIGHT we ate baked beans with salt pork, sweetened with maple sugar or molasses, and served with brown bread. Occasionally my mother added hot dogs (usually called frankfurters) to appease my sisters and me, and there was coleslaw or a molded Jell-O salad on the side. If one didn't like baked beans there was not much to eat at six o'clock on Saturday night. We were not alone in eating baked beans. All over town on Friday night, before they went to bed, women put beans in a pan of water to soak overnight. Yellow eye beans were the preferred variety, though soldier beans were acceptable. Pea beans, often used in Boston, were looked on as inferior in Vermont, and canned beans, usually packed in tomato sauce, were rejected out of hand. On Saturday morning the beans were cooked slowly for several hours on the back of the stove before they were placed in a bean pot and put in the oven for several more hours. After World War II we acquired an electric cooker with a timer that was used to bake the beans, but I like to remember the old-fashioned bean pot and the smell of the beans when the pot was taken from the oven. My sister recalls that our Grandmother Davis often made enough brown bread for both families. In an old cookbook I found her recipe: "1 cup corn meal, 1 cup rye, 1 cup graham, 1 cup sweet milk, 1 cup sour, ½ cup water, ¾ cup molasses, 2 teaspoons soda, 1 of salt. Steam three hours and bake for ½ hour. Before removing bread, place dish in cold water for a few moments. To cut bread while warm, use string like a crosscut saw."

In my childhood, baked beans were ubiquitous; they were a staple at church suppers, and when there was a death in a family and the neighborhood women brought in food, there were always several pots of beans. Baked beans even made an appearance at picnics, and they could be warmed up and used throughout the week. My father loved to eat cold baked bean sandwiches, a taste sensation I never appreciated. I now realize that the baked beans that were very much a part of my childhood had survived from an eighteenth- and nineteenth-century rural diet. Dried beans and pork, put down in salt brine, helped rural families survive in the days before reliable refrigeration. My father had a barrel of salt pork at the store, but in the nineteenth century the whole hog was often put down in brine, the exception being hams and bacons, which were smoked, and the odds and ends that were turned into sausage. We often ate fried salt pork or fried sausage for dinner, usually served with potatoes and milk gravy. We also ate salt cod cakes, and chipped beef with milk gravy on toast for supper. These were also meals that were legacies of an earlier age. We ate pea soup, always made with split peas, with a ham bone added for flavor. My family never used the whole peas, perhaps because that is the way the French-Canadians made their pea soup, a version I eventually discovered was far superior to the English variety.

We ate "Johnny cake," called cornbread in the South, but also a staple of rural diets everywhere in America. Only occasionally did we have New England boiled dinner, and it was not my favorite meal. A legacy from the one-pot meals prepared in the fireplace, before the days of the cook stove, New England boiled dinner usually consisted of potatoes, cabbage, turnips, carrots, and corned beef or ham. The New England boiled dinner was overcooked, like most of the food I ate while growing up.

Immigrants coming to America brought their recipes, and often their cooking utensils, with them. My family was far removed from the immigration experience, but they still passed on traditional meals and foodways from generation to generation. The food my family ate and the way it was prepared recalled a nineteenth-century rural past, but when we ate was even more significant. We had dinner at noon and supper in the evening. There was no concept of lunch in Hardwick until after World War II. The exceptions were those who worked in the granite sheds, but they carried their lunch to work in a "dinner pail." School children and businessmen walked home at midday. My father came from the store and my sisters and I walked from school. Dinner was on the table at twelve o'clock exactly. We usually had meat, potatoes, and home-canned vegetables, bread and butter, water and milk, and always dessert.

Supper, which was served soon after my father closed the store at six, was somewhat lighter than dinner. It might be a casserole (a word that described a variety of one-pot meals) or leftovers disguised one way or another. Meat could be ground with potatoes to make hash and with beets it made "red flannel" hash. Leftover beef could be ground in the hand grinder and combined with a potato crust to make Shepherd's pie. We rarely ate salad. In summer we had fresh lettuce, tomatoes, and cucumbers out of the garden, but they were not usually combined. In winter a wedge of iceberg lettuce, or, more likely, Jell-O and fruit, passed for salad. We often had macaroni and cheese, but never from a package. We ate spaghetti, made with tomato sauce, hamburger, perhaps an onion, all mixed together. The sauce was never placed on top of the spaghetti, Italian-style. Pasta was not a word I heard until I left home, despite the dozen or more first- or second-generation Italian families in town. They had originally moved to Hardwick to work in the granite industry, and they were so thoroughly assimilated that most went to the Methodist, and then to the United Church, perhaps because the Catholic Church was dominated by the Irish and the French-Canadians. The Italians probably cooked Italian at home. Several Italian families did preserve one aspect of their culinary heritage; they made dandelion wine, choke cherry wine, even rhubarb wine. In the boom years of the granite industry there were many Italians who were arrested and fined, not for making wine, but for selling it. They contributed to Hardwick's reputation as the "wettest dry town in Vermont."

My family didn't drink wine, and the Italian presence in town did not influence my mother's cooking, which could be defined as bland New England style. Salt and pepper shakers were always on the table, but spices were used sparingly or not at all. A small amount of onion was occasionally added for flavor, but never mushrooms or thyme, oregano or bay leaves. Sage was used to season the stuffing for chicken or turkey. Horseradish, which we grew in the garden, was made from the ground roots and served with meat, especially in the spring. We ate cheese, always Vermont cheddar, with pie, but my mother rarely added it to food, not even to make a hamburger into a cheeseburger. My mother, especially after the war, experimented with more exotic recipes, but my father announced that he liked old-fashioned cooking.

We ate more pork than beef, and I don't remember having veal or lamb. I am sure the meat markets in town sold these meats, but we ate what my father sold at the store. Most of his beef was tough, so my mother turned it into pot roast.

We ate great quantities of pork chops, pork roasts, sausage, and ham. We ate liver, both pork and beef, but we did not eat kidneys, hearts, or brains, although I do remember eating tripe, and cold sliced beef tongue. I did not realize that sweetbreads were a delicacy until years later.

Everything was cooked "well-done." I did not eat a rare steak until I worked in a summer hotel when I was seventeen. At dinner there was always potato—boiled, baked, fried, mashed, occasionally scalloped—and the potato was usually accompanied by gravy made by combining the meat drippings with milk and flour, or corn starch. Rice was never a substitute for potato though we occasionally had chicken-à-la-king, salmon wiggle, or Welsh rarebit on toast. Whatever my mother cooked for dinner or for supper, she always prepared more than enough for the family, even after seconds. To have barely enough food, or to ration the proportions, was a sign to my mother of living on the margin, and she never knew who might drop in and be invited to stay for a meal. To run short of food would be to admit you were poor, or at least a poor neighbor. Always, I had to clean my plate.

The chicken we ate was usually called stewing chicken, meaning it was a hen old enough to be retired from the duty of laying eggs. The chicken was cooked for several hours until it fell apart. Occasionally we had a more expensive and younger roasting chicken for Sunday dinner, but all the chicken we ate would today be called "free-range," and it was tough. Chicken in the 1930s was often more expensive than pork or beef. When Herbert Hoover campaigned for President in 1928 on the slogan of "a chicken in every pot," he was saying that everyone should be middle-class. I raised chickens for a few years and became hardened to the task of chopping off the head, plucking the feathers, and removing the intestines. But I watched in horror one day as I observed a woman in the neighborhood select a chicken from her hen house and then wring its neck with her hands before taking it into the house to prepare it for dinner. As a youngster

I witnessed two men slaughtering a pig. The sounds of the pig's squeals and the sight of the blood spurting out of its throat stayed in my dreams for days, but it did not stop me from eating pork. I also watched my father cut up a side of beef at the store, so I was not protected while growing up from the realities of the slaughterhouse.

No one in our family was a hunter. My grandfather must have used a gun when he was a farmer, but when he moved to town he gave up his gun along with other rural ways. A few of my friends were hunters, but I did not experience the thrill or the horror of killing a deer, nor did we supplement our diet, as many people did in Hardwick, with venison, rabbit, or partridge, though occasionally a successful hunter would give my father a venison roast.

My family did have a long tradition of fishing, and in the days before catch and release, we ate what we caught—brook trout, lake trout, and, especially yellow perch. During the summer, at camp in Greensboro, we often had a platter piled high with perch rolled in cornmeal and fried in butter or bacon grease. Many years later at an elegant London restaurant, when I first tasted Dover sole my initial thought was, "Its taste and texture are just like perch," but I kept that thought to myself. Another use for perch was in chowder, and I have fond memories of the perch chowder that my mother made usually at camp in the spring. Perch chowder and homemade bread fed several families for supper after a day of fishing in Caspian Lake.

During the winter in Hardwick we had fresh fish on Friday. I recall walking "down street" with my mother on Friday morning (I must have been under six) to buy cod, haddock, or flounder at the fish market, or at a meat market that sold fish. The large Catholic population in town was forbidden to eat meat on Friday, which explains why fresh fish was available. The joke around town was that only Protestants ate fish on Friday because the Catholics hated fish so much they ate macaroni and cheese.

At both dinner and supper we always had dessert—pies of all kinds, cake cookies, fresh or canned fruit. Because my family liked pie better than cake, my mother often recycled old cake by adding lemon sauce. She called it "cottage pudding." We often ate pie that was a day or two old, but I knew one demanding husband in town who insisted on having fresh pie every day. My mother made rice pudding with raisins in a double boiler on top of the stove. The rice pudding sold in the New York delicatessens and the rice pudding I have eaten in London, Amsterdam, Stockholm, and in other parts of the world tasted good, but not quite as good as my mother's rice pudding. She also made bread pudding, Indian pudding, tapioca, and custard. Another taste memory that I have never been able to duplicate is my mother's filled cookies, which were like little individual pies. When my sister and I cleaned out my father's house I discovered my mother's handwritten recipe for filled cookies: "one cup sugar, ½ cup butter, 1 egg, ½ cup sweet milk, 3-½ cups flour, 2 teaspoons of cream tartar, 1 of vanilla, a little salt. Roll thin, cut and put in filling on each one and cover with another cookie and press down edges. Filling: 1 ½ cups raisins (chopped), ½ cup sugar, ½ cup hot water, 1 teaspoon flour. Cook until thick, being careful as it burns easily."

My father sold ice cream at the store—vanilla, chocolate, strawberry, maple walnut—and occasionally he would bring a quart to the house for dessert. We had to eat it all at one meal, because, until we got a refrigerator after the war, there was no way to keep it over night. My favorite flavor was maple walnut, but nothing could surpass the taste of vanilla ice cream with maple syrup on top. When I was a youngster, one of my mother's rules was that I could not have dessert until I drank my milk. I never liked milk, but I did like dessert, so I drank my milk as rapidly as possible, hoping I could quickly wipe out the taste of the milk with something sweet.

Breakfast was my least favorite meal. We didn't have the typical Vermont farm breakfast of steak, eggs, fried potatoes, and apple pie, but my mother thought it was important to eat a substantial breakfast, by which she meant oatmeal or some other hot cereal. I hated oatmeal as well as Ralston, Cream of Wheat, and all the dry cereals which became a sodden mess when cold milk was added. I preferred a homemade doughnut or two, or a piece of homemade bread with raspberry jam. But one of my favorite radio programs, "Jack Armstrong, the All-American Boy," was sponsored by Wheaties, so occasionally I had to eat Wheaties to obtain the box top, which, together with ten cents, earned me some special ring or badge. Even more disconcerting, my other favorite program, "Captain Midnight," was sponsored by Ovaltine. In order to get my special decoder badge I needed a label or two. I found Ovaltine almost as undrinkable as Postum, the coffee substitute marketed by temperance advocate, C. W. Post. Coffee was supposed to be an adult drink, but I liked the smell when I was growing up. My parents drank coffee for breakfast and sometimes after dinner. The percolator, which bubbled on top of the stove, sent a wonderful aroma up through the register to my bedroom above. But when I stole a sip the taste disgusted me. It was only years later that I learned to love coffee. I discovered that if I left the sugar and cream out and drank it black it was wonderful. I also learned many years later that the French, the Dutch, and much of the rest of the world had the kind of simple breakfast that I preferred as a youngster.

Breakfast in our house was different from the other meals because we did not all eat together. My parents ate at six or six thirty before my father opened the store at seven. But Sunday breakfast was more leisurely. We often had pancakes (or griddle cakes as we often called them), waffles, or French toast with maple syrup. Or we had eggs with bacon or sausage. The bacon was maple sugar-cured, cut thick, and fried until it was crisp. The eggs were fried, but not sunny side up. Everyone in the family disliked runny eggs. Breakfast, like all other meals except Sunday dinner or when we had guests, was served on the kitchen table. By accident or design, we all had our special places. My mother, who was in command of the kitchen, sat on the side of the table closest to the stove. She served from the stove or placed serving dishes on the table. We always had bread and butter (never margarine) with each meal. Usually the bread was homemade although occasionally we had soft, spongy, "store-bought" bread, which nobody liked. There was a glass of water at every place, but no wine or beer and no cocktails before supper, even on special occasions. My family's total abstinence was probably the result of the Protestant temperance movement extending from the 1830s into the twentieth century. With no cocktails in our family there was no cocktail hour. We ate as close to six o'clock as possible. We used cloth napkins, but my grandmother was the only one who had a napkin ring. The kitchen table was covered with an oil cloth.

We were not a very talkative family, but we did converse at the table, not serious discussions about politics or religion, but we did talk about books and movies, about local gossip, school and church affairs, and sometimes about the local high school sports teams. There was little conflict and few arguments at the table that I remember, but everyone was expected to be there for meals, and I was not allowed to bring a book to the table, something I tried from time to time. In spring and summer I often desperately needed to hear the baseball scores. I would dash from the table to catch my favorite sports program. Our only radio was in the living room. Occasionally my father tolerated my brief exit from the table, for he also was a baseball fan, but when I returned to the table he announced "in no uncertain terms" that leaving the table during the meal was a rare exception. I learned not to talk with my mouth full, and to ask my sisters to pass the butter rather than to use what my father called a "boarding house reach." My sisters were enlisted to set the table and they often washed and dried the dishes after supper. But I don't remember their helping with the cooking; that was my mother's domain. Occasionally I was pressed into service to "do" the dishes and to "set" the table, or to peel potatoes, shell beans, or to help with other tasks. Usually I got away with more masculine chores—bringing in the wood, mowing the lawn, and shoveling snow.

We always ate Sunday dinner in the dining room. The big table, which during the week was piled with school work, sewing projects, newspapers, and magazines, was cleared, and the table was covered with a white tablecloth. We used the best china and silverware, and for this meal my father was in command—at least he carved and served the roast or the chicken, and he passed the plates around the table. On Christmas, Easter, and other occasions, when my grandparents joined us for dinner, my grandfather always said "grace." He was brief and direct: "Bless this food to our use, and us to thy service." I don't recall my father ever offering a prayer. It was obviously an aspect of playing the role of *pater familias* that he did not enjoy.

Sunday night supper was also special, though less formal, than dinner. Often my parents would have oyster stew, something my sisters and I did not appreciate, so we were allowed to have hot dogs. It was many years before I learned to eat oysters, first fried, then in stew, and finally on the half shell. I also learned how to eat lobster, clams, and mussels only after I left home. The oysters used in my mother's stew came from the store, shucked and packed in two-gallon cans, shipped, I suppose, from Long Island or the Chesapeake Bay. Sometimes my father ate crackers and milk for Sunday night supper, or for a snack at other times during the week. It was another survivor of nineteenth-century ways. He used the hard, dry crackers (Montpelier Crackers was the local brand) that were long a staple, whether for soldiers in the field or those on long sea voyages. I disliked crackers in milk just as much as Wheaties and milk, so I would raid the icebox for cold chicken, meat loaf, or, if I could find nothing else, cheese to make a grilled cheese sandwich, one of the few meals I learned to make for myself when I was growing up.

In the spring we sometimes had a special treat on Sunday evening. We had "sugar on snow," a Vermont tradition. In late March or early April, when there were still piles of snow at the corner of the garden, we would gather the granular snow in dish pans and then boil maple syrup down until it turned to sugar. When it "haired off the spoon" my grandmother announced that it was ready. Then we would pour the molten sugar over the snow. It would turn it into a kind of maple candy that we could pick up with a fork. Whatever was left we would stir into maple sugar cakes. We often ate plain doughnuts and sour pickles with this special treat in order to take the sweet taste of the maple sugar out of our mouth, so we could eat more. I understood when I was a youngster that eating too much sugar or candy was not good for you, but somehow maple sugar was exempted from that rule.

Caught up in the romance of sugaring when I was quite young, I tapped the four maple trees in the front yard and with my mother's help, boiled the sap into syrup on top of the wood stove. It takes forty to forty-five gallons of sap to make one gallon of syrup, so the kitchen was filled with steam for a few weeks in the spring. Somehow the ritual of sugaring meant the arrival of spring, and I would rush home from school on warm spring days to see if the sap was running. At first I used quart jars, then my Uncle Lovell gave me some regulation sap buckets from his sugar place in Craftsbury. Not content with the four trees in the yard, for a year or two I tapped additional trees on Buffalo Mountain and hauled the sap for at least half a mile. In remembering, I marvel at my energy and commitment, but at the time it did not seem like work. Sugaring was not only a spring ritual in our family, but maple sugar was used as the favorite snack and sweetener. Each year we purchased a ten-pound wooden pail of hardened maple sugar. My mother would use pieces to sweeten beans or other dishes, and I would often chip out chunks to make maple sugar sandwiches—a source of quick energy and a taste delight.

Holidays called for special food and routines that gradually became tradition. On Easter morning we rose early and attended the sunrise service at the United Church and then stayed for a breakfast of scrambled eggs and sausage, prepared by the young people's group. For dinner on Easter we always had baked ham. On the Fourth of July we were at camp in Greensboro and ate the traditional New England Fourth of July meal of new peas and potatoes, but instead of salmon we substituted trout or perch. And we always had wild strawberry shortcake and homemade ice cream. My fondest memories of homemade ice cream come from summertime visits to my uncle's farm. My Uncle Lovell would get out the ice cream maker which consisted of a wooden bucket and a metal canister. The cream, eggs, sugar, and flavoring (usually vanilla) were placed in the canister, and chipped ice and salt filled the space between the metal container and the wooden bucket. A hand crank, attached to the canister, turned a dasher or float to assure that the mixture froze uniformly. It took twenty to thirty minutes of cranking to make ice cream this way. It was a proud day when my uncle allowed me to crank and to decide when the ice cream was done. It was even more important to be allowed to lick the ice cream from the float after we pulled it out of the canister. Homemade ice cream was softer than the commercial variety, and it always seemed to taste better.

Most of my friends had roast turkey for Thanksgiving, but in my family the tradition was to go a few doors down to my grandparents' house where we always ate chicken pie prepared in a huge pan. I have vivid memories of the smell of my grandmother's kitchen, especially the smell of boiled onions, but I also recall the pumpkin and mincemeat pies. Christmas dinner was always at our house and we ate turkey, baked slowly all night in a low oven. My mother cooked for days preparing far too much food, but while most of my friends opened their presents in the morning, in my house, in part because relatives traveled from out of town, we did not open presents until we got up from the table at about 2:30 P.M. When I think of Christmas I think of the mixed nuts, Brazil nuts, pecans, almonds, and walnuts that I helped to crack. I also think of celery (a treat in the middle of the winter) and the taste of my mother's divinity fudge. My sister and I hung up our stockings on Christmas Eve, long after we had ceased believing in Santa Claus, and one thing we always received was an orange. For my mother, growing up on a farm early in the century, an orange in the middle of the winter was a special treat, but to us in the 1930s, finding an orange in our stockings on Christmas morning was not exciting. I now realize it was my mother's attempt to keep her family tradition alive, as she did with her cooking.

My family only rarely ate in restaurants. We never ate a meal in the restaurants in Hardwick that I can recall, but we ate dinner or supper out when we went on shopping trips to Barre, Burlington, or St. Johnsbury, and we usually ate in diners or diner-like restaurants when we took weekend trips over Labor Day. Occasionally a visiting relative took us out to eat. There is a family story, that when my Aunt Carrie from Boston took the family to a hotel dining room in Waterbury when I was about four, I took one look at the table covered with a white tablecloth with china and silverware and asked in a loud voice, "Why do they have two spoons?" I later learned to use a great variety of spoons and forks, and I learned to appreciate great restaurants, but that was after I left home.

While we didn't often eat in restaurants when I was growing up, we did go on many picnics. When we went on Sunday drives we often stopped by the side of the road to eat our picnic lunch. I remember an elaborate picnic basket that fit on the running board of the 1928 Willys-Knight. It came complete with plates, cups, silverware, and two thermos bottles. We searched for a picnic table, but if we could not find a table we spread a blanket on the ground. We often joined other families for picnics at state parks, at a public beach in the summer, or along an abandoned road in the fall. Sometimes we met relatives or friends who had moved out of town at a convenient midway spot for a picnic, and we went to Caspian Lake in spring and fall, even in the winter when we built a fire on the ice and cooked hamburgers and hot dogs. For these multi-family picnics the women apparently conferred ahead of time—one agreed to bring baked beans, another potato salad or dessert.

My family and friends in Vermont were not alone in enjoying picnics. It was an upper class thing to do in both Europe and America during the Victorian age. The auto extended the picnic to the middle class. My parents' photo album, documenting their honeymoon in 1924, shows them having a picnic on the beach with their car in the background. Another photo in a family album captures my sister and me having a picnic in the backyard of our house about 1935. I am sure that one of the reasons we took a picnic lunch on our auto trips was to save money. A picnic basket made for a flexible schedule allowing us to eat almost anywhere. Some of my fondest memories are of picnics in the summer at Long Pond in Greensboro or Big Hosmer Pond in Craftsbury, that combined fishing with eating around a campfire. Freshly caught yellow perch, rolled in cornmeal and fried in a skillet on an open fire, were superior in my mind to baked beans and potato salad. Those picnics seemed like great adventures. They had little resemblance to the elegant Victorian and Jazz Age picnics that featured fine crystal, vintage wine, and gourmet fare. Still, I have fond memories of the picnics of my youth. To this day, when I eat deviled eggs or stuffed olives, I am reminded of the picnics of my childhood.

Our style in picnics revealed the rural, small-town nature of my life in the 1930s and 1940s, but so did our large garden in the backyard. I did not think it unusual to have a garden a few feet from our back door, for most of my friends had gardens as well. It was a way to stretch our dollars during the Depression and the war, and it didn't take much intelligence to realize that fresh vegetables were better than those that came in cans. In our family the garden season started in February, when my parents, especially my mother, began to study the garden catalogues that came in the mail. Then in March we began to plant seeds in pots. We started tomatoes, cabbage, melons, and other vegetables indoors in an attempt to lengthen the short growing season in northern Vermont. The first real sign of spring, however, came in April, when enough snow had melted from a corner of the garden that we could dig up parsnips that had been left in the ground all winter. I never liked the slightly sweet taste of these carrot-like vegetables, but when my mother boiled them before frying them in butter, I ate them eagerly because they were a harbinger of spring. Shortly after the parsnips were harvested I began to dig in the garden to find fish worms in preparation for the opening of trout season on May first. About the same time we began to harvest young dandelions. My mother cooked them, or overcooked them, like spinach. I did not really like the slightly bitter taste, yet I ate them, and I even made a few extra cents by digging them and selling them by the peck to my neighbors. Everyone in town ate dandelion greens in the spring; they were free for the taking. My father had an expression that helped him define social class: "They are so poor," he would say, "that all they have to eat is dandelion greens."

The next thing we harvested after dandelions was rhubarb, which grew in one corner of the garden. My mother quickly made rhubarb sauce and combined it with strawberries to make strawberry rhubarb pie. For some reason we didn't grow asparagus, but our neighbors kept us supplied. The asparagus was also overcooked before it was served. Sometime in early May, my father hired a farmer to plow and harrow the garden in our backyard. With the garden ready we could start planting peas, lettuce, radishes, then beets, carrots, and several kinds of beans and squash (but never zucchini). On Memorial Day, following local Vermont tradition, we completed the garden by planting corn, the rest of the beans, and we set out the tender cabbage and tomato plants. During the war we enlarged the garden to be patriotic. My mother and I experimented successfully with growing potatoes and strawberries, and not so well with cauliflower, Brussels sprouts, and several varieties of melon. We did not grow broccoli, eggplant, or peppers.

I enjoyed helping to plant the garden, and I even liked hoeing between the rows to keep the weeds down. My fondest memory is of pulling up young carrots, wiping them on my pants, or running them under the outside faucet and then eating them one after the other. New peas could also be eaten raw, sometimes pods and all. One of my favorite meals consisted of new peas and potatoes cooked together and served in a bowl with a little milk and butter. That signaled the real beginning of summer. I also like to eat red currants and blackberries from the bushes beyond the garden. I had forgotten the wonderful tart taste of fresh currants until, when living in Amsterdam some years ago, I purchased a box at an outdoor market, stripped them of their stem in my mouth, and suddenly I had a Proustian moment as I was transported back to my childhood and to the garden in my backyard.

The cultivated blackberries, big and plump, eventually got choked out by weeds and small trees, but some migrated over the bank. A few summers ago I stopped behind the house, climbed the bank near a telephone building, which now occupies much of the back lot where I played as a child, and there I discovered a few bushes, descendants of those blackberries I picked long ago. They tasted just as good as I remembered. Raspberries are another matter; wild raspberries are much better than the cultivated variety.

I have always believed that the world could be divided into two kinds of people: those who like to pick raspberries and those who don't. I realized rather early in life that I was one of the former when I went with my family, or more often with my mother and sisters, in quest of the wild raspberry. Neither of my sisters liked to pick berries. They picked a few, ate most of those they picked, or found an excuse to quit early. But I approached the job with enthusiasm and competitively tried to fill my pail faster than the adults.

Wild raspberries are ripe and ready for picking in northern Vermont in late July or early August. They grow everywhere, especially where a wood lot has been cut over. They appear mysteriously and come back every year until they are choked out by young poplar and fir trees. Some of those we picked were turned into jams and jellies, others into pies, tarts, and filled cookies. The kitchen was transformed into a factory to create these preserves, and because raspberries and currants ripen about the same time, many jars of raspberry currant jelly were put up for the winter. My family preferred jam to jelly and we especially liked to eat wild raspberries crushed with a little sugar on vanilla ice cream. I still pick wild raspberries each summer in Vermont, not only because of their taste, but also because I like the process. I tramp around a wild raspberry patch having great fun as I watch my pail fill up. Alone with my thoughts in a beautiful spot, I make a link to my past.

Not long after the raspberry season, other vegetables became ripe—string beans, shell beans, sweet corn. My mother put up jar after jar of corn and especially succotash, a mixture of corn and beans. But the corn was best when eaten fresh, right out of the garden. My mother would put a pot of water on the stove, then she would go into the garden and pick a dozen ears of corn. After the corn was shucked, a task that I was often assigned, she placed the corn in the boiling water for exactly three minutes. Eaten with butter and a little salt, this corn on the cob marked the culinary high point of summer. It has made me dissatisfied with much of the corn I have eaten since. In retrospect, it seems odd that, in a household where most vegetables were overcooked, the corn was done so precisely.

The growing season in northern Vermont was stressfully short. There might be a hard frost in early June, and for many years there was a killing frost in mid-September. It is a wonder that any vegetables had time to ripen. During the first cold nights in September we would rush out to cover tomatoes and other tender plants with old blankets. Soon the threat of a hard frost sent us out to harvest tomatoes, both green and ripe, cucumbers, cabbages, squash, and other vulnerable produce. The kitchen smelled of vinegar as my mother made pickles of various kinds—bread and butter pickles, green tomato pickles, and sweet cucumber pickles. Eventually the weather turned cold, and the first snow flurries found us digging up carrots, beets, and turnips, which were placed in the vegetable cellar in the basement. Here they were joined by several bushels of apples—Macintosh, Cortland, Winesap, Northern Spies—that we had purchased on a visit to a relative who ran an orchard near Lake Champlain. We were repeating the rituals of the harvest season that had been going on for centuries, but I found the desolate and destroyed garden a sad reminder that winter was coming.

My mother was an excellent New England cook. She learned from her mother and grandmother on the farm where she grew up, using their recipes. After World War II she experimented with new recipes, but most of what she cooked and the way she prepared food had been passed down for many generations. She often baked on Saturday morning, and she could turn out two loaves of bread, a couple of dozen doughnuts, a batch of cookies, and a pie before I got out of bed. My mother had a few cookbooks, and she frequently cut out recipes from magazines and stuck them in the books, yet I can only recall rare occasions when she consulted these books. Still, when my sister and I cleaned out the house after my father died, we found a well worn 1919 edition of the

Fannie Farmer Cookbook. She swapped recipes with friends, and she had a democratic sense that good food should be shared with all. She had little sense that food was related to social class.

One of my good friends in college was Rodman Rockefeller, the oldest son of Nelson Rockefeller and the great-grandson of John D. Rockefeller, the richest man in America. Rodman and two other college friends spent a weekend at my house during my senior year at Dartmouth while we skied at Stowe. Years later, my mother's best friend, Leone Cobb, told me that my mother remarked to her, "Well, I was going to serve them baked beans before I knew a Rockefeller was coming, and I am still going to serve them baked beans." Baked beans were our traditional meal, and her attitude, consistent with her philosophy of life, was that if they were good enough for us they were good enough for a Rockefeller. In any case, she could not imagine anything better than baked yellow eye beans with salt pork for Saturday night supper.

Chapter 6

GREENSBORO: A DIFFERENT WORLD

I USUALLY ARRIVE in Greensboro in mid-May. I get away from Philadelphia in the early afternoon, drive across the Delaware River on the Walt Whitman Bridge, and go north on the New Jersey Turnpike, through the suburban sprawl of factories, shopping malls, and fast food restaurants, until I reach Exit 11, where I take the Garden State Parkway. I work my way north along the Hudson Valley on the New York Thruway, which, like all the interstate highways, slices artificially through the landscape, avoiding towns and cities. Sometimes, when I have the time, I abandon the interstate and drive through the small towns and the countryside so I can admire the vernacular architecture—the barns and farmhouses from another era. When I finally reach Albany, I take the Northway to Saratoga Springs where I stop for the night at the Roosevelt Inn, a motel where I have stayed many times before. There are several ways to drive from Philadelphia to Greensboro; perhaps the fastest is to brave the traffic on the

George Washington Bridge and the Cross Bronx Expressway to Interstate 95 and then take 91 up the Connecticut Valley, but somehow I prefer the Hudson Valley route.

It is almost 500 miles from Philadelphia to Greensboro, and many times I have done it in one day, but it is more civilized to break the trip in half. After a martini and a light supper in the Silver Bullet Lounge I sleep well. The next morning I rise at seven, excited to be on my way. I enjoy driving especially if I am not pressed for time, and I often stop for coffee or to explore an antique store or a bookshop. I leave the Northway at Route 197 and slice over to Fort Edward, then I follow Route 4 through Fort Anne and Whitehall, where a sign claims it is the birthplace of the U. S. Navy. The forts, now only names, are left over from the French and Indian War and the Revolution.

It is good to be off the interstate and to drive on a two-lane road, rather than the impersonal superhighway. Already the landscape looks familiar. I pass two old barns that have a medieval look. I have watched them crumble over the years. As I approach Rutland, Vermont, there is suburban sprawl that includes big box stores—McDonald's and Pizza Hut—that turn certain stretches of road into Anywhere, USA. I think of other trips to Greensboro. When my sons, Greg and Paul, were young and I was teaching at the University of Missouri in the 1960s, it was a three day trip to Greensboro with two stops at Holiday Inns where I could use my Gulf card, the first credit card I owned. One of the reasons I moved from the University of Missouri to Temple University was that Philadelphia was closer to Greensboro. Sometimes when the boys were older we would leave Philadelphia at five in the morning and drive straight through. I no longer rise before dawn, but I am still eager to get to camp.

In mid May the fields are green and the leaves nearly full-grown on the maples and birches. I take Route 4 over Mendon Mountain, past Pico Peak ski area where a few gray snowdrifts still survive on the trails. I turn on to

Route 100, then I take Route 107 to Interstate 89 at Bethel. Soon I am in Barre and heading north on Vermont Route 2 and finally 14. I drive through Woodbury Gulf and into Hardwick, my birthplace and the town of my youth. I pass the building that had been the Davis Store and the house that I once called home, but I do not linger. I drive up Slapp Hill on my way to Greensboro. Driving along the center road I look at the northern Vermont landscape of plowed fields, pasture, rolling hills, and a mixture of hard- and softwood forest. The leaves here are barely the size of my little finger. The Northeast Kingdom, and especially the area around Hardwick and Greensboro, is a special world, and a place where the growing season is as short as anywhere in Vermont. As I pass the four corners and drive down the long, gentle hill (now called Breezy Avenue) into the little village of Greensboro, I spot Caspian Lake to the left and I remember that my sisters and I always tried to be the first to announce that we could see the lake when we drove the seven miles from Hardwick to Greensboro. I pass Willey's Store, the only store in the village, and continue north for a mile, my heart racing with anticipation. Just beyond Perron's farm, I turn into the familiar driveway. I am back.

I feel the same thrill that I felt many times as a child. The camp is still there; the lake is still there. It is like having an anchor against the unpredictable things in life. I walk around the camp looking for winter damage. Sometimes there is a tree down or a shingle or two missing from the roof, but this time I spot no immediate disaster. The dock is still in place. The wind is roaring down the lake from the north, and I am reminded how important the wind direction and velocity is here. In the city I am rarely aware of the wind, but here even a slight breeze in magnified by the lake. I unlock the back door, a door that is always left unlocked during the summer. As I enter the kitchen there is a slight smell, hard to define, a mixture of old wood, stale air, and a hint of mouse droppings—a comfortable and familiar smell. I walk through the camp, opening the curtains on the windows in the dining room. I remove the canvas coverings from the front windows in the living room, open the porch door, and move the porch furniture from the living room. (At camp the front is the side toward the lake.) I go upstairs and I inspect each of the five bedrooms. Later, I will sweep up the dead flies and the dust that has accumulated. Most of my neighbors hire a cleaning service, or a local person, to get their camps ready for arrival, but I prefer to clean myself; it is part of the spring ritual. That ritual once included the difficult task of lighting the pilot lights on the ancient gas stove and water heater, but a few years ago I had the kitchen remodeled; now I am all electric and it is much easier in the spring, though more complicated on the frequent occasions during a storm when the electricity goes out. I search around in a round wooden box on top of the bureau in the dining room and come up with a key ring with a half dozen keys. After a few tries I manage to open the garage door and locate a rake and the wheelbarrow. My first task tomorrow will be to rake leaves, and then there are two trees that my professional tree man, Tracey St. Louis, has taken down, a yellow birch and a balsam fir. They are blocked and ready to split, but now I just glory in being back in a familiar place, a place that gives the illusion of never changing.

My camp was built in 1923 on land my grandmother, Florence Haines Davis, bought in 1913 for $300. I have the original deed framed and on the wall. Before 1923 the Davis family camped in tents for two weeks on the shores of Lake Champlain. They took the train with all their gear to Essex Junction, where they were met by a farmer with a horse and wagon who hauled them to the beach near the mouth of the Lamoille River. Sometime about 1915 they hired a professional photographer to record their adventure. I have a series of photographs showing women with long skirts and men in old business suits in and around their tents. If it rained, as it frequently did, or if the weather was unusually hot, living in the tents must have been oppressive. They were participating in the hiking, camping, outdoor-adventure boom of the early twentieth century. They were part of the generation that believed that camping out was good for one's health and one's soul. My own interpretation is that my grandmother (who died before I was born) got tired of this outdoor life and bought the land in Greensboro, as she looked forward to a summer cottage rather than a tent. The deed is in her name alone. Unfortunately she did not live to use the camp, built in 1923, the year she died.

The camp is constructed of spruce boards, which, according to family legend, were sawed from logs taken in trade by my grandfather at the store. Those boards have mellowed over the years to a honey color. The camp (no one in Greensboro calls them cottages) sits on cedar posts instead of concrete because the land is swampy and there are little springs everywhere. There is no indication that the camp was designed by an architect. My grandfather probably made a sketch, based on my grandmother's idea of what a camp should be, and a local builder executed it. My father recalled that some of the clerks at the store were pressed into service to help the carpenters. The porch, which extends across the front, has a cedar rail made of small logs and twigs in Adirondack style. The living room, which also extends across the entire front, is dominated by a brick fireplace, which is not just ornamental; on many cold days and nights the heat from the fireplace becomes a vital necessity. There is a large dining room and a kitchen on the first floor. The stairway, which leads from the living room to the floor above, takes a sharp ninety-degree turn, using four triangular winders to make the turn. It can be treacherous for the very young and the very old. There is a trap door that can be pulled at night to prevent the sleepwalker or the unwary from falling down the stairs. It gets very dark in Greensboro; at some point an opening was cut in the stairwell to let heat circulate from the kitchen. That window has long been a favorite place for children to sit on the stairs and look down on the adults gathered in the kitchen. A few years ago a distant cousin came to visit and the first thing she wanted to do was to see if the window was still there.

There are five bedrooms because, again, according to family legend, my grandmother had four sisters, and she wanted to entertain them all at the same time. The partitions between bedrooms consist of only the width of one board, and originally they only extended about twelve feet so one could look from each bedroom all the way to the rafters and the pointed roof. This arrangement limited privacy, and if a light was turned on in the middle of the night it illuminated the whole upstairs. My grandfather used to say that you could hear what people were thinking at camp. A few years ago I had ceilings put in, but the upstairs is still rustic, and some of the partitions still contain an occasional knothole that inspire adolescent boys to peep into the next bedroom. Instead of windows, the bedrooms have barn doors that can be rolled open to let the wind blow through the entire camp. For my grandfather, the camp was just one step removed from the tent, and he wanted the feeling of sleeping outdoors. Probably inspired by the outdoor and strenuous life movements of the early twentieth century, he slept with the window open even on the coldest nights. It may also have had something to do with the fear of tuberculosis and the sense that fresh air would cure all ills. In other ways my grandfather believed that camping should be primitive. He never wanted to cut down a tree or remove a shrub unless absolutely necessary. Even though there was an icebox, he preferred to keep his milk and butter cold by digging a hole and letting the ground water do the cooling. Later, there was a contest between my grandfather and his second wife. She wanted to turn the camp into a Victorian cottage, and he wanted to keep it as primitive as possible.

One of the attractions of camp is that it is not a house. There are no plastered walls and no wallpaper. There are simple rugs but no carpet. The wood-burning range and the icebox survived longer at camp than they did at the house in Hardwick, but they were finally replaced by a gas stove and a refrigerator. The advantage of a camp, especially one only seven miles from home, was that old furniture and other things no longer used at home could find new life at camp. My dining room table was purchased by my grandparents in 1889, the year they were married. When they bought a new table for their house in the 1920s, they brought the old one to camp. Many of the beds come from the early twentieth century, although the mattresses and the springs have been replaced. My grandfather believed that an old bed that sloped toward the middle was fine for camp, because one didn't need the comforts of home at camp. The fire tongs and shovel I still use were made by my great-great-grandfather, who was a blacksmith. There are old Windsor chairs, wooden tables, and a blanket chest that have some value today as antiques. I like these old things. They have much more sentimental than monetary value.

I walk around the camp, inspecting each room. Memories come flooding back, but in no chronological order. The things I did last summer mix with memories of my childhood. Several generations of children have had their yearly growth recorded on the kitchen walls. My first mark is from 1932 when I was a year and a half, but nearby are my grandchildren carefully recorded as they grow taller each year. In the bedroom where I slept as a child I can still see the knots in the spruce boards that I transformed into fish or birds or monsters in my imagination. In the garage I find a toy sailboat I made when I was about ten, but right next to it are signs created by my sons. They read "Night Crawlers" and "Minnows," and they survive from a project to sell bait to fishermen. My grandchildren are the fifth generation of the Davis family to use the camp; they already have their own projects, their own memories.

I vault up the stairs, placing my hand automatically on

the edge of the fifth stair, and instantly I am a child again. I work on a writing project on the dining room table and suddenly I recall a family meal around that same table. I hear the wind whistle through the trees and the waves crash against the shore; I'm transported back to my youth and I remember the exhilaration tinged with fear that I felt when a storm raced across the lake. The late-afternoon sun creates the same flickering shadows on the wall over the fireplace that I remember. Everything seems so utterly familiar that I can't date or sort out all my memories. To hear the rain on the roof, to sit on the deck drinking coffee in the morning sun, or read on the dock in the late afternoon, sipping a martini and watching the lake, is to believe that some things stay the same in a changing world. Some things do change, even here; photographs reveal trees that were once small, and are now large, and a few have come down in windstorms, but enough stays the same to give the sense of permanence. Joyce Carol Oates writes that our earliest memories are likely to be of a particular place, a special space. "We carry imprint of this memory through our lifetime." For many people, the magic space of their childhood exists only in their memory or in their dreams. But for me that magic space is the camp in Greensboro, and I go there every summer as I have done every year of my life, except one year when I was in the Army. Even today, when I have a difficult time getting to sleep in a strange hotel or in my townhouse in Philadelphia, I imagine myself at camp, and it usually works better than a sleeping pill.

Taking a break from unpacking, I walk up the driveway to the road. I turn left and walk a few hundred yards to a swampy spot where I fill a small bag with fiddlehead ferns, which are the new tops of the ostrich ferns cut just as they poke through the ground. I never ate them while growing up, but recently I have discovered that they are good in salads, even better sautéed and served with trout. Across the road is the Perron Farm with beautiful hay fields and pastures climbing up the hill. The open land is punctuated by several copses, mostly sugar maples, which create a contrast in the landscape. The Perron Farm, until last year, was one of eight or ten remaining operating farms in Greensboro, which, in 1880, had more than 150. Oscar Perron moved from Quebec to Vermont about the time of World War I to work in the granite industry, but he soon abandoned that for farming. He was part of a large migration of French-Canadians into northern Vermont until, by the 1930s, they had taken over most of the farms from the English and Scots, who had abandoned the rural life for the city or to move west searching for better land and a longer growing season. As a youngster I watched Oscar Perron turn a cedar swamp into usable land. He cut down the trees, pulled out the stumps with a horse and chain, drained the land, and picked out the stones one at a time. I had no clear idea what he was doing, but he was creating farmland that looked like a park. Some have called it a vernacular landscape. Oscar's son, Ted, told me that his father had no plan as he created the landscape, only intuition and a respect for the land. Last year Ted died and the family was forced to sell their cows. For the first time in more than a hundred years there are no cows grazing on the land. It is difficult to make a living on a small farm in Vermont. I would hate to see a row of condominiums sprout on the ridge.

I often take visitors on a tour of the back roads and neighboring towns. They are always attracted to the carefully restored farms with white Greek revival farmhouses and high-drive barns painted red. However, if we look closely it is obvious that this is not a real farm, but the summer home of someone from New York, or Boston, or Princeton, New Jersey. The few remaining working farms are not as neat and orderly; they have trucks and tractors scattered about, and the new milking parlors have none of the charm of the old barns. There are other houses in need of repair whose occupants no longer farm but commute thirty or even sixty miles each day to work. As we drive along a back road we come across several trailers, or mobile homes, the new Vermont vernacular architecture. My guests usually don't notice because their eyes are on the beautiful landscape, but hidden away there is a part of Vermont that is much like Appalachia. There remains a certain tension and divide between those who use Greensboro as a summer resort and those who have to struggle to make a living in an unforgiving place.

Greensboro, like all the towns in the northeastern part of Vermont, was chartered during the American Revolution. During the war, a military highway, the Bayley-Hazen Road, was constructed from Newbury, on the Connecticut River, through Peacham, Hardwick, Greensboro, and Craftsbury toward the Canadian border. The plan was to use the road to attack Montreal, but the war ended before the road was finished. The military leaders also discovered that the road could be used in reverse by British troops and their Indian allies to attack New England towns. The road's main usefulness was to open up the territory to settlers after the war. There is a monument near Caspian Lake that reads: "Near this spot by a Block House guarding Hazen Road, two scouts, Constant Bliss and Moses Sleeper, were killed by Indians and buried where they fell." The monument was erected in 1941 during another patriotic time.

Greensboro, chartered in 1781 and settled in 1789, had 566 residents in 1810 and then reached a peak population of a little over 1,000 in 1860. The year-round residents now number a few over 700. There is some good farmland in the town, especially along the upper reaches of the Lamoille River, but the growing season is short and the winters long and cold. Many settlers left the rocky hill farms after a generation or two and moved west. Greensboro had one advantage over neighboring towns; it had Caspian Lake. The glacial lake is over a mile and a half long and a mile wide. It is deep and cold and very clear. On a quiet day you can see the gravel bottom at twenty-five feet. In the early years, the lake was important because the outlet brook provided sites for a grist mill and a sawmill. But in the late nineteenth century the lake was discovered as a place to fish, to camp, and to relax. Especially after the railroad came through the valley, four miles from the lake in 1872, Greensboro became accessible to travelers from Boston and New York. Two enterprising and shrewd local businessmen convinced the railroad builders to loop several miles from the direct route to create the village of Greensboro Bend. In 1886 there was a hotel in Greensboro Bend and two more in Greensboro, in addition to four boarding houses. There were also several fishing camps on the lake.

According to local legend it was Bliss Perry, a literary scholar from Princeton University, who "discovered" Greensboro in 1897. Actually he learned about Greensboro from his sister-in-law, who had come the year before with her husband, Peter Snyder, a minister in Burlington. The Snyders were joined by Celan Landon, the principal of Burlington High School. In any case, Perry, who later moved to Harvard University and became editor of the *Atlantic Monthly*, fell in love with Greensboro and began to tell his friends about a wonderful little town in northern Vermont where the air was cool and where Caspian Lake, which was 1,400 feet above sea level, was beautiful and unspoiled. It was a good place to write, and read, and to escape the pressures of the academic life. Among the Princeton group who were lured to Greensboro were art historian E. Baldwin Smith, Dean Luther Eisenhart, and Dean Christian Gauss, the mentor to both F. Scott Fitzgerald and Edmund Wilson. John Hibben, who had succeeded his friend Woodrow Wilson as president of the university, was constantly promoting the glories of Greensboro to his faculty. Yale was represented by Albert Stanborough Cook, chairman of Yale's graduate college of English, Clive Day, professor of economics, Robert Corwin, director of admissions, and George Parmly Day, the founder of Yale University Press.

When Bliss Perry moved from Princeton to Harvard (to be closer to Caspian Lake, he claims in his autobiography) he spread the word about Greensboro. Philosophy professor William Ernest Hocking, one of the Harvard contingent, built a camp on Caspian Lake, but he left for Madison, New Hampshire in 1925 when he decided that Greensboro was getting too crowded. Hocking encouraged Wesley Clair Mitchell and his wife, Lucy Sprague Mitchell, to come to Greensboro, and they built a camp at the north end of the lake in 1913. Wesley was a professor of economics at Columbia, an expert on business cycles, and an advisor to Franklin Roosevelt. Lucy was a pioneer in progressive education. She was the founder of the institution that became Bank Street College in New York, and she was a leader in the development of child-centered and experience-based learning. She wrote many books for children and many books and articles about the way children learn. Lucy Sprague Mitchell was not the only professional woman who spent summers in Greensboro. Agnes Hocking was the principal of the Shady Hill School in Cambridge, a school she had founded on her porch in 1915. Elizabeth Day was the director of a private school in New Haven, while Amy Watson, whose husband taught at Haverford, had a Ph.D. in sociology from Bryn Mawr and was the executive secretary of the Parents Council of Philadelphia, organized to "promote child study and effective parenting." In her autobiography, *Two Lives* (1953), Lucy Sprague Mitchell calls Greensboro "our one continuous home," and the gyroscope that kept the family on course. She also argues that it was their camp in Greensboro, where she had her own study in a separate building, that enabled her to have a career. The Mitchells arrived in Greensboro with at least one, and sometimes several maids, and that made writing possible during the summer for many of the academic visitors.

A directory of more than a hundred camps around the lake in 1915 revealed about a quarter belonged to professors and school teachers, and there were seventeen ministers and a number of doctors and lawyers. Reverend Alfred H. Barr of

Union Theological School built a camp early in the century, and his son, Alfred H. Barr Jr., the genius behind the Museum of Modern Art in New York, hid away in a camp on Caspian Lake writing books on modern art. John Gunther, the journalist, traveler, and author of *Inside USA* and many other books, found Greensboro a convenient place to work and to play. Often, in the 1930s, Greta Garbo, perhaps Hollywood's most seductive star, would visit the Gunthers. She called herself Helen Brown in Greensboro. There are still a few men in their eighties who claim to have canoed near a certain rock at the north end of the lake to observe Garbo sunbathing in the nude. In some ways the most able of the Greensboro authors was Wallace Stegner, novelist, Pulitzer Prize winner, and distinguished teacher of writing at Stanford University. He first discovered Greensboro in the 1930s, and he often retreated to his study or "think house" on Baker Hill to write stories and novels about the west. But his last novel, *Crossing to Safety,* is set in Greensboro. For many, Greensboro is still more a retreat than a resort, a place to combine work and play. Some Greensboro summer residents still find it difficult to believe that I grew up in Hardwick.

When I was a youngster and spent summers in Greensboro, I was aware that some of the campers had more money than we did. The Turrells from New York owned several camps and boathouses, and they had the only inboard motorboat on the lake, but most of the cottages, even the bigger ones, were rustic and simple in design. Except for having maids, most families lived simply on Caspian Lake in the summer. One didn't come to Greensboro to dance in casinos or to go to parties that would be written up in the society pages of the urban newspapers. Greensboro was a long way in style and appearance from Saratoga Springs, Nantucket, or Bar Harbor. Still, the ministers and professors occasionally acted or spoke differently than the Vermonters. I remember overhearing a woman complaining in Willey's Store that it was impossible to buy pasteurized milk in town. Another urged Mr. Willey to stock S. S. Pierce canned goods; something he eventually did. Very few of the camps had telephones in the 1930s and 1940s; if you absolutely needed to make a phone call you had to line up at Telephone Central, which was in a house on Main Street. I remember once going there with my father, perhaps during the war. He had to call the store in Hardwick for some reason. As we were standing in line a man rushed up and barged in ahead of us saying that he needed to call Washington, D.C. No one in line was impressed. In Greensboro you waited your turn, even if you were calling the president. We sometimes laughed at the youngsters from away who had to go to church on Sunday, and who often looked silly trying to catch fish out of the lake. But I shared with them a passion for the ice cream sodas served at the soda fountain inside Willey's, and I sometimes saw them in the tiny little library in Greensboro where I went to find books for rainy days at camp. I began to meet some of the young people from away in 1945 and 1946, and if I hadn't escaped to work in a boys' camp and then in summer hotels I might have become part of the Greensboro social set, but avoiding employment in my father's store was more important.

My family lived only seven miles away from Greensboro, enabling us to go to camp not only in the summer, but also in spring, fall, and even winter. In early spring we often went to Greensboro to fish, clean the camp, and put the dock in the lake. In fall we had to close the camp, pull up the dock, and do other chores. At least once during the winter we joined a couple of other families to have an outdoor picnic on the ice. We often brought our sleds so we could slide all the way back to Hardwick. It was almost all downhill, but one of the men would follow us in his car and, with the aid of a rope, pull us up the few hills or along the flat spots. As I got older I discovered that camp was a good place to take a girlfriend, and even in early spring when the waters of Caspian were truly cold, a group of brave-hearted souls would plunge into the lake. Once, with several friends, I went swimming in early May with chunks of ice still floating around. Many years later, while attending a conference in Tampere, Finland, I went to an oldfashioned, wood-burning sauna on the shores of a lake, but it was April and the lake was still frozen. Many of the Finns left the steaming sauna and walked down a path to jump into a hole chopped in the ice. I declined by saying that I had once gone swimming in Caspian Lake in May, and I did not have to prove my manhood.

That lake in Finland reminded me of Caspian Lake, and I have often been reminded of Greensboro and the northern Vermont landscape as I have traveled in various parts of the world—Scotland, northern Italy, even Austria. Others share a similar affection. In 1975, while attending an American Studies conference in Japan, we were taken by bus from Tokyo to a government conference center near Mt. Fuji. We stopped on the way at a beautiful lake for what the Japanese called barbecue. I was sitting next to a professor from Australia. I looked out at the lake and at the mixed hardwood and softwood trees along the hills. I remarked to my companion that it reminded me of northern Vermont. "Where in northern Vermont?" he asked. "A little town named Greensboro," I responded. "You have to be joking," he said. "I spent the summer of 1962 staying in a rented camp on Caspian Lake trying to finish my dissertation."

When I was growing up in Hardwick, we packed up and moved to camp as soon as school was out in June. We stayed until near the end of July, when my grandparents moved to Greensboro to remain well through September. I was always excited when we moved to camp. Even as a youngster I stored up memories from one year to the next. Memories are one of the important results of going to the same place each year. Now, I listen to my little grandchildren talk about the fish they caught, or the lean-to they built, or the adventure they had last year or the year before.

Over the years there have been rare occasions when I have had visitors who complain that there is nothing to do in Greensboro. I never remember being bored there. There were stones to skip, toy boats to play with, the big boat to row, fish to catch, minnows to trap, walks to take along the shore to the village, or hikes up Baker Hill to pick wild strawberries. On rainy days we often played Monopoly or card games, or we labored over a jigsaw puzzle. Miss Martin and Mrs. Lock, two elderly sisters who had the camp next to ours, worked all summer on very difficult jigsaw puzzles, and I spent hours talking to them and helping to find the right pieces. Perhaps those jigsaw puzzles taught me patience, or possibly it was just busy work, but to this day when I pass a jigsaw puzzle in progress I can't resist stopping to find a missing piece.

Summer at camp meant various rites of passage. I learned to swim using water wings when I was about five. One year (was I six?), my mother allowed me to row the boat alone. About the same time I swam out to the raft. A year or two later I swam all the way to the point and back. I was a strong, if not a graceful swimmer and I loved to explore the bottom of the lake, and I would spend hours poking around the rocks on the shore. At some point I was allowed to walk along the path alone (a distance of about a mile) all the way to Willey's Store. In 1946, the summer I was fifteen and in training to play football, I ran the seven miles around the lake. Most people thought I was crazy, but now runners routinely make that loop, and some even do it twice.

The large brick fireplace in the living room was the social center of the camp. On cold days we would sit close to absorb the warmth. After swimming we would rush to dry off in front of the fire. I loved to build fires, to chop wood, and to keep the wood box full, and I still do. There was no bathtub at camp. Why do you need a bathtub when you have the lake, my grandfather asked? Now and then we would take a cake of soap with us in swimming; we would scrub a little and call that a bath.

Camp was also a good place to read. My favorite spot was the hammock on the porch, but on rainy days I could curl up in a corner chair in the living room. One summer, when I was perhaps ten or eleven, I discovered the Boy Allies series at the Greensboro Free Library, and during the early days of World War II, I fought in all the battles of the Great War. We did many things together as a family at camp, but in my memory I was often alone, living in my own special world.

We usually returned to Hardwick on Saturdays to allow my father to work at the store on the busiest day of the week. We hoed the garden at home, did laundry and other chores, and returned to camp after the store closed at 9:00 P.M. Hardwick seemed like a different world. It was always exciting to return to camp at night, and sad, when all too soon, we had to pack up and return to Hardwick for the last part of the summer. Often during August, especially on a hot Sunday, we would drive to camp to take a swim and to visit with my grandparents. I would change into my bathing suit in "my room" only to discover that someone else was living there. It was always a little depressing and sad. While we were staying at camp we often had relatives or friends who came for a few days, and if there was an excess of children I sometimes had to share my bed, or even worse, had to sleep in one of the other bedrooms. I was always glad when those guests left and I could go back to my familiar routine. But I looked forward to the arrival of my Uncle Herman. My father's older brother, Herman, was more gregarious and outgoing than my father. He owned insurance agencies in Concord and Nashua, New Hampshire, and he always arrived with a new, black Lincoln Zephyr. He usually came alone because his first wife did not like Greensboro, and in my family we did not take kindly to those who did not like camp. I did like his daughter, my cousin Barbara, who was a couple years older than my sister Florence, and six or seven years older than I was. She led us on expeditions to find snakes and frogs. Sadly, she stopped coming after Herman and his wife divorced. He came alone and that was fine with me, for I liked the presents he brought me and the stories he told about fishing expeditions of the past. When Uncle Herman was at camp we usually went fishing every day in the lake or went on an expedition to Long Pond.

I walk along the unimproved road into Long Pond several times each summer. The pond is about four miles north of Caspian and about two hundred feet higher. The road, about a mile long, goes downhill most of the way. It cuts through a forest of balsam fir, spruce, white cedar, yellow birch, and an occasional maple. The woods appear deep and primeval, even though they have been cut over many times. Wallace Stegner once remarked that "Vermont wants to be woods." He also was impressed that in Vermont, unlike on the Western Plains, the land heals itself. The *Beers Atlas* of 1878 shows farmland, pasture, and sugar orchard extending to the edge of the pond and in the woods there are the remains of stone walls, a reminder that there were many more farms in Greensboro 130 years ago. As I approach the pond there are wild roses. Are they wild or did they escape from somebody's front yard more than a hundred years ago? The pond, much smaller than Caspian, covers about a hundred acres. It has a swamp at one end and there are lilies, cattails, and wild irises. Across the pond I can see Blueberry Rocks, a granite outcropping that rises from the shore. There are no cottages and I cannot even see a farm or a house from the shore. I am alone in the wilderness. Only a beer can or two and a plastic wrapper are signs that other people have made the same hike to the pond.

Every time I hike into Long Pond I am reminded of other adventures. Sometimes, when I was a child we drove in along the same road where I now walk, and at least once, we got stuck. We usually rented an old flat-bottomed boat from a farmer, but once, we got lost trying to find it, and another time the boat leaked so badly that we didn't dare take it more than a few feet from shore. We brought a picnic lunch, which we ate on a sandy beach at the upper end of the pond, but occasionally we built a fire and fried perch for lunch. After a day of fishing we had often caught over a hundred perch, enough for a giant fish fry. Occasionally we drove in the other side of the pond and parked our car near an abandoned farm that my father called "the Rutledge Place." After the war, Russ Dawley, an Army veteran, bought the farm and improbably turned it into a Vermont version of a dude ranch. Not many guests came, and after a couple of years he gave up the dream of Tamarack Ranch. A few years ago I walked along the old road. I became disoriented by the deep woods, and I found neither the Rutledge Place nor the pond. The land around the pond is now mostly owned by the Nature Conservancy and there is no danger that a developer will build condominiums along the shore. The pond seemed like a wilderness paradise when I was a child, and it seems even more remote today.

Long Pond triggers many memories of trips there with my father and with my sons. I have one snapshot, taken just a year before my father died, of three generations of Davis men fishing in a boat at the pond. Long Pond also reminds me of my Uncle Herman. He smoked cigars, and to this day, when I smell cigar smoke, I think of him and the exciting adventure we had when he visited at camp. While I was at Dartmouth he would often visit me and take me out to eat at the Hanover Inn. He came to my graduation, and after the speeches and awards and the congratulations, he took me aside and offered me the chance to work for his insurance agency and eventually take it over. I am afraid, in retrospect, that I rejected his offer too quickly and offended him by announcing that I was going to study history in graduate school.

When my Uncle Herman arrived at camp we always went fishing; in fact, most of my memories of Greensboro are somehow related to fishing. I can recapture the way I felt as a youngster on a Sunday in May, having to sit through a church service knowing that as soon as church was over we were going to camp. The sermon and the hymns seemed endless and the hands on my watch barely moved, but finally I was released. I raced home, changed my clothes, and put my fishing pole and a can of fish worms in the car. I had been digging worms from the moment the snow melted from the garden. Digging worms and trapping minnows were almost as exciting as fishing; it was the sense of preparation and anticipation. I used fish worms, or angleworms as my father called them, to catch both brook trout in the streams and perch out of the lake. Eventually, I discovered fly fishing, but worms were still preferred for perch. My father, even my mother and sisters, seemed as excited about going to camp as I was. My mother has prepared enough food for both dinner and supper. Often we joined another family at our camp or theirs for these spring fishing trips and picnics. We could usually catch perch from the shore in the spring, and later in the summer we would anchor in twenty or thirty feet of water in "our bay" and be confident of catching enough perch for a meal in an hour or two. But catching fish also meant cleaning them. When I was no more than six or eight my father taught me a special way to dress perch, a technique he had learned from his father and that I passed on to my sons. Perch fishing was a family affair, and at least in my family my sisters and my mother also participated.

Catching perch from the shore in the spring brings to mind two childhood adventures, or misadventures. The first occurred when I was perhaps six. I went with my grandparents to camp early in the spring. They planned to clean the camp and I expected to fish. I went immediately to the vacant lot next to our camp, owned by Oscar Perron, the local farmer. He had been clearing and draining one of his fields, and in the process he picked out the stones and deposited them in a pile extending into the lake. This made a perfect place to fish, because the water was deep and I could look down into the clear water and watch the fish bite. I caught two or three small perch and then watched with great excitement as a gigantic perch headed for my worm. Fish look bigger when magnified by the water, but it was still a large fish. As I leaned over to get the baited hook in just the right place, I tipped too far, and the next thing I felt was the cold water. Soaked from head to toe and disappointed that I had scared the fish away, I raced back to camp. My grandfather comforted me, built a fire in the fireplace, helped me strip off my wet clothes, and found an old shirt for me to wear. One of the things I remember about the incident is the way he showed me how to dry my back with a bath towel by grabbing both ends and moving it like a saw back and forth. Sometimes, even now after a shower, I grab a bath towel and dry my back, and I think of my grandfather and that early spring day in Greensboro. He was not always as understanding. When I was quite small he gave me a toy drum for Christmas. I was quite excited. I beat it with the drumsticks and it broke. He seemed angry that I had broken "his" drum. I prefer to remember how he rescued me and helped me dry off after I had plunged into the frigid waters of Caspian Lake.

The other incident I recall vividly probably happened a year or two later, but my memory has no dates or chronology. It was another spring Sunday picnic in Greensboro, this time not at our camp but at the Lane/Taylor camp on Black's Point, in part, I suspect, because the fishing was better off the point. The men had set out lines hoping to catch a lake trout, and the women were in the kitchen preparing dinner. I told my mother that I would be fishing for perch from the Parker boathouse next door. One advantage of visiting Greensboro during the off-season is that one can "trespass" on other people's property, even peek into windows, without fear of being detected. I fished for a while from the boathouse without much success and then decided to move up the shore fifty feet or so. There, by a big rock and an overhanging tree, I had better luck. Completely absorbed, I lost track of time. Suddenly one of the Lane boys, several years older than I, disturbed my fishing odyssey, and informed me that there were search parties out looking for me. I was angry that my fishing was interrupted, and even more concerned that my mother thought I had drowned. I knew I was in no danger, and I had a hard time understanding why the adults were upset. But even now, when I pass that spot on the shore, I remember, and I think about the good fishing and about how I frightened my mother. Why do I remember these two events? Perhaps because my image of myself even as a youngster was of being independent and in command, and these adventures revealed that I was vulnerable and dependent.

There are still perch in Caspian Lake, but they are not as easy to catch. The ecology of the lake has changed; perhaps the water is cleaner with the elimination of agricultural runoff and the improvement of septic systems, or perhaps it was the accidental introduction of cray fish into the lake some years ago. For whatever the reason, one can no longer catch perch from shore in the spring, nor can one anchor in our bay and expect to catch enough fish for dinner. Still, despite my memories of fishing for perch, even while I was growing up, fishing for lake trout, rainbows, and brown trout was more romantic and somehow carried more prestige. On the wall in the living room at my camp are the outlines of two large lake trout caught by my father and carefully traced on the wall; one is a ten-pound trout caught by my uncle and father on June 3, 1934, and the other is an eight-pounder caught in 1941. I also have a "Fishing Register" kept sporadically by various members of the family. The first entry is June 15, 1925: "Harold F. Davis and Fuller Mitchell, 14 lb. laker, 35 inches." There are other success stories, including those that are traced on the wall, but most of the trout are smaller—though sometimes, before the two-trout-per-person daily limit, ten or twelve trout might be caught in a day or two. But fishing was not always good. In 1935 my father wrote in the Fishing Register: "Regarding the trout fishing, we are at a loss to understand why the depression should have made the trout grow smaller. We had only two trout to eat, but if HFD could have had pay-per-hour for the time spent trolling, we would be driving a new car." The economic downturn is probably as good an explanation for poor fishing as excuses I hear today, which tend to emphasize ice fishing and big boats equipped with depth finders and down riggers.

Trolling has always been the preferred method of catching trout out of the lake. The technique I learned from my grandfather and father (and still use) is a combination of lead-core line, Dave Davis spinners (no relation), and a minnow threaded to spin naturally. Just how to thread a minnow, the proper size to use, and how to make it spin has been a family secret for at least four generations. Some fishermen refuse to use minnows and swear by Mooselook Wobblers, Record spoons, or Sutton spoons. There are dozens of sizes and variations, but the secret is to get the lure down near the bottom. There are still a few old-timers who can be seen early in the morning trolling with a handheld line, using a rhythmic motion alongside their boat as they bounce a Sutton spoon off the bottom.

Another way to catch trout in Caspian Lake, especially the big ones, is to still-fish near the islands. The experts anchor their boat in shallow water near a ledge so they can place their line in very deep water. The experienced fishermen often use two boats, one anchored and one free, to play the big trout once it strikes and to move away from the other lines. While they wait, the fishermen often play cards, sleep, or read, or some combination of the three. Setting a line out from shore, especially early in the spring, was another way of taking trout. We never had much luck doing that from our dock, but Clyde Lane caught trout all summer from his camp on Black's Point without even leaving his porch. He wrapped the line around an old tobacco can (the kind they now sell as antiques), and when the can rattled on the rocks he knew there was a fish on.

Trolling was the favored method in my family for catching trout: we did not have the patience to sit all day, and we rarely had any luck setting a line out from the shore. When I was growing up, anyone could catch perch, even girls. Trolling for trout, on the other hand, was a man's sport. It was an important rite of passage when I was allowed to go fishing with the men and to hold a trolling pole (we never called it a rod). My grandfather recognized this when he wrote in the Fishing Register the year I was six: "The men went trolling (including Allen) and caught two nice trout." We usually went fishing in the early evening, although we occasionally got up at dawn to see if we could get a strike (perch bit, but trout always struck). My father made elaborate preparations for these fishing expeditions. We carried extra jackets and pillows, a minnow bucket, landing net, and a tackle box filled with extra hooks, lures, and spinners, many never used. We always rowed. We finally purchased a motor in 1955, but it never worked very well for trolling. I still row, but now mostly for the exercise, and because I like the silence. I remember trolling with my father one morning in the early 1940s out near the islands, not too far from where several boats were fishing for the big ones. We had a solid strike, and about the same time, Aquinaldo (Pop) Barr in one of the anchored boats began whooping and yelling as his pole bounced up and down. He thought he had hooked a huge fish, but it soon became obvious that we had hooked his line. After everyone realized what had happened we all laughed, but there was a lingering disappointment because there was no big fish. Barr was one of the many devoted fishermen from Hardwick who fished regularly and successfully in Caspian Lake. He also gave famous fishing parties at his camp on the lake. On one occasion during World War II, one of the men staying at his camp, perhaps a little groggy from the late party, forgot to attach the outboard motor properly, and the motor, irreplaceable at any price during the war, flipped off in about forty feet of water. Despite several days of diving and using grappling hooks, they never recovered the motor.

There were many famous fishermen on the lake who caught many legendary, even mythical trout. There was Bruce Young, who rowed his flat-bottomed boat, with a peculiar jerky motion so one could spot him from a great distance. There were many stories about how he sank a dead calf in the lake and then fished over it, or how he set lines attached to syrup cans anchored just below the surface. No one ever caught him and the stories are probably apocryphal, but such are the tales that fishermen tell.

There was also "Indian Joe," who lived in a shack near the lake. We heard that he could do magical things, but I never saw him do them. He could make a basket out of birch bark and catch fish with his bare hands. There were always stories about how much better the fishing was in the past than it was in the present. My father told of visiting his aunts, who had a camp on the lake, about 1910, and they would go out in a boat and in about fifty feet of water, they would catch a trout or two for supper as easily as if they had gone to the fish market. And I heard over and over again how my father and my uncle got a ten-pound trout on a troll.

I learned when quite small that trolling was about more than catching fish. It was a time to think and plan, to tell stories and to appreciate the lake, the hills in the distance, and the beauty of the sunsets. Going trolling with my father was one of the few times we had real conversations. We talked about fishing, and he told me stories of fishing successes and failures in the past, but he also talked about more personal matters. He was a very private person who rarely shared his thoughts, but when we were trolling he asked questions, even shared his worries and his plans. The summer before I went into the Army he came to me one day and suggested that we go trolling one more time. We rarely fished late in the summer, but I quickly realized this was about more than fishing. He told stories that I had heard before about his own Army experience, and then he told me how worried he was about my mother, who was fighting the breast cancer that would take her life a few months later. It was probably the most personal and meaningful conversation I ever had with my father. I remember it often as I troll today, using the same pole and the same boat that we used that day.

Bernice S. Allen and Harold F. Davis about a year before they were married in 1924.

Allen helping his father wash the family car, a 1928 Willys-Knight, in the driveway in front of of the South Main Street house, probably about 1935. In the left background, is a saw mill operating in what had once been a bobbin factory. This is an indication of the mixed neighborhood in the south part of town in the 1930s.

The Davis Store on South Main Street in Hardwick, circa 1905. Charles F. Davis, my grandfather, purchased the store in 1902. It became the C. F. Davis Department Store, then C. F. Davis and Son in the 1920s when my father, Harold F. Davis, joined the business. It became the H. F. Davis Store in the 1930s and my father finally sold it in 1968. The building remains but is now an apartment house.

Charles Freeman Davis, Harold Freeman Davis, and Allen Freeman Davis, May, 1937, with a six-pound lake trout caught at Caspian lake. The photo was taken in front of the Hardwick house. Charles Davis, born in 1864, was named after his uncle, Charles Freeman, who died at Andersonville Prison during the Civil War. Freeman, as a middle name, has now continued for five generations.

Formal family photograph taken at the Spaulding Studio, Hardwick, Vermont, circa 1942. From left to right: Bernice Allen Davis, Allen, Marjorie, Florence, and Harold F. Davis.

Allen Davis at about age 4 riding a tricycle on the sidewalk in front of Davis House on South Main Street in Hardwick before the house was remodeled and the porch removed. In the background is an apartment house soon to be demolished.

Allen Davis as skier, circa 1943. Notice the long, wooden, ridge-top skis, the bamboo poles, the snow-covered woolen jacket.

Most of us were born in 1931, a low birth year. Still, there were thirty-two of us who gathered in October, 1937, in front of the Academy building to have our first grade photograph taken. I am in the back row, second from the right with hair uncombed. Eleven of us persisted to

graduate from high school in 1949. Others dropped out, or moved out of town with their parents. Some were "kept back" a grade or two. A few students joined us to make a class of twenty-three graduates in 1949.

Florence, Allen, and Marjorie on our dock c. 1941.

Davis camp on Caspian Lake, Greensboro, Vermont. Build by Charles F. Davis in 1923, on land purchase by Florence Haines Davis in 1913.

Hardwick Academy where I went from Grade 1 to graduate from high school in 1949. Next door was the "new gym," built in 1940, giving Hardwick one of the best basketball courts in the state as well as a place for dances, plays, and other events.

Junior prom, Spring 1948. I am in the middle in the dark suit and bow tie. My date is Connie Lavertu. The "New Gym," built in 1940, served as basketball court, but also as a place for meetings, plays, and dances.

Hardwick Academy basketball team, 1946-47, my sophomore year. I am in the front row on the left.

The Jeudevine Memorial Library, built in Romanesque Revival Style in 1897, where I spent many hours reading magazines and searching for books.

Auction at the home of Harold F. Davis, July, 1978. Photo taken from cemetery across the street. Buffalo Mountain is in the background.

Chapter 7

THE GREAT DEPRESSION

IN MY MEMORY, Hardwick during the 1930s was sepia or gray. Perhaps that is because most people did not have the money to paint their houses, or perhaps it is because I have studied so many black and white photographs and snapshots of the 1930s that I remember it as a black and white and brown decade. Hardwick was a declining industrial town. The granite industry had reached its peak of prosperity about 1915 and the town had not participated in the national prosperity of the 1920s, so my sepia memories may be accurate. I was born in the depths of the Depression. My memories are framed through the eyes of a child, but filtered as well by what I have learned about the decade through years of study.

Looking at family photos I see few indications of the Depression. The collective memory of the Depression years is influenced by images of breadlines and soup kitchens and by John Steinbeck's story of the "Okies" in *The Grapes of Wrath*, and the movie version that came out in 1940 starring Henry Fonda. Yet, I have no memory of this kind of poverty in Hardwick. Images of the 1930s are even more influenced by Farm Security Administration photographs—Dorothea Lange's *Migrant Mother*, Arthur Rothstein's Dust Bowl photos, and images from the Southwest do not help me imagine the Depression in Hardwick. A few of Walker Evans' stark interiors—tables covered with oil cloth, iron beds, and simple bureaus and chairs—trigger memories. For many, the Depression in Hardwick meant houses in need of paint, vacant lots that stayed vacant, wood stoves rather than electric, linoleum rather than carpet on the living room floor, cast iron rather than enamel sinks, and two or more children sleeping in the same bed.

There is one famous FSA photograph of Hardwick taken by Carl Mydans on a fall day in 1936 (and reproduced on the cover of this book). The photo is dominated by political banners because 1936 was an election year. There were banners promoting Franklin Roosevelt and his Vice President, John Nance Garner, and Republicans Alfred Landon of Kansas and Col. Frank Knox of Illinois. Another sign strung across Main Street promotes the Townsend Old-Age Revolving Pensions Plan originated by Dr. Frances E. Townsend of Long Beach, California. The plan (which was never enacted) promised to pay all unemployed Americans $200 a month if they were over sixty years old and if they promised to spend it all in the month they received it. The sign proclaims: "Quick national recovery, permanent old age security. It is up to you to get it enacted into law. Work for it. Vote for it." There was a Townsend Club in Hardwick, though I have no memory of it, nor do I recall the political campaign. I do remember the fall of 1936, however, because that was the year many of my friends went off to first grade and I had to wait until the fall of 1937.

The Mydans photograph captured Hardwick's busy Main Street about noon on a warm fall day. There are both trucks and cars parked on the street. A few look like they might be 1936 models, but most are ancient survivors from the 1920s. In the foreground, a farmer talks to a businessman.

Farmers dressed differently from those who lived in town in the 1930s, but all men wore hats. Hardwick in 1936 has a slightly shabby and run-down look, and Main Street betrays the haphazard way the village was built between a steep hill and the river. But there are new electric lights and a recently poured concrete pavement. Hardwick is a gritty town, but it appears more prosperous than many towns recorded by the FSA photographers.

The Mydans photograph, of course, does not capture the sounds of Hardwick during the 1930s, but they still exist in my memory. There were bells—church bells and school bells and a clock on the Methodist Church that struck the hour. The United Church bell was a little deeper in tone than the Catholic Church bell if my memory is correct. It struck once at 9:00 P.M. to signal a curfew and to warn those under a certain age to return home. It must have been a relic from an earlier time because no one took the curfew seriously. The United Church bell also served as a fire alarm. When it struck a certain number of rings or combinations everyone in town raced to their chart that told them the location of the fire. I remember when a fire broke out on Sunday or in the evening, we would jump into my father's car and race to the scene. Tragically, in the summer it was often a barn on fire. Sometimes we even beat the firetrucks.

In addition to the bells there was the high-pitched whine of the saws at several sawmills in town and a whistle at the granite sheds, which blew every morning at seven and every afternoon at four, to signal the beginning and the end of the work day. There were no whistles on Saturday and Sunday, except the train whistle that marked the arrival of a steam locomotive pulling several cars on the St. Johnsbury and Lake Champlain Railroad as it crossed the road near the depot. At the depot the *click, click* of the telegraph key indicated a form of communication still prominent in Hardwick in the 1930s. A telegram usually meant an emergency, though travelers could keep in touch by wire and fathers could send money to a son in a distant city using the telegraph. During the Depression decade, one could hear trucks and cars, but also the *clop, clop* of horses and the ping of metal on metal in the two or three remaining blacksmith shops in town. Hardwick was a town in transition in the 1930s.

By the time I was six or seven I roamed all over town, either with my friends or alone. I loved to look in the store windows, and I especially liked the news store and the five-and-dime stores, which apparently were not affected by the Depression. Everyone knew who I was, so if I misbehaved someone could easily call my mother to report on my activities. Before I went to school I often walked "down street" with my mother when she went shopping. About once a month I went with my father in the evening to the barbershop and then often to the bowling alley. Sometimes in the winter my father and I went to the "old gym" to see a high school basketball game. The old gym, replaced in 1940 by an impressive "new gym" next to the Academy building, was a remodeled granite polishing shed located at the corner of Maple and Church Streets. It was tiny with low ceilings and very little room between the walls and the basketball court. The only place for fans was in the balcony, where they were protected by chicken wire. Basketball was an important sport in Hardwick during the Depression. I loved to go to those games with my father and I dreamed of becoming a star player when I grew up.

My grandfather, like many others, lost money when banks failed after the stock market crash. He died in 1951, and those settling his estate discovered that he had small accounts in more than a dozen banks. He spread his money around; he was not going to be fooled again. I once asked my father how the Depression affected him and he said that he went to work in the store everyday, but some of his customers couldn't pay for their groceries. I talked to one of those customers a few years ago, and she told me that my father carried her family for three years during the 1930s, but she said,

"I'm proud to say that I eventually paid every penny." I recall the older brother of one of my friends going off to work for the Civilian Conservation Corps, and I remember others working for the Works Progress Administration (WPA). My father was a faithful Vermont Republican, and there was much criticism of Roosevelt and the New Deal in my house. My father did not approve of make-work programs and he thought most of those employed by the WPA were lazy. He said that WPA stood for We Putter Around, and he complained about government red tape, but he thought that the Rural Electrification Association that brought electricity to remote Vermont farms was a good idea. And many years later he was proud of his Social Security check.

My father was influenced by the Depression, but probably more by the New England work ethic. His philosophy of life included: don't go into debt, pay your bills on time, save for a rainy day, don't gamble or squander your money or talk to others about your investments or bank accounts. It was important, he said many times, "to know the value of a dollar." He was meticulously careful with his money, but he was thrifty, not stingy. He had a wallet with three sections. In one he kept money for the store, in another for house expenses, and the third was for his car. I remember once we stopped to get gasoline, and he discovered that he didn't have enough money in the car compartment so he made a loan to himself from one of the other sections. When he died I found many notebooks in which he had written down every personal expense. Perhaps this careful accounting of money was the product of a lifetime habit of a small businessman and had nothing to do with the Depression, but the economic downturn made him even more cautious with money and more careful about investments. My grandfather invested in stock and owned several rental properties. My father was much more cautious and took fewer risks. Still, he bought a house in 1931. He paid $2,400, one half down with the balance due in one year. Yet, because of the economic collapse, he was forced to renegotiate the loan several times. He finally paid it off in 1943. In his neat hand he wrote across the loan document: "Total interest, $427.03." I am sure it was not a happy moment. He hated to pay interest.

My father drove his cars for at least ten years before he traded them, and he always paid cash. He was proud of his car. During the 1930s he drove a 1928 Willys-Knight four-door sedan. Even during the Depression we went on Sunday rides, and unlike some in town who put the car up on blocks for the winter, we took trips in both the summer and the winter. I loved to ride in the front seat with my father, though usually I had to sit in the back with my sisters. In the winter we placed a car robe over our knees to help ward off the cold because the heater in the Willys-Knight didn't work well. I liked to sit in the front seat, in part, because I could study the map and trace our route. It seemed magical to me that the maps actually matched the real towns and route numbers. I acquired a large collection of road maps that were given away free by the gasoline companies. I had not only Vermont and New Hampshire, but also New York, Michigan, Massachusetts, Pennsylvania, and, for some reason, California. Later, I acquired *National Geographic* maps for much of the world. I dreamed of traveling to far away places, to New York and Chicago, to Paris and Rome, and also to the Arctic, and the tropics.

Our usual Sunday afternoon drives did not take us to exotic places, but to Craftsbury, Cabot, Glover, Waterbury, and to other nearby towns to visit relatives. We went to Barre, where I was outfitted with my first sports coat. Or we went to Lancaster, New Hampshire, where my father's cousin, Ellen Davis, owned a dress shop. We always went on Sunday because that was the only day my father did not work at the store. Ellen would open the dress shop so my mother and sisters could shop for clothes. I was bored and begged to be released to walk around the town. Few stores were open on Sunday, but I did discover a drug store that sold magazines and a few cheap paperback books. They were much more exciting than the dresses.

We went most frequently to St. Johnsbury, a town of seven or eight thousand people about twenty-five miles east of Hardwick. It seemed like a city to me. There were several five-and-dime stores, several restaurants, and two movie theaters. It was here about 1937 that I saw my first movie, *Snow White and the Seven Dwarfs*. St. Johnsbury was the home of the Fairbanks Scale Factory. The Fairbanks family had given several impressive buildings to the town including an athenaeum and a museum. I loved to linger in the athenaeum to study the art, especially the huge Albert Bierstadt painting, *The Domes of the Yosemite*. I also looked at the books, but it was the museum down the street that fascinated me. There were collections of stuffed birds and animals, geological specimens, and Indian artifacts. There was a main floor and a balcony where I loved to inspect the exotic specimens in glass cases. Many years later, on a rainy day at camp, I took my two sons to the same museum. As we walked in the door it suddenly occurred to me that it was this museum and my childhood visits that had created an image in my mind of the way a museum should look.

Sometimes on our Sunday drives my father would take back roads that were not on my map. These roads were unpaved, and they sometimes had grass growing in the middle. My father seemed to know exactly where these roads would come out, but on a couple of occasions I can recall we got stuck in the mud. My mother was not amused, but I thought of it as just another adventure. After jacking up the back wheels and using rocks and tree branches to improve the traction, my father would give up, walk to the nearest farm, and hire the farmer to come with a horse to pull the car out of the mud. Nothing was more embarrassing to the early car owner than to have to rely on a horse to rescue him, but my father never seemed disturbed. He had been driving since he was sixteen and had been pulled out of the mud many times. During the spring "mud season" many of the unpaved roads were impassable, and that included the main road from Hardwick to Montpelier.

Once a year in the summer when we were staying in Greensboro we made a trip to Burlington, Vermont's largest city with a population then of about 20,000. The excuse, as I remember, was that my father had to visit some of the wholesale grocers who did business with him. I recall once visiting the McKenzie Meat-Packing Plant. We watched the production of hot dogs. The smell alone ruined my appetite for hot dogs for several months. Burlington seemed like a metropolis to me and I would break away from my family and arrange to meet them later in the day. I wandered around the city visiting sporting goods stores and news stores where I browsed through the magazines and paperback books, which cost I think twenty-five cents. They had colorful covers encased in cellophane. My mother considered them "cheap" and not worth reading, but on one trip I bought Howard Fast's, *The Unvanquished*, the story of Washington's Army during the Revolution. I loved to wander around the city alone. I still find exploring a strange city by myself and browsing in bookshops among the most pleasurable of all activities.

Every August we went to the Barton Fair. My father must have taken a day off from the store, for we went for the entire day and stayed into the evening. Occasionally, we went to other fairs, in Lyndonville, Lancaster, New Hampshire, and other towns, but it was the Barton Fair that was, for us, an annual event. It was always exciting to ride the Ferris wheel, to look at the fair grounds from forty feet in the air. It was even interesting to view the displays of vegetables and flowers and farm animals raised by young people or to watch the horse pull. But the Midway, with games, restaurants, hot dog stands, and other attractions, was the best part of the fair. I quickly learned that the games of chance, knocking down bottles with a baseball, throwing darts at balloons, and the others games were rigged, or if I won a prize it was often worth less than the price I paid to play. Still, it was exciting to walk the Midway and at one end were sideshows—the bearded ladies, 400-pound men, and other freaks. Outside the shows the criers tried to entice the unwary in to see the show. One come-on that is fixed in my memory is the advertisement for a woman who apparently bit off the head of a chicken. "She's hungry: she must be fed," the crier announced. I did not give up my quarter for that show. But on one occasion, at the very end of the midway I came across a "girlie show." Just as I had convinced my parents that I should be allowed to wander around St. Johnsbury or Burlington, on my own so I insisted that it was all right for me to do the fair by myself as long as I agreed to meet them at a certain time and place. So I was alone when I came upon the girls in front of a tent promoting their show. They were carefully wrapped in capes or bath robes, but the crier promised that they would "take it all off." I was perhaps ten and I am sure the ticket seller would not have allowed me to buy a ticket, and I had little interest in any case, only curiosity. But as I walked away a man from the show offered me a quick look through the side of the tent. I could not resist. I got only a glance, but there was a woman, hardly a girl, naked, going through various contortions. It wasn't sexy or provocative. It was frightening, but at the same time compelling. The image of that naked woman stayed with me for years.

The Barton Fair was more than the Ferris wheel, the midway, more even than the girly show. It was about horse racing, and my Aunt Myrtie (second wife of my Uncle Lovell) raised and trained harness racers. She moved to the Barton Fairgrounds in early July, where she lived in a trailer and trained her horses. After the Barton Fair she moved to various fairs in New Hampshire and finally completed her circuit in Maine where betting on horses was legal. We always sat in the grandstand and watched her horses race at the Barton

Fair. The horse I remember best was Cocatella's Colt, and in my memory, it always came into the stretch in third place, and it always won. We would cheer and then go to the barns where my aunt and uncle held forth. My uncle was an expert at shoeing horses and probably should have concentrated on that rather than on farming. In the barns after a race, he was in his element, and I was proud of him. But the horses made me sneeze, my eyes water, and my breathing become difficult, so I quickly left the barns and returned to the midway.

Over Labor Day, the only time my father had a long weekend, we went on slightly longer trips, and we stayed in ovenight cabins, the forerunner of the motel. On these longer trips we played various games as we traveled. We looked for various objects such as a cemetery, a grindstone, and ever-present Burma-Shave signs. The red signs designed to be read at about thirty-five miles per hour were humorous and to the point. One that sticks in my mind went like this: "A Man. A Miss. A Car—A Curve. He Kissed the Miss and Missed the Curve." Burma-Shave. In our game each object was assigned a value and those on one side of the car played against those on the other. The side that got the most points won. Another game consisted of identifying different makes of autos, with unusual cars such as the Pierce Arrow or the Essex counting for more points.

In 1937, the year I was six, we went to Old Orchard Beach, Maine. It was my first visit to the ocean; even though it was cold I went in for a swim. One of my disappointments was that all the overnight cabins were full, and because my father had not made a reservation, we had to stay in a tourist home. A few years ago I drove out of my way to find Old Orchard Beach, now a favorite summer destination for those from Quebec. To my amazement I found many things that looked familiar, though I never found that tourist home.

In 1939 we traveled to the Rangeley Lakes in Maine. We had a cabin this time near a lake. But because there were two double beds, one for my parents and one for my sisters, I was the odd man out, and I had to sleep on a cot. I remember this trip over Labor Day 1939 because that was the weekend Germany invaded Poland, and Great Britain and France declared war on Germany. It was the beginning of World War II. It was cold that weekend, and on Labor Day morning we ate breakfast on the screened porch of a restaurant while my parents read the newspaper and talked in worried tones about the war. A few years ago, I drove through the village of Rangeley Lake. I stopped and walked around, but I could not find the overnight cabins, and even the lake triggered no memories. Yet the beginning of World War II in Europe is still associated in my memory with an overnight cabin, cold weather, and eating breakfast on a screened-in porch.

In 1941, a few months before Pearl Harbor, our Labor Day trip took us to Bennington, Vermont, Ausable Chasm, and Fort Ticonderoga. Exploring the restored fort was exciting to me because I had been reading Kenneth Roberts' novels and other books on the Revolution and the French and Indian Wars. There is a surviving photograph of that trip, taken by my mother. My two sisters and I, along with my father, are posed in front of the Bennington Battle Monument. I am wearing shorts. We all look windblown and tired, but I am pouting and appear unhappy, an image that contrasts sharply with my memory of that trip as the first time I realized that the history I had been reading had actually happened.

In 1941 we had a new car, a 1940 Packard that my father had bought the summer before. I remember the exact moment when we drove to St. Johnsbury and traded in the twelve-year-old Willys-Knight for the new car. A Packard, which my father always insisted was the least expensive model, had the reputation of being a rich man's car. My grandfather criticized my father for buying it because he thought the customers at the store would get the impression that his business was too successful. This purchase was a little out of character for my father who usually economized and believed in shopping locally. Because there was no Packard dealer in Hardwick we had to go out of town. But he remained true to his philosophy in another way—he wrote a check for the entire amount. He paid, if my memory is correct, a little over $1,000 in a year, when a Plymouth or Chevrolet would have cost about $650. It proved to be a fortuitous purchase because after 1942 no American cars were produced until 1946. Many of my friends were fascinated by cars—they haunted the garages, learned from the mechanics, and by the time they were twelve or fourteen they could make some repairs and dreamed of restoring an old car. I had little interest in cars; the oily smell of the garages and the greasy feel of automotive parts did not inspire me. Even today I can open the hood of my car and look in, but beyond that I am helpless, and I have no desire to restore an antique car.

I don't remember feeling poor when I was growing up in the 1930s, but one of my high school classmates recalls being embarrassed because she had only one dress to wear to school. Another friend says that she still goes around the house and turns off the lights, a habit she acquired during the Depression. My generation did not have firsthand experiences with the worst aspects of the economic downturn, but our parents used the Depression to warn us about the importance of saving money and of looking for a secure job. My mother urged me, when I was at Dartmouth, to take a few education courses in case I someday needed to teach in high school. And my father advised me against taking a thirty-year mortgage. He was horrified when some close friends got one of the first twenty-year FHA mortgages in the late 1930s. To him mortgages meant debt, and that was to be avoided. He never made a long-distance phone call unless there was a family crisis. He worked hard all his life, was never late for an appointment, and never stayed home when he was sick. And he expected others to do the same.

My parents taught me the value of money when I was

quite young. In my memory, I got an allowance of sixteen cents a week and was expected to save a portion of that. I had a little metal bank for my coins, and one of my earliest memories is being lifted up at the Hardwick Trust Company so I could see the teller count the coins for deposit in my savings account (started by my grandfather with one hundred dollars on the day I was born). I recall arguing with my playmates, Bill and Harry Pilbin, over whose father had the most money. Their father, who owned a garage, had a cash register, as did my father at the store. Our argument was over who had the most coins. We had not yet graduated to dollar bills, let alone fives, tens and twenties. A fifty-cent piece with an eagle on the back seemed like a fortune, and a buffalo nickel was much prized and carefully saved. When the Jefferson nickel came out in 1938 we weren't quite sure that it was really worth five cents. Our favorite coin was the standing liberty quarter with a flying eagle on the back. If you placed your thumb in the right place the eagle's head seemed to form an erect penis. It was perhaps the first sexy joke I learned.

When I was seven and my playmates nine and ten, their father died suddenly. They had to sell their car and the garage. They moved into a smaller house. Their mother had to find a job. They were forced to sleep in the same bed. They were poor. Because they needed the money, they invented all kinds of ways to earn a few cents. We searched along the side of the road hoping to find a small soda bottle that could be redeemed for two cents, or the big bottles that were worth five cents. Sometimes we competed with unemployed men or tramps for the bottles. In the early spring we dug dandelion greens and sold them, if my memory serves, for twenty-five cents a peck. And we hiked halfway up Buffalo Mountain to pick blueberries and then peddled them around town. Before Christmas, we cut evergreen branches, vines, and small trees for decoration. For a few years I made Christmas decorations out of a small birch log, candles, and evergreens and sold them in the neighborhood. I was quite shy as a youngster, and without my playmates I can't imagine that I would have had the courage to rap on a neighbor's door to offer something for sale. Yet, I did have my own projects. I subscribed to a magazine called *Open Road for Boys*, and one day I saw an ad there that suggested that I could make a lot of money by selling Cloverine Salve. I sent away for several boxes, but despite my efforts, I couldn't convince my neighbors that they should use the salve. I am sure my pitch was not very effective. Finally, my grandmother bought one tin and I mailed the rest back to the company. I learned in the process that I did not want to be a salesman.

My first real job was delivering flyers for my father after school on Monday. He belonged to the Nationwide group of independent grocers, and the Nationwide flyers I delivered all over the south side of town announced weekly grocery bargains. It was easier than trying to sell salve because I didn't need a sales pitch, but much of the year it was cold work. I remember on dark, winter afternoons how welcoming and warm my mother's kitchen seemed when I returned home from walking my route.

If we weren't exactly poor, there were others in Hardwick who were. Unemployment was high. Some people survived by taking marginal or seasonal jobs. One of my friends had a trap line and made a little money by selling muskrat, mink, and otter pelts. Some men set up cedar stills in late winter and sold the cedar oil to companies that made furniture polish. For those who were truly down and out, or too old to work, there was a poor farm just outside of town up a hill from the main road to Craftsbury. It was an institution left over from the nineteenth century that housed the indigent and elderly poor who had no family to care for them. I remember going with my father when he delivered groceries to the farm. In my memory I can see the elderly men and women sitting on the porch, staring blankly toward the hills on a warm summer day. When I heard adults say "I hope I never have to go to the poor farm," I knew what they meant.

Most families who suffered during the Depression were treated as hardworking citizens down on their luck. They were the worthy poor, and they could be helped by the church or by the town. But a few families, some living in ramshackle houses on the edge of town, were considered lazy and shiftless. They were the unworthy poor. They often drank too much, at least that was the usual explanation. Their children never had enough to eat or the proper clothes to wear. Some of the children, in the euphemism of the day, were "not quite right." My father often criticized these families, but he gave credit at the store and other forms of help to those he considered worthy, down on their luck, or victims of the Depression. My mother, on the other hand, was more sympathetic to the most forsaken, and she often reached out to help the women who were trapped by poverty, even if she had little good to say about the men. She often brought food to one of the desperate families, or she passed on clothes that my sisters and I had outgrown.

There were others in town who were not only poor, but also eccentric, or perhaps they were "grotesque," to borrow a word used by Sherwood Anderson to describe some of the characters in his *Winesburg, Ohio.* The Ainsworth brothers, Guy and Llewelyn, lived in a primitive camp without running water or electricity near an abandoned road a few miles from Hardwick. They had black beards, dark clothes, and carried dirty feed sacks over their shoulders as they walked into town for supplies. They were perhaps in their forties, but they seemed like old men to me. We called them "the black crows" and we made fun of them. But they were harmless characters who rarely spoke and never seemed to work. I secretly admired their simple lifestyle.

We also made fun of "Happy" Weeks, a man in his twenties or thirties who smiled all of the time. Only later did I realize that he was mentally challenged (we used a crude term that was in use at the time). "Happy" Weeks was harmless and childlike, but there were others in town who were frightening. On one of my attempts to sell Cloverine Salve, or perhaps I was delivering flyers for my father in a poor section of town, I was welcomed into the kitchen by a woman I knew slightly. While I was talking to her a creature came crawling and barking from another room. He was, I decided later, a mentally retarded adult, hidden away by the family. The woman seemed embarrassed, and I was terrified. I had nightmares for many months.

Another of the characters who lived on the margin during the 1930s was a woman we called "the mountain queen." She lived on Buffalo Mountain with her commonlaw husband and young daughter. She was always unkempt and dressed like a man. She had the reputation of being a hard-drinking, tough-talking woman. She came to town on Saturday night with her family. Usually they bought groceries at my father's store and then tied their horse and wagon behind the store while they went downtown to drink and party. At some point early in the morning when they were drunk or exhausted, a friend would take them to the wagon, kick the horse, and the horse would take them home. They were among the more picturesque of the Hardwick characters, but my mother always worried about the daughter.

"Sissy" Bridgman, whose real name was Everett, lived alone in the biggest house on West Church Street. He was descended from one of the oldest families in Hardwick. We called him "Sissy," because he was a little effeminate in the way he talked and walked. He was probably gay, but we had no concept of that term in the late 1930s; we just knew he was easy to taunt. His house backed up on the railroad tracks and there were several apple trees in his backyard. In the fall we would walk down the tracks, climb a fence, and steal a few of his apples, not so much for the apples, but because he always responded. He would yell and shout, call us names, and chase us out of his yard. We would escape through a hole in the fence and run down the tracks to disappear into the woods or into someone's backyard. Yet Bridgman, even though he was bald, overweight, and effeminate, could run well enough to catch up with the youngest or the slowest boys. The fact that he chased us made the adventure of stealing apples more exciting. During the war he invited a group of us into his house. We were conducting a scrap paper drive for the Boy Scouts and discovered that he had two rooms filled from floor to ceiling with copies of the *Boston Globe* going back for thirty years, which he contributed to the war effort. Sissy Bridgman was eccentric, but he was also talented. He was an accomplished musician who gave violin lessons, and his oil paintings are now in great demand. A few years ago I discovered his gravestone in the Hardwick cemetery. He was born in 1884 and died in 1948. He would have been in his early fifties when he chased us down the tracks. I now own a couple of his landscape paintings and I wish that I had gotten to know him better. To our gang he was not an artist or musician—he was just Sissy Bridgman.

May Foote was one of the most formidable and bizarre of the eccentrics that I knew in the 1930s. She lived alone in a tarpaper shack several hundred yards behind my house, beyond our large "back lot." She seemed old but she also may have been in her forties or fifties. She had black hair, which we thought was a wig, and she pretended to run a store in the front room of her house. She had a few loaves of stale bread, candy, and some canned goods for sale, but I don't remember anyone actually buying anything from her. She was also an FBI agent, or that is what she told us. She showed us her badge and told us stories about how she had broken a spy ring, and how she had to travel frequently to Washington to confer with J. Edgar Hoover. She did leave town occasionally, but it was usually because the state authorities had picked her up and taken her to the state mental hospital in Waterbury. Several other people in town made frequent visits to Waterbury, and I suppose there were some who resided there permanently. May Foote, however, always returned to

Hardwick, usually with a story about a special assignment for the FBI. We called her crazy and insane and we made fun of her. But in the end she had the last laugh.

The Pilbin brothers and I had built a club house on the back lot that sloped toward her house. One day while she was away on one of her trips we thought it would be fun to bounce stones off her roof. Her shack was just out of our range, but with our BB guns we could reach her house. I don't remember whose idea it was. I was perhaps ten or eleven and I was usually the follower. Our air rifles were not very accurate beyond about thirty feet, and it was at least sixty yards to her house. By using our guns like mortars we discovered that we could lob BBs onto her roof and even into her windows. After we tired of the game we sauntered by her house, only to discover, with mixed pleasure and remorse, that there were five holes in her front window. We vowed that no one would tell. In our childhood code of honor there was nothing worse than a "tattle tale." But when May Foote returned it didn't take her long to discover who the culprits were. My father eventually found out and forced the three of us to pay for a new window. It wasn't the money so much as the humiliation that stuck with me for years.

It was hard to get away with anything in Hardwick, for it was a small town and there were no strangers. Several times I recall my father or mother saying to me over supper, "You were observed this afternoon throwing stones at Johnny George's barn," or, "I had a call from Lloyd Beede who says you and your friends took lumber from the wrong pile this morning." It could work the other way as well, with praise for a touchdown scored or a good deed performed, but I rarely heard about the good reports until weeks or even years later. The observation and judging continued even after I grew up and moved away. Sometime in the early 1960s, when staying at my camp in Greensboro, I would go to the Hardwick Trust Company to cash a check. I was a college professor with a family of my own. Happily, most people in town still knew who I was and who my parents and grandparents were, and greeted me warmly. Even though I had worked hard to get out of town, it was fun to be back. In the days before ATM machines, writing a check was the only way to get cash. I would stand in line to wait my turn. One day I found myself presenting my check made out for one hundred to Cathy Drechsler, a bank clerk and one of my neighbors while growing up. We talked about our families and the old neighborhood and she gave me my cash. I don't remember what I did with the money, but it disappeared quickly and the next day I was back at the bank. Quite accidentally I once again got in Cathy's line. When I presented my check for one hundred dollars, she looked at me sternly and said: "What did you do with the hundred dollars I gave you yesterday?" For a brief moment I felt guilty.

There was little sense of social class when I was growing up in Hardwick. There was no big house on the hill that was occupied by the richest and most powerful family, as there was in many other towns. Even West Church Street, considered by many to be the most desirable residential street in town, consisted of modest frame houses. The George Bickford house, owned by the president of the Woodbury Granite Company early in the twentieth century, was, by the 1930s, part residence and part farm machine business. Perhaps the wealthiest man in town was W. W. Marshall, a flamboyant entrepreneur who had made a fortune and then lost a fortune in Florida real estate. But he lived with his wife in a modest house. The president of the bank, the two doctors, one dentist, store owners, and car dealers all lived in similar dwellings, comfortable, but not palatial. There were small houses in town, and several tenements, built for granite workers. The place you lived did matter but there were also subtle distinctions made. There were those who owned their own house and those who rented (though as a youngster I did not know the difference). There were those who had a second home or camp on a nearby lake (with Caspian Lake in Greensboro having more cache than other lakes). There were those who owned a car and those who did not, but even this distinction was muted by the fact that most people walked to work and to shop. There were some who could afford to take trips to Boston or Montreal. A sociologist might have decided that there were poor (both worthy and unworthy) and there was a lower-middle class and a middle class, but no upper class, though even those distinctions had been made fluid by the Depression. Although my family was solidly middle class and well respected in town, I discovered when I went to college that almost all of my classmates came from families with more money than mine, and they had a sense of class distinction that was foreign to my experience. My lack of class consciousness was reinforced at every turn by my mother who insisted that, intrinsically, everyone was alike. It was hard work and what you did with your talents that mattered. This attitude that I absorbed while growing up, I now realize, enabled me to become a friend of Rod Rockefeller, Nelson Rockefeller's oldest son. I treated him like a person while others viewed him as a Rockefeller. I had no hesitation to invite him to my home and I felt no awkwardness when I visited his family at 810 Fifth Avenue.

Hardwick was a long way from Fifth Avenue and I recall many abandoned farms and empty buildings. Farmers were hard hit by the Depression and by the agricultural downturn of the 1920s. Many simply gave up and left their farms. Some of those farms were sold by the bank, which held the mortgage, for a few hundred dollars, and in the next decades some were restored to make elegant summer homes. Others, especially those marginal places many miles from town, were allowed to rot and fall apart. There were cellar holes in the woods everywhere, marking a place where a farm had been abandoned in the nineteenth century, but these were more recently given up. I remember going on fishing trips and coming across a farm now overgrown with weeds but with the buildings still standing. It was a strange feeling to walk into a farmhouse with some of the furniture still in place even though the plaster was falling down. The house was now occupied by raccoons and squirrels, but outside a lilac tree, rose bushes, and a couple of apple trees were reminders of the family that had once called the place home. One of these abandoned farms was in Greensboro on the north side of Long Pond. We would dig fish worms near what had once been the barn and then walk the remaining distance to the pond. I passed another decrepit place when I walked up Corkscrew Road to fish in a remote stream. This farm was much nearer collapse than the Rutledge farm near Long Pond, but one day among the broken furniture I found several beer bottles and a used condom, a sign that unknown lovers had discovered a new use for a farmhouse that had once sheltered a family.

While I was growing up in the 1930s, there were whispers around town of family violence, of men beating their wives, and in some cases, their children. There were stories of at least one murder and several suicides. The suicide that I remember best comes from after the war when I was in high school. The police came to the school one day in the fall to ask for volunteers to search for J. C. Spaulding, the town photographer. His wife had reported him missing and, because he had been depressed, she was afraid he might be at risk. I went with one of the search teams but we found nothing. Later in the day I heard that Spaulding's body had been recovered in the Lamoille River. He had carefully placed his umbrella on a rock before he jumped.

Hitchhikers seemed to be everywhere during the 1930s. Those men who could not afford a car just stood by the side of the road, stuck out a thumb and accepted a free ride from a passing car. A woman would occasionally hitchhike with her husband or boyfriend, but rarely would a woman hitch a ride alone. My father often stopped to pick up a hitchhiker, usually someone he knew, and my friends and I learned that hitchhiking was easier than walking if we wanted to go to

Greensboro, to a remote trout stream, or to a neighboring town for a baseball game. When I was sixteen, I hitched to Burlington with a friend in February to watch a basketball game at the University of Vermont. We stayed overnight in one of the dorms, borrowing the beds of Hardwick students we knew were away. On the return trip, it was bitterly cold, and to this day when I pass the spot in the road where we waited for a ride, I think of that winter hitchhiking adventure.

When I was in college, I always hitched home from Hanover, New Hampshire. It never occurred to me to take the bus. Standing beside the road especially in winter was no fun, but frequently I met interesting people. Often those who gave me a ride told me stories how they hitchhiked everywhere during the 1930s. One man told me he had graduated from college in 1930 and the only job he could find was driving a truck filled with bootleg whiskey from Montreal to New York. He picked up hitchhikers, he said, to have someone to talk to and someone to keep him awake.

There were no African Americans in Hardwick. I did not meet a "Negro" until I went to a boys' camp the summer I was twelve. In high school I took part in a minstrel show where we preformed in black face. Innocently, we did not think of our disguise and our antics as being demeaning to Blacks. When Billy Conn fought Joe Louis for the heavy weight championship we cheered for Conn. Was that because Louis was black or were we just going with the underdog? The year after I went to college an African-American family moved to town. The girl, in my younger sister's class, was quickly elected the class president and when she graduated she was voted the most popular girl in the class.

There were a few Jewish residents in Hardwick, but no Synagogue or Jewish culture. The only people we identified as Jewish were Oscar Schlarman and his wife. He was the junk dealer. At least one other Jew, married to a gentile, went to the Protestant Church. Hardwick had a greater ethnic mix than most Vermont towns of its size, largely because of the granite industry. There were Italian, Scotch, Irish, and Spanish families, but I grew up with little sense of ethnic differences. The Italians were so assimilated they went to the Protestant Church. Many had initially joined the Methodist Church because they didn't feel comfortable in the Irish and French- Canadian-dominated Catholic Church. Many of the French-Canadian families had migrated to northern Vermont about the time of World War I. Some worked in the granite industry, but many purchased farms. I later learned that the local Hardwick bank would not give them mortgages, forcing them to go to other towns for loans. There was some prejudice against them not only because they were Catholic (and they took their religion seriously), but also because many families retained their language and customs. There were a few French-Canadians in the village. The Racettes lived next door and Dr. Beaupre was the only dentist in town. There was a Gauthier and a Robarge in my first grade class, and Lavertu, Tremblay, Michaud, and Brochu were familiar names. Many more French-Canadians joined my class in the seventh or ninth grade after they attended a rural one-room school near the family farms. Those in my age group were second-generation and a few spoke with a slight accent. We called one boy "Froggie" and another "Pea Soup," but we would have denied that they were derogatory terms. My father sometimes referred to someone as "The Frenchman," but "Canuck," we all realized, was a term we shouldn't use. My mother argued that everyone should be treated alike. But the French-Canadians were Catholic and when I dated a French Canadian girl in high school my mother took me aside and suggested that it was fine to go out with a French girl, but I should not think of marrying one because then the children would have to be raised as Catholics. Even for my tolerant mother, somehow, that seemed like a terrible fate.

Despite some prejudice, the relationship between Protestants and Catholics in Hardwick was more cordial than in the larger towns and cities. French-Canadians, for example met much greater prejudice and rejections in mill towns like Woonsocket, Rhode Island or Lewiston, Maine. There were no Catholic schools in Hardwick and no Catholic Boy Scout troop. Catholics went to the Knights of Columbus and Protestants to the Masonic Temple, but both groups were members of the American Legion and the Kiwanis Club. When there was a death in town both groups rallied to support the family. Catholics came to Protestant Church suppers and Protestants played Bingo at the Catholic Church. Occasionally a Catholic girl was a bridesmaid in a Protestant wedding. Some of the cooperation can be credited to the presence of two powerful and respected clergymen—John Chester Smith, a Baptist, at the United Church and Father Arthur LeVeer at the Catholic Church. Occasionally I went with friends to the Catholic mass on Christmas Eve. I was impressed by the elaborate symbolism and by the presence of Father LeVeer. Tall and dark, he had a sonorous voice. He delivered the sermon first in French and then in English. In Hardwick everyone knew Father LeVeer. He came to all the home basketball games and he cheered just as loudly when I scored as he did when one of my Catholic friends hit a basket.

In my family when we spoke of "the church" we meant the United Church of Hardwick located only a couple hundred yards from our house. The United Church had been formed in 1931, the year I was born. The Methodist, Baptist, and Congregational Church churches decided to merge because of financial difficulties in the depth of the Depression. The Congregational Church was selected as the main building partly because of its superior organ while a splinter group of Baptists refused to go along with the merger. There was also a small Episcopal Church, a Seventh Day Adventist congregation that met in a private home, and a group we called the Holy Rollers, but most people went either to the United Church, or to the Catholic Church, located directly across the street from each other.

Most of my family had been members of the Congregational Church for generations, but the Wylies were Scots-Irish Presbyterians in the beginning, and the Davis family had joined the Methodist Church sometime after the Civil War. My grandfather once explained how he became a Congregationalist. Moving to Hardwick in 1901 he set off on the first Sunday to walk to the Methodist Church which was nearly a mile away on the other side of town. "I walked by the Baptist Church," he recalled. "Then I walked by the Congregational Church, and then I stopped and I said to myself, 'I'm not going to walk by two churches every Sunday in order to go to a third.'" So he returned to the Congregational Church. That was his story, but the Congregational Church was also the most prestigious church in town and getting acquainted with the members would be good business for one just opening a store in town. By selling his farm and moving into town my grandfather moved into the middle class, by joining the Congregational Church he solidified that status. Still he retained some of his Methodist ways. He never allowed card playing on Sunday.

The Congregational Church in Hardwick may have displayed some of its Calvinist roots when my grandfather joined in 1901, but by the time the three churches joined forces and I came along in the 1930s few remnants of Calvinism remained except for the work ethic and a certain sense of guilt. The theology, such as it was, was liberal, I now realize, and the ministers had accepted Charles Darwin's theories and adopted modernism in other ways. There was no hint of predestination or original sin, little attention paid to heaven and even less to hell. The religion of my childhood promoted the goodness of man and was optimistic about the state of the world. God was kindly and not wrathful and Jesus was supposed to be a friend, a concept I had a hard time grasping as a youngster. During the monthly communion service the minister announced that the bread was the body of Christ and the grape juice his blood. I knew better because my grandparents were in charge of the communion trays. I watched them cut Wonder Bread into little squares and fill the tiny wine glasses with Welch's Grape Juice. Such complicated concepts as the Virgin birth and the trinity were not stressed in the church I went to. When I asked my mother about the various miracles in the Bible, the parting of the Red Sea or Christ turning water into wine she explained that they were symbolic. I did get in the habit of reading the Bible and of praying every night. But I quickly became disillusioned with the power of prayer. When at camp in Greensboro, at about the age of six, I prayed that I would catch minnows in my trap. I was about ten when I decided that my prayers had nothing to do with the minnows' habits.

The church was important as a social center. We walked to church every Sunday and for special occasions, a midnight service on Christmas Eve, a sunrise service on Easter, and for a variety of church suppers and special events. Occasionally a missionary spoke and showed slides about exotic lands in Asia or Africa. And after John Chester Smith arrived as the minister in 1938 he promoted folk and square dances in the meeting room on the lower floor. I have a Bible given to me when I was eight for "perfect attendance at Sunday School," but I have little memory of Sunday School except an older woman reading Bible stories and pictures of a feminized Jesus on the wall. I have a more vivid memory of sitting in church and being impressed by the quiet eloquence of John Chester Smith. For a brief time some years later I thought I would like to be a minister like Mr. Smith, to preach to a big congregation and to have a book-lined study in my house just the way he did. That career goal faded quickly, but the church did give me an opportunity to act in plays, to sing in the junior choir, even though I could not carry a tune. It gave me a chance to take a leadership role in the young people's group, and in many ways the United Church was my social center while I was growing up in Hardwick.

I entered the first grade in the fall of 1937 (there was no kindergarten in Hardwick). I remember the first day of school. My mother offered to walk me to school, as she had apparently done for my sister Florence a few years before, but I announced that I was going with my friends Bill and Harry Pilbin. I had been waiting anxiously for a year to go to school, because I had missed the cut by nine days the year before.

School was held in the Academy building on Main Street. Grades one to six were on the first floor, grades seven to twelve on the second and third floors. Constructed in 1893, Hardwick Academy was old even in 1937 with well-worn, wooden floors, desks with names carved by former students, and varnished wainscoting on all the walls. Students and teachers walked to school and then they walked home for dinner at noon, back to school for afternoon classes and finally home when the bell rang at 3:10 P.M. I have a group photograph of my first grade class taken in the fall of 1937 in front of the Academy building. It is probably October because there are carefully colored, dancing jack-o'-lanterns on the windows. There are thirty-two in the class, nineteen boys and thirteen girls. We all stand at attention with hands to the side. We have already begun the process of socialization and we know how to obey the teacher. The girls wear dresses with cotton stockings. Several of the boys have short pants and the same kind of stockings that the girls wear. (I have a vague memory of wearing such stockings.) Hardwick was still mired in the Depression in 1937, but everyone looks neat, if not affluent. I am in the back row with hair uncombed and a shirt that looks a size too small. I don't look very happy. I have another photo taken when we were in the third grade and I still don't look happy. Except for a couple of boys in the back row who are repeating the first grade, I am one of the tallest boys in the class. Many of the little boys in the front row later grew to be much taller than the five foot eight inches that I eventually achieved. Perhaps my early growth, or because I started school nearly a year late, prevented me from feeling short. In fact I never knew I was short until I went to college.

Several in that first grade photo did not graduate with the class. Some moved away, some dropped out and others were "kept back," and made to repeat a grade. There were no social promotions and the news that one was being "kept back" was delivered in a cruel fashion. One the last day of school in the spring the whole class would go on a picnic and at some point the teacher would hand out report cards. I remember sitting next to a girl who opened her envelope and discovered that she was not promoted. She burst into tears. A few boys failed to be promoted over several years. There were no special classes for children with learning differences. Some of these big boys (whose names were always Buddy or Buster in my memory) ruled the playground during recess and after school. One of these bullies challenged me to fight after school (was I in the second grade?). Encouraged by my "friends" I reluctantly agreed to the confrontation. I couldn't complain to my mother because I knew she would encourage me to confront the bully. Because I was frequently ill as a youngster she feared I might grow up to be "a sissy," or at least that was my interpretation. I can recall vividly the fear and the dread that engulfed me during the afternoon classes. We met somewhere away from the school and beyond the playground. Buddy (if that was his name) and I squared off surrounded by a group of interested observers. I have no memory of the fight but I must have swung for I do recall that my opponent's nose began to bleed and that ended the fight. And because I had proved my manhood (if that is what it was) that ended the harassment at least for the year, but it didn't end the need to fight.

My usual tactic was to avoid wrestling with the big boys, but rather to get in one or two blows and then run. I discovered rather early that I could outrun most of my friends. In my neighborhood the only person that could beat me was a girl a couple of years older. On one occasion while playing with the Pilbin boys, I got into an argument with Bill who was three years older. I have no memory of what we argued about, but I threw a stone at him and then ran up the hill from his house. He picked up a stone and hit me in the head as I retreated. I continued to run home "bleeding like a stuck pig," according to my grandmother, who almost fainted. She died when I was nine so I must have been seven or eight. Many years later I asked Bill Pilbin if he remembered the stone throwing incident. He not only remembered but said he was terrified and afraid that he had killed me. Despite the wound Bill and I remained good friends.

Before and after school and at recess we played games. The girls played hopscotch and they jumped rope. The boys played baseball or kick the can. When spring arrived we played marbles, which we called "alleys." We didn't play in a circle and flip the marble into a hole or try to hit another marble. We stood upright and aimed our alley at another placed in the mud or snow. To hit the alley was to win it. We had an elaborate grading system that told the worth of each marble. Size, color, and clarity counted but I have forgotten the scoring system. When I cleaned out my father's house I found a leather bag filled with my prize marbles left over from the days when recess meant games in the schoolyard.

I went to the same school for twelve years, but my memory of what I learned in the classrooms is fleeting. I was a good, but not an enthusiastic student. I learned rather early how to be obedient and I discovered that it wasn't wise to admit that I knew the answer to the teacher's questions or I would be denounced by my classmates. My only rebellion in the first grade was to color outside the lines, but I soon learned to stay within the lines because that was what the teacher expected. I have an image in my mind of a classroom with desks lined up in rows and bolted to the floor (progressive education with its movable seats had not arrived in Hardwick). There were pictures of both Abraham Lincoln and George Washington on the classroom wall. There was also an American flag and, I think, a piano. Every morning we said the pledge of allegiance to the flag and repeated the Lord's Prayer (the Protestant version.) In fact we said them so close together that it was not until the second grade that I realized that they were separate and different. We saluted the flag with our arms outstretched in a salute as we faced the flag. But as war approached we were told by the superintendent to place our hand over our heart during the pledge. There were blackboards around two sides of the room and the white powder from the chalk was ever-present. Above the blackboards were examples of the correct way to form capital and small letters in cursive. We never learned to print and I struggled to form the letters neatly, first with my Ticonderoga Number 2 pencil, and then with pen and ink. But even with the aid of a penmanship teacher who came in on Friday afternoon to teach the proper Palmer method, I never learned to write neatly, to my father's dismay. Worse still I always seemed to get ink stains on my clothes whether I used a straight pen or a fountain pen. The ball point pen, which came along many years later, was invented for me.

My memory of grade school consists of a few snapshots. We would line up, boys on one side, girls on the other, before morning recess to go to the basement to use the toilets. The boys' room had a long urinal and reeked of a combination of disinfectant and urine. On winter days the wet wool jackets hung outside the classrooms gave off an aroma that combined with the faint odor from the oiled floors and mixed with the steam heat to create the special smell of school. In the days before light weight, water resistant fabrics, it was wool that kept the cold away. In grade school I wore wool knickers and a wool jacket, purchased on an annual trip to the woolen mills in Johnson, Vermont. Wool mittens, wool socks, and a wool knit hat, that we called a "tuque," completed my wardrobe. Despite "long john" underwear it was impossible to keep the wool away from skin, and the wool made me itch. My itchy pants made me squirm in my seat as

I tried to complete my assignments in the early grades. I also remember the endless task of getting those winter clothes on and then off. Especially difficult were the overshoes with their buckles, almost impossible to hook and unhook in the cold with hands encased in mittens.

Other things remind me of school. I can recall the aroma, even the taste, of the white paste that we used for various projects. I loved the look and feel of school books covered with brown paper, and I liked the special smell of the printed pages. I also remember the joy of a freshly sharpened pencil. I especially liked the big geography book that we got in the fourth grade that had wonderful maps and pictures of far-off places. Miss Morgan, my fourth grade teacher would go into the closet and smoke. She must have thought she was fooling us but we knew because the smoke curled out of the cracks. Miss Lambert, my fifth grade teacher, had us construct a giant relief map of Europe using flour and water and perhaps something else to make it hard. I still remember the mountains and rivers of Europe because of that map. Miss Lambert was a good teacher, but she had little patience with those who did not learn quickly. I can see her with her pointer trying to explain fractions, but when Armond Gauthier would not, or could not learn she crashed the pointer on his head breaking it into three pieces. Armond did not change expression. All the teachers had rubber hoses in their desks, which they threatened to use on unruly students, and rulers that they sometimes did use to crack a recalcitrant student on the knuckles.

I have no memory of learning how to read. Before I went to school I could read simple stories perhaps because my sister Florence liked to play school and I was a convenient pupil. Or I could have absorbed the sounds and symbols from my mother who constantly read to me and to my sisters. I do remember looking at books that were scattered everywhere in the house and inventing stories to go with the pictures. And I remember being frightened by a picture that was half human and half chicken. When my younger son had a difficult time learning to read, I consciously tried to recall the process by which I learned, and I came up blank. I do remember how agonizing it was to listen to some of my classmates stumble over words, as we sat around in a circle in the first or second grade and read a sentence or two in turn from a book. I don't know what method, if any, the teachers were using but I am sure we did not learn phonics.

I learned to read easily and just as quickly I fell in love with books, but I had a difficult time learning to spell. Even today I am not a confident speller and I constantly look up words to check the spelling even if my first effort is correct. In the second grade we had a spelling test every Friday. I think we were given twenty words to learn and then Miss Anair gave us ten of those to spell on the test. I devised a way to get those ten correctly spelled each time. I wrote all the words out on a slip of paper which I somehow attached to my pencil box which I placed between my legs. If I was not sure whether or not it was "receive" or "recieve," I simply looked down at my list. But one day Miss Anair caught me at my scheme (I never thought of it as cheating). After that I memorized the words. I usually got an "A" and then promptly forgot most of those that I memorized. No one realized I couldn't spell, though my mother must have guessed because I was constantly asking how to spell a word. Years later, I decided that the reason I couldn't spell was that I didn't see words. Somewhere along the way I learned to read phrases and lines. Even now I have a difficult time reading page proofs and a number of errors escape me. Probably today I would be classified as being "neurodiverse," but my handicap enabled me to read rapidly. By the age of about ten I was racing through books. Or perhaps it was the other way around, by reading books rapidly I increasingly learned to read phrases rather than words.

The books and stories assigned by teachers did not excite me, but I found reading material around the house. I was fascinated by *The Book of Knowledge*, a twenty-volume encyclopedia that my parents had purchased at some point. Unlike most encyclopedias it was organized topically rather than alphabetically and it had wonderful illustrations. It would entertain me for hours as I read about famous people, scientific experiments, and exotic places, but it was Horatio Alger who helped me fall in love with the printed page. I don't remember where I first discovered an Alger novel, but it probably was in the Jeudevine Memorial Library, an impressive Romanesque revival building in Hardwick. I don't remember exactly when I first went to the library. I probably went first with my mother, but about the time I wast ten, I trudged there after school on Tuesday afternoon and again on Saturday. The librarian was Gladys Hooper, tall, gray-haired, and very stern. I don't remember that she ever recommended a book, but I probably never asked. She tolerated my presence, allowed me to browse endlessly in the stacks, and to hide away for hours on the balcony where the back issues of magazines were kept. She also cheerfully checked out the books I selected to take home. For a time the books I checked out were written by Horatio Alger. I worked my way through the *Ragged Dick* series and then the *Luck and Pluck* series. I sometimes read as many as four books a week. Of course they all had similar plots usually featuring a young boy living with his widowed mother who achieves success, if not fame and fortune, through hard work, perseverance, and luck. In recent years I have often tried to read an Alger novel and after being appalled at the stylized, sentimental prose and the predictable plots I have wondered why as a boy I was attracted to these books. The only thing I can conclude is that they introduced me to an urban world, and a world where the hero was always working hard to get ahead, and where he always outwitted the villains. I shall always be grateful to Alger, for those books introduced me to the printed page, at a time when many of my friends were fascinated by comic books. My mother worried for a time about my addiction to

Horatio Alger, but I soon moved on to Tom Swift, and the Frank Merriwell books, and then I discovered the Boy Allies Series. I followed these heroes as they fought World War I in the trenches, on the high seas and even in the air. I read books indiscriminately sometimes because they were on the same shelf in the library as the novels of Kenneth Roberts and Howard Fast, biographies of Benjamin Franklin and Thomas Jefferson.

Those of us in the lucky generation were influenced by the Depression, but it was mostly second-hand. We were too young to feel the horror and despair of losing a job or watching a savings account disappear as the bank failed, but we heard parents and grandparents tell stories about defeat and despair. We learned about the man who made a fortune in Florida real estate and then lost it all, or about the man who lost money when the bank failed and after that kept all his money in his mattress. We listened as parents and grandparents used the Depression as a lesson or a club to urge us to seek a secure job or to save our money in case there was another Depression. We may not have learned the lesson but at least we heard the stories. The Baby Boomers, another generation removed from the Depression, thought of the 1930s as simply part of history.

My Depression experience, both first- and second-hand, was in a small town where church and community rallied around to support those out of work or in need of help. There were no soup kitchens or bread lines in Hardwick, and most people had a garden and raised a few chickens. Even though times were tough no one went hungry. My family and my hometown protected me from the worst aspects of the economic downturn. Still the Depression had its impact on my world view even though I was born in 1931—especially because I was born in 1931.

Chapter 8

WORLD WAR II

MEMBERS OF THE LUCKY GENERATION can tell you exactly where they were when they learned of the Japanese attack on Pearl Harbor, the death of Franklin D. Roosevelt, and the assassination of John Kennedy. These were defining events for those of us born in the late 1920s or the early 1930s. I was one month short of my eleventh birthday on December 7, 1941, and I was sitting at home on a gray, overcast day reading and listening to the radio when the announcement came of the attack. I don't remember the book I was reading or the radio program I was listening to, but I know it was not the Washington Redskins football game that seems to be part of the collective memory of that event. The war in Europe had been raging for more than two years. I had been vaguely aware of the quick German victory over France, the disaster at Dunkirk and the Battle of Britain. I was fascinated by the war in the air. Most of my information came from newsreels that were shown before the main feature at the Idle Hour Theater, and an occasional magazine article and newspaper. My parents talked in worried tones about the war in Europe. I remember my father working his way slowly through Adolf Hitler's *Mein Kampf* and talking about how Hitler threatened the world including the United States. I don't remember hearing much about the war in the Far East. I was shocked, as were most Americans, by the attack on Pearl Harbor. I had no idea of the exact location of Pearl Harbor. I went immediately to my collection of National Geographic maps to find out. Within days I was looking for Wake Island, Bataan, and Singapore. I was in the fifth grade when the United States entered the war and I remember walking to school with my friends on Monday, December 8. The war was exciting. We could talk of nothing else.

The outbreak of war did not immediately change our lives, but it did change our games. Instead of playing "cowboys and Indians," or "cops and robbers," we played war. We shot "Japs" or Germans with our imaginary machine guns, though most of our hate was aimed at the Japanese, influenced (I now realize) by the images of the Japanese soldiers in the press and the movies as sub-human brutes. There was only one problem. In our earlier games it was possible to convince a few boys to play the role of robbers or Indians. In fact it was fun to be an Indian because you could hide, crawl around in the woods, and then attack the white settlers while making war whoops. But no one wanted to be a Japanese soldier, and few could be convinced to play a German. Consequently our enemies were usually imaginary. Most of my playmates were boys of various ages, but two girls often joined our games. We assumed that they would be nurses, but Jo Racette, my next door neighbor, always insisted on being a soldier.

We went on long expeditions especially on Saturdays. We dug foxholes, and pretended to parachute behind the enemy lines. We carried Kool-Aid in our canteens and we made grenades by putting stones in tin cans. We lobbed them into imagined machine-gun nests. In the fall we picked up slightly rotten tomatoes from the garden and pretended that they were grenades. They were better than the tin cans because they splattered when they hit. In winter we became ski troopers, inspired by the Finnish ski troopers who held up the Soviet advance, and by the formation of the American 10th Mountain Division. We went on cross-country hikes and now and then we would drop down in the snow to fire on the enemy with our wooden M-1 rifles. But our favorite place to play war was in an old auto that had been abandoned in an alley on the south side of town. We turned that old car into a tank, a truck, a PT boat, or a submarine often depending on the last movie we had seen. But most of the time the car became an airplane, a P-40, or a B-17. The war in the air somehow seemed more romantic than the war on the ground.

At the end of the Korean War, after the shooting had stopped, I was drafted into the Army. I fired a real M-1 rifle, hurled a real grenade, and actually became a ski trooper in Alaska. But all the time I was in the Army, my mind kept flashing back to those times when I played war with my childhood friends in Hardwick.

The war altered life in America in many ways. The war created jobs and effectively ended the Depression, but not in Hardwick. There was no war industry in town, except for a small granite shed which hired a few men to manufacture surface plates used in the manufacture and measurement of precision tools. The whistle on the granite sheds still echoed through the town during the war. But many Hardwick families moved to Springfield, Vermont, Hartford, Connecticut and to other wartime boom towns where suddenly there were jobs. My fifth grade girlfriend, whose name I have forgotten, left town with her family without even saying goodbye.

Hardwick had no war industry. Still it was a lively regional shopping center especially on Saturday nights in the summer. Farmers and residents of the surrounding small villages came to town to shop and to meet friends and perhaps to find some excitement. Hardwick residents, young and old went downtown to take part in the action. Young women walked back and forth on Main Street looking for young men, while young men cruised in cars (if they could find the gasoline) or they sat on the wall in front of the gymnasium looking for young women, but many were too shy to admit it. All the stores stayed open until 9:00 P.M. and the Idle Hour Theater always had a double feature. Some of the men lingered at Art Bacon's barber shop waiting to get a hair cut, but also catching up on the latest rumors. They drank beer and talked at Bruno's Cafe, or they went to Charlie Morris' pool room, perhaps to play pool, but also to hang out. Neither the barber shop nor the pool room welcomed women, but at the bowling alley both men and women could bowl, trying their luck using small balls and candlepins. There were no automatic pin setters, but high school boys worked efficiently to set up the pins. Other young people, especially girls, danced to the juke box, which played the latest hits if someone fed it nickels. There was another juke box at Drown's Restaurant, but not enough room to dance. At the Cox Drug Store and at Ashley's Cut Rate teenage youngsters and those older and younger sat at the soda foundations and consumed ice cream sodas, sundaes, banana splits, or cherry cokes served up by "soda jerks'" who were usually high school students. Some of the women shopped at Racette's Dress Shop or at the Ben Franklin Store or at Bemis Variety Store. As the stores began to close at nine some of the young people, especially in summer, looked for a ride to the dance at Cole's Pond or at Joe's Pond Casino. "Saturday night is the loneliest night in the week," according to a popular, wartime song, but not in Hardwick, where Saturday night, even during the war, meant action and excitement.

Some of the men who gathered in Hardwick on Saturday night were not satisfied with the beer served in Bruno's and a few other bars. Hardwick had no state liquor store so these men depended on Al Stratton to buy them bottles in Barre.

Stratton ran the "stage" to Barre and Montpelier. He carried the mail, but he also brought "packages" for a number of customers. Not all the people in Hardwick were happy with this service. Stratton's daughter, Ann, recalled that several wives arrived at the Stratton house before the stage hoping to intercept the "package" that their husbands had ordered.

Early in the war there were air raid drills in Hardwick, even though there was no realistic chance that northern Vermont would be attacked by enemy planes. The older men in town became air raid wardens and when the siren at the United Church went off, their duty was to patrol around town to make sure that every house had its dark curtains pulled tight. There was an airplane spotter station on top of Cannon Hill in back of the Academy building. There, early in the war, volunteers, including high school students, stood watch to give early warning of enemy planes on their way to attack Montreal or Boston. I was too young to serve, but I visited the Cannon Hill shack frequently and memorized the silhouettes of enemy planes posted on the wall. I learned to identify the Messerschmitt ME-109, the Heinkel HE-111, and a dozen other planes. But no German bombers appeared over Hardwick; the only excitement was an occasional Piper Cub from the St. Johnsbury airport. By 1943 or 1944 the urgency of the early war panic had subsided and the air spotter station became mostly a place for a romantic rendezvous, but I was too young for that, too.

The young men, and a few young women in town began to enlist within days after Pearl Harbor and those of us too young to serve envied them, especially when they returned home on leave in their new uniforms. They were participating in a great adventure that we were missing. I was even too young to join the Junior Home Guards organized by some of the businessmen in town to train those from fourteen to seventeen to defend the village. They practiced marching and doing close order drills with their wooden rifles and they gave the businessmen a sense of participating in the war effort. Still, those of us who were too young to join took part in the war vicariously. Our Boy Scout camping trips became like military training exercises, encouraged by the fantasies of our leaders. We spent hours constructing balsa wood models of war planes. When I smell a certain kind of glue I am transported back to my bedroom in Hardwick where I laboriously cut and glued balsa strips. I made a P-38 with its twin fuselage, a B-24 Liberator and a B-17 Flying Fortress. I even made a Japanese Zero in order to set it on fire and watch it go down in flames. But my favorite was the P-40, the most dependable American fighter plane early in the war. I fantasized about being a P-40 pilot shooting down Japanese Zeros one after the other. I even drew pictures of P-40s in my school notebooks. Only years later did I learn that the Zero, with its greater speed and maneuverability, was far superior to the P-40. I assumed during the war that all things American were better than anything made by the Japanese or Germans. The United States was innately good and the enemy entirely evil. And in the end good would triumph over evil. The war that I experienced growing up was a sentimental and romantic war. I didn't learn of the Holocaust or of the imprisonment of Japanese-Americans until after the war was over. I failed to appreciate the irony of fighting for freedom with a segregated Army. I didn't question the saturation bombing of German cities or the dropping of atomic bombs on Hiroshima or Nagasaki. I was an ardent supporter of the American cause.

In Hardwick everyone enthusiastically supported the war effort. My friends and I searched out old tires and flat irons, even old water bottles and pieces of iron fences, to contribute to scrap drives. My Boy Scout troop collected old newspapers, and we saved war stamps. Each week in school we purchased a twenty-five cent stamp and pasted it in a little book until we had $18.75, enough to buy a $25 war bond (redeemable in ten years.) No one warned us that because of almost certain inflation the $18.75 in 1943 dollars would be worth more than the $25 in 1953 dollars. We "licked stamps to lick the Japs," and we believed that each stamp bought twelve bullets. We even became itinerant farm workers to help the potato growers harvest their crop. During the war many farmers near Hardwick planted hundreds of acres of seed potatoes. With the usual pickers in the Army, or working in war industry, the potato growers convinced the superintendent and the school board to dismiss students from junior high and high school for two days a week to harvest the crop and aid the war effort. Trucks pulled up in front of the Academy building at 6 A.M., to pick up the volunteers. It was often below freezing and the grass was covered with frost, but it was exciting to be released from school and to go with friends to the potato fields.

The farmers paid six cents a bushel. We were given a half-bushel basket which had to be filled twice and dumped into a burlap sack. A potato digger pulled by a tractor went down the rows plowing up the vines and laying the potatoes out on the ground. Picking potatoes was hard and dirty work. You crawled around and ended the day with swollen and bruised knees, or you bent over and developed a painful backache. By steady, methodical work one could pick as many as 100 bushels a day, but many of the students quit after lunch, started potato fights or simply drifted away. Some of us persisted and tried to compete with the few remaining older pickers. I remember a couple of older women who always beat me by at least twenty bushels. By working three days including Saturdays, I made as much as eighteen dollars a week, more money than I had ever seen before. The potato season was only about three weeks long and I probably picked for only two or three years. Yet the experience remains vivid in my memory. I have always had great sympathy for all migrant farm workers.

We planted Victory Gardens, which were somewhat redundant in Hardwick, because almost everyone had a garden even before the war. My plot was in a vacant lot on

Wolcott Street. I raised cabbages and green beans and a great many weeds. I sold the cabbages to my father at the wholesale price. He used the occasion to instruct me on the difference between wholesale and retail, and the margin that enabled him to make a profit at the store. We saved tin cans, cutting off both ends and then stamping on them until they were flat. We even collected the tin foil from cigarette packages and formed them into a ball before turning them in. Did we get paid for it as we did for scrap metal? I'm not sure. But I do recall that we thought we were aiding the war effort. One day in July, 1942 I was in Greensboro when I heard that there was a special scrap drive. I gave up a day at the lake, returned to Hardwick and spent the day collecting old pots and pans, old tires and other scrap metal to aid the cause. We even helped our mothers save grease and we believed that the government turned that old bacon grease into bombs, and we collected the silk-like fibers from milkweed because we heard that the government was using them in life jackets. Was that true or just a war story?

We endured rationing during the war. One needed ration stamps (issued in little books based on the size of the family) to buy sugar, coffee, meat, butter, shoes, and other items. The customer presented the necessary coupons and sometimes got little red and blue tokens as change. My job on Saturday mornings was to sort out the various ration coupons for my father at the store because he had to return them to the wholesalers with his next order. It was dull and repetitive work, made easier by convincing myself that I was helping to win the war.

Gasoline was also rationed. An "A" sticker displayed on the windshield meant an allotment of two gallons a week, while a "C" sticker indicated you worked in a vital war industry and could purchase more gasoline. Every farmer had a "C" sticker and everyone in Hardwick knew a farmer so few went without gasoline. But auto trips became shorter and new tires almost impossible to obtain near the end of the war. My family still went to Greensboro in the summer, but we no longer took overnight trips. Everyone sacrificed to some extent during the war, but I don't remember any real hardship. My father always made sure we had enough meat and sugar and, because he hated oleomargarine, we had butter on the table throughout the war, even if it was sometimes almost rancid.

When I visited the Smiths on West Church Street, I was introduced to margarine. In Vermont during the war, you could not purchase yellow margarine; it came white in a plastic bag with a little pellet of dye. You had to work the bag with your hands until all of the contents turned yellow, but Betty Smith did not have the patience to get the entire pound of margarine a proper yellow so she served what seemed to me like lard with dark yellow streaks in it. To put that striped mess on my bread seemed like a real contribution to the war effort.

The high school basketball team had a reduced schedule during the war and they played only teams within a limited radius in order to save gasoline. Still, basketball remained important and loyal fans found a way to get to out of town games. A local farmer contributed a truck. Hay made the ride more comfortable and the sub-zero weather gave couples an excuse to cuddle in the corner to keep warm. When I watched the high school games, I dreamed of playing myself. I did play on the junior high team, but most of our play was disorganized. There were few places to practice in Hardwick. There were no outdoor courts, but we did play in Jenkins' barn across the tracks on Maple Street. George Jenkins, the Superintendent of Schools, had three sons and a makeshift basketball court upstairs in his barn. There were no lines marked on the court and the ceiling was low, making it difficult to shoot anything except a layup. The baskets were a little less than the regulation ten feet, the front rims drooped a bit and there were no nets. The basketballs we used were often under inflated and they had laces on one side making dribbling difficult. Worst of all, in the winter the barn was cold. Yet after school we chose up sides and played there anyway.

Some of the gyms we played in when I was in junior high and high school were not much better than Jenkins' barn. My junior high team played against East Hardwick in the basement of the elementary school. There was a sewer pipe over one basket, making only lay ups possible at that end of the court. In Craftsbury, the gym was a remodeled church. The balconies that hung over the court made it difficult to pass the ball in from the sidelines and impossible to shoot from the corners. There was a hot air register in the middle of the floor forcing the players to dribble around it or risk an errant bounce. The Craftsbury court was so small that the foul line circle intersected the center circle. The court was so narrow that a tight zone defense (taking advantage of the overhanging balconies) was almost impossible to penetrate. The ceiling was low in Craftsbury, and in many of the other remodeled structures we played in, which made it especially difficult for me because I had a high-arching one-handed shot that often rattled off the ceiling or off the wire cages that protected the electric lights. Many of the courts were poorly lighted with dark corners and most were cold, but as spring approached some became unbearably hot. In Stowe, there was no basement under the court so during an early spring thaw the floor was covered with moisture and the players slipped and slid around. In Greensboro the court was on the second floor of the high school building; on a fast break you could feel the floor moving up and down. In Morrisville, we played in a swimming pool, or on a court originally designed as a swimming pool. There was no space under the baskets. Despite the padding on the concrete walls, going up for a lay up often meant being checked into the wall as if it were a hockey game. In Littleton, New Hampshire, we played on a stage with a net protecting the players from flying out into the audience.

Hardwick had one of the best gyms in northern Vermont and we were proud of our "new gym." We scrambled to find ways to practice and to play there. But as we perfected our shots and experimented with hook shots and behind-the-back passes we had few role models. In the days before television we did not have college or professional ball players to emulate. We studied the high school players when we were in junior high, and we watched the town team and an occasional college game. We also listened to games on the radio. Through static, sometimes late at night, I listened to Marty Glickman broadcast New York University and City College games from Madison Square Garden. He had a special, clipped style. When a player, especially a New York player, made a free throw he announced: "It's good: like Nedicks." It was years before I learned that Nedicks was the name of an orange drink and also a hot dog franchise in New York. Glickman also sometimes called a successful shot by saying "swish" to imitate the sound of the basketball dropping through the net without hitting the rim. I quickly adopted "swish" to the imaginary play-by-play that ran through my head as I hit shot after shot in my room using a rolled-up sock and a waste basket in the corner to simulate the game. As I listened to basketball on the radio, I imagined myself a star.

Radio played a crucial role in other ways during the war. We heard the war news first on the radio—the surrender of Corregidor, the disaster at Kasserine Pass, the victory at Midway, the invasion of Normandy. I huddled close to our upright Philco, listening intently to Lowell Thomas at 6:45 P.M., and to Gabriel Heater ("Ah, there's good news tonight!") at 8:45 P.M. Late at night after the rest of the family was asleep, I would sometimes creep downstairs and twist the radio dial, picking up WWVA in Wheeling, West Virginia, even KMOX in St. Louis, or KDKA in Pittsburgh. I became expert at adjusting the dial and listening to programs through the static. I also learned to read while I listened to the radio and to concentrate on both the words on the printed page and the words coming over the airways. On the shortwave band I could sometimes pick up BBC from London. I listened faithfully to "Captain Midnight" and to "Jack Armstrong, the All American Boy," that is if I could get the radio away from my sister who preferred to listen to "Stella Dallas" and "Young Wider Brown." We often listened as a family to the radio on Sunday night and at the same time we played cards—whist, contract rummy, or occasionally bridge. My family never adopted my grandfather's belief that playing cards on Sunday was a sin. Sunday was prime time for radio programming. At seven there was Jack Benny with Mary Livingston, Rochester, Dennis Day, and the whole gang. Then at eight came Edgar Bergen and Charlie McCarthy. We also listened to the Aldrich Family and the Great Gildersleeve. I think it was Tuesday that I listened to the Lux Radio Theater and on Wednesday I never missed the Lone Ranger. The sound of the radio permeated our lives during the war, and provided background for everything we did. We listened to music, to the chatter of the baseball play-by-play announcer, even to the advertisements. I would sing: "Super Suds, Super Suds. Lots More Suds with Super Suds;" or: "I'm Chiquita Banana and I've come to say, bananas have to ripen in a certain way." When Lucky Strike changed the color of its package from green to white, the slogan, "Lucky Strike Green has Gone to War," became almost as famous as "Remember Pearl Harbor."

With no television to give instant visual images of the war we depended on *Life* and *Look* and sometimes *Time* to print the photographs of the major battles and other events. I didn't realize at the time that these photographs were censored, but I rushed to the library every Saturday, and sometimes on Tuesday afternoon, to read the latest issues and to learn about the Battle of Stalingrad or the sinking of a Japanese aircraft carrier, the invasion of North Africa or Guadalcanal. There were also stacks of old *Life* magazines, as well as *Argosy* and *Esquire* at Art Bacon's barbershop next to the Idle Hour Theater. Following the news of the war made me an eager reader of the newspaper, which in our household meant the daily *Burlington Free Press* and the Sunday *New York Herald Tribune*, and I followed the progress of the war on my *National Geographic* maps.

The war also stimulated my interest in collecting stamps. I became an avid collector when I was only seven or eight largely because my older sister and her friends were collectors. I loved to attach the hinge and place a new stamp in my album. I studied catalogues from H. E. Harris, the Mystic Stamp Company, and other dealers. I dreamed of owning the complete 1893 Columbian issue or the rare 1923 twenty-four cent airmail stamp with the inverted center. But I settled for ordering approvals from one of the stamp companies and selecting a few inexpensive stamps to add to my collection. The war expanded my horizon to include exotic foreign places, not just Germany, Japan, and Russia, but *Manchukuo* (the Japanese name for Manchuria), Persia, Mongolia, Danzig, French Equatorial Africa, French Guiana, Straits Settlements, and many other countries. On cold winter afternoons I enjoyed studying my collection, checking for watermarks and measuring the perforations. At the same time I dreamed of traveling to some of the places pictured on my stamps.

In June 1950 I was working at a summer hotel in the Adirondacks when the Korean War broke out. There were many other college students there, but I was the only one who knew instantly where Korea was because of my stamp collection and my fascination with maps. Maps, magazines, and the radio delivered war news, but nothing was more important during the war than the movies. The Idle Hour Theater on Main Street was the only theater in town until an enterprising businessman turned the town house into a movie theater during the last year of the war. But that experiment lasted only a year. It is the Idle Hour Theater that captured my imagination and lives on in my memory.

Those under twelve paid eleven cents (one cent was a federal tax added during the war) and were required to sit in the first five rows of hard seats. After twelve the admission was twenty-five cents and even at that it was a bargain. On a Friday night there would be a cartoon, a serial, with our hero or heroine left in a precarious position so you just had to come back the next week to see if they survived. On Friday and Saturday there sometimes was a live act, the very end of vaudeville, I now realize. There also was a news reel, usually Movietone News, and a double feature.

The Idle Hour Theater was tiny by most standards; it probably had a capacity of no more than a hundred. There was a small balcony in addition to the main floor. Also in the balcony was the projection booth. When I was in high school I knew the projectionist and watched as he would change reels. If he did it correctly the audience barely noticed the change, but occasionally the screen went dark during the reel change, and then there would be boos and hisses. At first I went to the movies with my parents, then with my friends and, by the time I was in high school, I went with a girlfriend, or I went alone. It was exciting, when after several minutes of anticipation the theater went dark, and on the screen came the MGM lion, the RKO beacon, or the Twentieth Century Fox search lights. It was preferable to see the movie from beginning to end, but it was possible to go into the theater in the middle and then stay to watch the beginning. It was an interesting intellectual exercise to put the two sections of the movie together in my mind as I left the theater. Even in Hardwick's little theater there was an usher with a little flash light to show you to a vacant seat and to make sure you didn't trip over another patron. At first I was not very fussy about what I saw; I liked them all, the cowboy movies, the mysteries and even the romances. Then I became more discriminating. The first-run movies were shown on Sunday and Monday. I don't remember when the Idle Hour Theater began showing movies on Sunday, but I do recall the argument my older sister had with my father and mother. They argued that she should go to the young people's meeting at the church and she wanted to go to the movies with her friends. By the time I came along the church had changed the meetings to late afternoon and then we all went to the movies afterwards. There was something magic about the movies. One could be transported to another world and then, on leaving the theater, the world outside seemed, for a brief few minutes, less real than the world on the screen.

The films I liked best were about the war: *Wake Island, God Was My Co-pilot, Burma Road, Casablanca, Mrs. Miniver, Wing and a Prayer* with Dana Andrews, and even *Desperate Journey*, with Errol Flynn and Ronald Reagan. The first time I saw *Casablanca,* when I was about twelve, I was not impressed because it didn't have enough action. But within a few years Humphrey Bogart, with his cool confidence, became my hero. He had the kind of nonchalance around women that I aspired to and never achieved. Yet I was hooked on World War II movies and I still watch them, even the bad ones, when they are replayed on television. The movies continued after the war was over, *Twelve-o' Clock High, Stalag Seventeen, The Great Escape,* and many more.

I have been so influenced by World War II movies that when I first flew into Tokyo in 1975 all I could think about was *Thirty Seconds Over Tokyo,* and Jimmy Doolittle's bombing raid on the city. When I was living in Amsterdam I took the train frequently into Germany. At the border a Gestapo-like German agent would check passports and I imagined that I was an American pilot trying to escape from a German prison. When I first visited Vienna it was not the great Hapsburg city that was in my mind, but the city of *The Third Man*.

During the war going to the movies usually made me feel more patriotic and I came away from the theater more determined than ever to join the fight and win the war.

Memorial Day was especially meaningful during the war, much more important as a patriotic holiday than the Forth of July, and patriotism was in fashion in Hardwick. The parade started at the Memorial Building on Church Street. In my memory it almost always rained, and the parade started late, but it was never canceled. I also associate Memorial Day with the smell of lilacs, because in northern Vermont lilacs did not bloom until near the end of May. The parade consisted of a ragtag marching band, a few floats, a couple of old fire trucks, assorted Boy and Girl Scout troops along with World War I veterans squeezed into their old uniforms or wearing American Legion caps. The old veterans contrasted with the slim World War II soldiers home on leave with their sleek, perfectly-fitted dress uniforms. The parade stopped at the bridge over the Lamoille River where, after a brief ceremony, a veteran tossed a wreath into the river to honor all of those who had died at sea. The entourage then moved slowly through the business district to South Main Street and into the cemetery where there were speeches and prayers. A bugler played Taps and the honor guard fired three volleys of blanks to honor those who had died in American wars. After each round small boys dashed to pick up the empty shells. But I was always with the Boy Scout troop; I had to stand motionless, and I missed out on the souvenirs.

The service in the cemetery became more poignant as 1942 turned into 1943 and 1944 and there were more tributes the Hardwick men who had died in the war. The first person to be killed in the war that I knew personally was Robert "Bobby" Jones, who lived on Pearl Street in my end of town. His father worked for my father at the store and he had been my teacher in a New Deal-sponsored summer program where we did arts and crafts projects. Trained as a bombardier on a B-17, he had been home on leave shortly before he was declared missing in action in the Pacific. In all, Hardwick lost six of its young men out of 296 men and women from town who served during the war.

On Memorial Day the war seemed profoundly more than a great adventure. It was during World War II that I got interested in baseball. I was a casual fan from the time I was about ten. My father would sometimes have the Red Sox game on the radio at our camp in Greensboro, and the ball game was always on at the store during baseball season. I also remember cheering for the St. Louis Cardinals when they played the New York Yankees in the World Series in 1942. Cheering against the Yankees was part of my heritage. But I did not become a real Red Sox fan until 1943. My addiction was caused by a brother and sister from Boston, Bobby and Gwendolyn Bupp, who spent summers during the war with their grandparents on West Church Street. Probably their parents thought that a small town in northern Vermont was safer than the big city. In any case it was exciting to have some new people in town when so many families were moving to the cities to take wartime jobs. Gwendolyn, a year older than her brother, was blond and I thought quite beautiful. She taught us all kissing games, but at twelve kissing was not nearly as important as baseball and Bobby was a passionate fan. He had actually been to Fenway Park and he could describe in great detail the left field wall—thirty-seven feet high, and the short right field fence, only 302 feet from home plate, and the way the wall curved around to the bull pens 380 feet away. Even more amazing, he knew the batting averages of often-obscure Red Sox players such as Roy Pardee the catcher, and George "Catfish" Metkovitch who alternated between first base and the outfield. He followed the standings in the newspaper, showed us how to read box scores and how to calculate batting averages and the pitcher's earned run average. He even taught us how to keep score.

Bobby Bupp regaled us with stories of past Red Sox triumphs, how in 1941 Ted Williams had hit .406. We knew that, of course, but he filled us in on the details, how he had gone into the final doubleheader of the season in Philadelphia against the Athletics, hitting .3995 which was technically .400. But he refused to sit out the games. In the first game he went four for five and in the second two for three to finish at .406, the highest average since 1930. But Ted Williams was not around in 1944. Along with Johnny Pesky and Dom DiMaggio, and the Yankee stars, Joe DiMaggio and Phil Rizzuto, he was in the service. Bobby Doer did play in 1944 and he became my favorite in part because he played second base. I also liked Eddie Lake, the shortstop. Despite my cheering, however, the Red Sox finished fourth in 1944 behind the pennant winning St. Louis Browns (of all teams), Detroit and New York.

I spent a good part of the winter of 1944-1945 (the year the war came to a climax in Europe and Asia) poring over baseball books, studying statistics, learning the history of the game. I did not realize it at the time but the 1945 season would prove to be the most pathetic in baseball annals. Almost all of the stars and even most of the minor leaguers were in the service. The sixteen teams in the American and National Leagues patriotically played a full schedule even though their players resembled the men in the World War I song where the love-struck young woman complained about the men in her life: "They're either too young or too old," she decided. The St. Louis Browns even played a one-armed outfielder named Pete Gray. He had to catch the ball with his good left hand, toss it into the air while he tucked his glove under the stump of his right arm, catch the ball and with one motion throw it back to the infield. My baseball encyclopedia indicates that he played in seventy-seven games, batted .218 one handed with six players, but many on their roster had been at their peak in the 1930s or they were 4F minor leaguers who never should have been playing in the major leagues in the first place. Bobby Doerr, who had played in 1944, was finally drafted, but Eddie Lake still played shortstop, "Catfish" Metkovitch was usually at first base, while thirty-eight-year-old "Indian Bob" Johnson, whose best years had been with the Philadelphia A's, played left field and led the team with twelve home runs. Dolph Camilli, an aging former star with the Brooklyn Dodgers, even played a few games while Joe Cronin, the manager, who had been an outstanding infielder with the Washington Senators, tried to play third base. After he broke an ankle in an early game, he retired as a player. The one bright spot was the arrival of a young pitcher, Dave "Boo" Ferris, who won twenty-one games and (in the days when pitchers actually batted) hit .267. But the Red Sox lost the first nine games of the season, and, despite a mid-season rally, finished seventh, beating only the Philadelphia Athletics while the Detroit Tigers edged the Washington Senators for the pennant.

In 1945 I learned to suffer with the Red Sox, an affliction that has lasted a lifetime. During the war, and for several years after the war, especially in northern Vermont, Major League baseball was a radio game, and I still think it remains a better game on the radio than on television. Listening to the play-by-play announcer I learned to imagine the action, to hear the crowd, to follow every pitch as I created my own virtual Fenway Park. I did not see a game there until 1950 after my freshman year in college, but I could imagine every angle, every configuration of the walls and the stands. I listened to the games on WDEV in Waterbury, Vermont, always in the afternoons with frequent double headers on holidays and Sundays. The station carried only the Red Sox home games, because they also broadcast the Boston Braves' games. I never cheered for the Braves (I don't know why) even though in 1945 they had a much better team than the Red Sox, with Tommy Holmes hitting .352 with twenty-eight home runs.

Occasionally, when there was a rain out or an open date, WDEV carried a telegraphic recreation of the Red Sox game. The announcer (in Boston and not Waterbury) received the details of the game via telegraph—strikes, balls hits, runs etc., then, with the aid of recorded crowd noise and the sound of bat hitting ball, he created a narrative that seemed real. But you could always tell that it was a recreation because in the background there was the constant *click, click, click* of the telegraph key (which was also recorded). Ronald Reagan, the future president, got his start in broadcasting by doing telegraphic recreations of Chicago Cub games from a station in Des Moines, Iowa, even though he had never seen a major league game. On occasion, when the connection to Chicago was lost he would have the batter foul off pitch after pitch until more information came over the telegraph wire. One scholar has argued that Reagan got so involved in creating and narrating the game that he came to believe that it was real, the beginnings of what became a habit of confusing fantasy with reality.

Willie Morris, in his memoir, *North Toward Home* (1967), writes of listening to telegraphic recreations of St. Louis Cardinal games while growing up in Mississippi. One day he discovered that he could pick up the same game on his father's short-wave radio, but the real broadcast was several innings ahead of the recreated version. For a brief time his friends thought he had special powers because he would check the game on the short-wave radio and then rush to the pool room, where his buddies were listening to the recreated version, and casually predict that one of the players was going to take two pitches and single to right. But his friends soon discovered what he was up to and his triumph was short lived.

My radio was not powerful enough during the day to pick up the real game from Chicago or St. Louis so I never found out whether or not there was a time lag. But live or recreated, I listened to as many games as I could, and I was not the only one in Hardwick for there were a lot of Red Sox fans. In the summer, in Greensboro, I could walk along the shore between my camp and Willey's Store and keep up with the progress of the game because enough people in their camps along the way had their radio tuned to the game. Some days, especially during a thunderstorm, I had to listen to the game through a great deal of static. That skill became useful after the war, when I acquired a portable radio and night games became more routine. I could lie in bed and listen to the game as it faded in and out.

Baseball was a radio game; it was also a newspaper game. Each morning in the summer of 1945 when the *Burlington Free Press* arrived I would turn first to the sports page to check the account of the previous days' game; only then would I check the war news. That summer I became an addicted newspaper reader, a habit that has lasted a lifetime. I studied the box scores and the descriptions of the other games as well as the league standings. Baseball scheduling was simpler in the days before expansion. There were only eight teams in the American League with none west of St. Louis or south of Washington, D. C. The teams traveled by train so it was not difficult to figure out that after Boston played the White Sox they moved on to play the St. Louis Browns. As I read about the game in the newspaper I would often be amazed at the situations or the plays that the writer emphasized, which conflicted with my memory. It was the beginning, I suppose, of my distrust of journalists and the realization, only half-formed, that truth is always subjective. I gradually realized that the writer was trying to tell a story and to make it as dramatic as possible. For a time I wanted to be a sports writer. Sometimes, especially after a big game, I was dissatisfied with the coverage in the *Burlington Free Press*, and annoyed with what I saw as the bias and the pro-Yankee slant of the Sunday *New York Herald Tribune*, I would spend a nickel and buy a copy of the *Boston Globe* or the *Boston Post* to glory in the detailed, and more partisan, accounts of a Red Sox game. But the Boston papers did not arrive in Hardwick until the two o'clock train. I sometimes made a special trip downtown to visit the Shattuck News Store, a fascinating place filled with magazines and even a few paperback books, and Freddy Shattuck tolerated my looking at the magazines without buying them.

I had already discovered the Jeudevine Library when I

became a baseball fan, but I learned that on the mezzanine there was a wonderful collection of old magazines including several sports journals. I would sit hidden away reading sports stories all afternoon. I was especially intrigued by the biographical profiles of the sports heroes, and in the days before Jim Bouton's *Ball Four* (1964) these heroes had no flaws. Looking back and trying to recall, attempting to sort out what I remember, and what I have read about since, I realize that becoming a baseball fan was the genesis of my lifetime habit of reading, studying, and doing research. And because I first got interested in baseball during the war I followed the sports news and the war news at the same time. In the spring of 1945 I would tune in to a Boston station (or perhaps it was a Vermont station that carried a Boston program) to listen to "Bump Hadley Pitching," which came on at 5:45 (or was it 6:15?). Hadley was a former major league pitcher who labored for a half dozen teams (none of them the Red Sox) and compiled a lifetime record from 1929 to 1941 of 161 wins and 165 loses. But in his radio persona he was an ardent Red Sox fan and he started his broadcast with the lead in: "This is Bump Hadley pitching, and the pitch is a good one," or if the Red Sox had lost, "the pitch is a bad one." A win made me feel good no matter what else had happened during the day, but a loss was depressing, and in 1945, there were many more losses than wins.

The next year, the first post-war baseball season, was special for the Red Sox. All the stars were back from the service including Ted Williams, Johnny Pesky, and Dom DiMaggio. It was a completely different team, though Dave Ferris survived from the 1945 team. I was depressed even before the season began when the Red Sox, in an era when most ball players stayed for an entire career with the same club, traded Eddie Lake, one of my favorite players, to Detroit for slugger and first baseman Rudy York. Ironically my favorite bat had always been a Rudy York model, doubly ironic because I used the bat not to hit home runs but to bunt. I quickly forgot about Eddie Lake (and his .200 batting average) and cheered as York hit balls over the left field wall at Fenway Park. "Pesky to Doerr to York," was the Red Sox double play combination in 1946. I rushed home from school and baseball practice on opening day that year to listen to "Bump Hadley Pitching," to learn that not only had the Red Sox won, but that "The Kid," Ted Williams had smashed a home run, one of many he hit that year. The Red Sox won the pennant so easily in 1946 that we all assumed that they would win the World Series against the St. Louis Cardinals. All the games were played during the day so we would sneak out of study hall and go down to the basement in the Academy building where Mr. Bradford, the janitor, would let us listen to the game on his radio. The principal, Chandler Mosher, tolerated our behavior because he was also a Red Sox fan. To everyone's surprise (at least in northern Vermont) the series went seven games and then Enos Slaughter scored the winning run all the way from first on a single as the throw from Leon Culbertson (who had replaced Dom DiMaggio in center field after the"Little Professor" pulled a muscle) came in late to Johnny Pesky. "Pesky held the ball," became the plaintive cry of Red Sox fans. I was disappointed, but assumed that they would win in 1947. As it turned out, although they came close a few times, it would not be until 2004 that they finally won the series. I learned as Bart Giamatti put it, that to be a devoted Red Sox fan was to understand, "that man is fallen and that life is filled with disappointment."

I not only listened to baseball and followed the pennant races, I also played the game and fantasized about being a major league, or at least a high school star. I don't remember when I first started playing, but it may have been as early as five or six for I played with a group of boys two and three years older than I. But I did not get seriously interested in the game until I was about ten. I remember my father taking me up to the attic to find a couple of old baseball gloves left over from his high school days before World War I. They were little more than two pieces of leather sewn together, and at first I had difficulty catching a ball with them. Eventually I acquired a new glove signed by Mace Brown, a journeyman pitcher with Pittsburgh, Brooklyn, and finally the Red Sox. I don't remember buying it, perhaps my Uncle Herman gave it to me; he often brought gifts when he visited. It had a little more padding, and a more definite pocket, than my father's gloves. I oiled it carefully, threw a ball over and over into the pocket to "break it in," and I even wrapped it with string with a ball in the pocket to make it conform to my idea (and my friends' idea) of what a glove should look like. Later when I was in high school I bought a better glove, but it is the Mace Brown model that I remember. It was an improvement over my father's gloves, but it was a far cry from the huge gloves with large traps that the modern player uses to snag throws and fly balls with one hand. I had to learn to catch the ball in the glove and then to clap my right hand over the ball so it would not escape. If one squeezed the ball too soon the ball squirted out, and if one got the right hand in too quickly it could be painful. The summer I was ten, the fingers of my right hand were black and blue most of the time

My father did not teach me how to play baseball; he was always busy at the store. But over the years we shared an interest in the game. We talked about the Red Sox, suffered with their defeats and held out hope for the next year. When my sister and I cleaned out his house after he died I discovered stacks and stacks of homemade scorecards that he had used to keep score when he watched the Red Sox on television. When the Red Sox finally won the World Series in 2004 I thought of him and how much he would have enjoyed that triumph.

It was Harold Leach rather than my father who taught me how to catch a fly ball, how to get back on it, how to catch it shoulder-high and off to the side so it wouldn't hit me in the face. Harold Leach, who was three years older than I, and an excellent athlete, also taught me how to catch a brook trout, another important masculine skill in Hardwick when I was growing up. Catching a high pop fly was not easy for me to learn, but I practiced and practiced. I threw a tennis ball to the roof of our barn and then tried to catch it as it rolled off, or I threw the ball against the barn door and tried to catch it on the fly, or to pretend I was playing second base and fielding it like a ground ball. All the time I had a play-by-play in my head, "There's a long drive to left field; Davis goes back, back, leaps, and makes the catch."

My friends and I played informal baseball games. There were no Little Leagues in the 1940s, and no organized baseball for youngsters in Hardwick. We tossed the ball back and forth on lawns and driveways, and we played in vacant lots. We also played on what we called the "circus grounds" and at Prospect Park, where the high school played. But our favorite place to play was the Chautauqua grounds at the end of West Church Street. I had no idea what a Chautauqua was or how to spell it at the time, but I later heard my parents talking about going to Chautauqua in the 1920s when a traveling troop came to town for a week in the summer, and about the time when a sudden thunderstorm blew the tent down. Hardwick, like a great many towns and small cities across the nation with a rail connection, was visited in the 1920s by the Redpath traveling Chautauqua, a mixture of culture, religion, and entertainment. But the traveling Chautauqua in Hardwick and elsewhere had fallen victim to the Depression and the popularity of the movies and the radio. Only the name survived in Hardwick when I was growing up.

The Chautauqua grounds made an imperfect and oddly shaped ball park. The railroad tracks cut across right field, and by common consent a ball poked onto the tracks was a ground-rule double. If someone hit a ball into the woods in left field that was a home run, but that almost always meant a lost ball and time out to search for it. We usually had only one ball to play with and it was often covered with "Bulldog tape." Out bats, often cracked, were also taped. We used pieces of cardboard for the bases and the distance between bases was far from standard. The field was part grass and part dirt and the outfield sloped in various directions forming hills and valleys. Even Prospect Park, where we played high school games, had a virtual gravel pit near second base. Between pitches I occupied my time digging out stones and throwing them away.

In our pick-up games we often played three against three, or six against six, rarely nine against nine. If we had only a few players someone from the opposing team became the catcher. Rules were flexible and negotiable, and often an argument would break out over who was safe or out. But there was a certain amount of order enforced by the older players. We started a game by choosing sides. Two of the bigger boys or better players (not always the same were selected by reputation or consensus to choose teammates. One threw a bat to the other who caught it with one hand somewhere in the middle, and then the two would alternate hands until one could get three fingers under the knob of the bat giving him the right to pick first. Each chose in turn until there was no one left. When I first started to play I was usually the youngest and the last, or near the last, chosen, but gradually I moved up the ladder until I became one of those who did the choosing. It was an important rite of passage, but someone always had to be picked last, like my friend, Paul Brandon, who had broken his arm as a child. Because it was badly set, he had a difficult time throwing and batting. But he still liked to play and he spent hours hitting fungoes to me to improve my skills. Others, like my friend Harold Leach, were always, without argument, one of the leaders. There were at least two girls that I remember playing ball with us. One was my neighbor Jo Racette, the other was a slight girl with pigtails who could run faster than most of the boys. I have forgotten her name. By the time they were twelve or thirteen the girls dropped out of the gang, but some retained the ability to talk about baseball, but playing the game, when I was growing up, was mostly a "guy" thing.

Our pick-up games were usually filled with errors and awkward play, but in our imagination the games were directly related to the major league games we heard on the radio. Because we did not actually see the games we had to imagine the way our heroes swung the bat and fielded the ball. We did mimic some of the high school players, but it was the major leaguers we most admired. Like Pete Gray, the one-armed ball player, we experimented with hitting and catching with one arm. In 1946 after Ted Williams hit a home run off Rip Sewell's high arching "ephus" pitch in the All-Star Game, we tried to hit balls into the left field woods off the best imitation we could muster of Sewell's famous delivery.

Baseball games on the Chautauqua Grounds were an important part of my growing up. In the spring and summer, on Saturdays or in the early evening, I would slip my glove over the handle bars on my bike and head out to find a ball game. It was after I arrived at the Chautauqua Grounds in the early evening on April 12, 1945, that I learned that Franklin Roosevelt had died. We had no game that day.

The day that Roosevelt died was unusually warm in Vermont, but April was often too cold for baseball. The Red Sox always opened their season on Patriot's Day, the same day as the Boston Marathon, April 19, but in northern Vermont there were often patches of snow still on the ground, and occasionally even in May, the opening day of trout season, there was snow. The high school team started to throw in the gymnasium in late March, but even when the team went outside sore arms were routine. I remember one high school game in Johnson (or was it Morrisville?), when I chased a foul pop-up beyond first base from my second base position, and just as I was ready to dive for it, I crashed into a pile of snow that had been plowed off the field a few days earlier.

My fantasies of becoming a major league pitcher ended with a jolt the summer I was twelve, I attended Royal

Ambassador, a boys' camp in Ocean Park, Maine, for two weeks that summer, and in one baseball game I gave up eight runs in one inning. But I did reasonably well at second base; I got a few hits and discovered that I could run faster than all but one or two of the campers from Boston. It is a softball game that I remember best from that summer. I hit a ball over the cabins in right field for what I thought was a home run. Many of my hits went to right field because I had a hitch in my swing. That would prove fatal when later in high school I faced tall, rangy farm boys who could throw hard, but it had a certain advantage for the softball field at Royal Ambassador had a short right field. When the ball soared majestically over the cabins, I dropped my bat and went into my home run trot. I knew about home run trots only because the week before the entire camp had seen *The Pride of the Yankees* with Gary Cooper. In that movie both Babe Ruth and Lou Gehrig go into a slow trot after belting the ball out of the park. In Hardwick, a home run was often hit so far that it rolled beyond the outfield, allowing the player to score by outrunning the throw to home plate, often with a dramatic slide. In that far-away softball game, I should have run faster because the outfielder went behind the cabins, retrieved the ball and threw it back into the infield. The relay made it a close play at the plate. The umpire who was also a counselor, and a minister (it was a Baptist camp), turned to me as I cleaned the dust off my pants and said, "Son, do you think you were out or safe?" I hope I said "safe?" but I don't remember what I said. What I recall is my anger that my long drive had not been immediately declared a home run, and the umpire who refused to rule one way or the other.

In my memory I hit well until I was about thirteen or fourteen and then suddenly I started to swing and miss frequently. About the same time an eye exam revealed that I needed glasses, a humiliating blow to my athletic fantasies. I was diagnosed with myopia, and my left eye was much worse than my right eye. Unfortunately, because I was a right-handed batter, my left eye was crucial in locating the ball. I refused to wear my glasses when I played (despite my admiration for Dom DiMaggio, who was called "the little professor," because he wore glasses.) My inability to get the bat on the ball may also have had something to do with the improved pitching I faced in high school, including some tall youngsters who could break off a curve ball to my complete bafflement. I did make occasional contact, and my best weapon was my speed. If I could lay a bunt down the third base line I could usually beat it out for a base hit, and then I could steal second. But unfortunately I could not steal first.

In my senior year I once struck out four times in one game prompting my team mates to call me "whiff." Even more humiliating, my younger sister, Marjorie, acquired the nickname "breeze." My baseball career ended with high school, but I continued to play softball; the bigger ball and the slower pitching enabled me to convince myself that I was still a ball player.

Baseball is about memory. I remember exactly where I was when I heard that the Red Sox had clinched the American League championship in September 1946. I was getting ready for football practice when I heard that the Red Sox had lost a playoff game to Cleveland in 1948, and I was driving around with friends on a beautiful fall day when a Yankee bloop hit meant defeat for Boston in 1949. I even recall that I was in Amsterdam listening to the play-by-play on Armed Forces Radio, out of Frankfurt, Germany, when Bill Buckner let a ground ball go through his legs in 1986. I can also remember a high school game in 1947 when I got the winning hit, although it is not the hit so much as heartache that I recall, because I had just broken up with my girlfriend.

I not only discovered baseball during the war, I also discovered sex, although I was more an observer than a participant. The war years coincided with my adolescence. I discovered girls, and I also absorbed the romantic and sentimental wartime music and movies. I fell in love, hopelessly, head-over-heels in love, usually with older girls who more or less ignored me. I was in the sixth grade when I noticed that some of the girls in my class were developing breasts. I was aware that girls had breasts, for after all I had an older sister, and I had observed her and her friends, but it was astounding to see the transformation in my classmates and friends. Classmates were not the object of my fantasies, at least not in beginning. First there was Joanne, slender, vivacious, with dark hair. I was captivated by her, by the way she played "Battleship," by the way she laughed. Sad to say she was from out of town, her father was in the Army and she visited her aunt and uncle in Hardwick only occasionally, and when she did visit there were several other boys who followed her around. My relationship with Joanne was fleeting and mostly in my head, but from her I learned a life-long lesson: whenever a beautiful and intriguing woman appeared there were always several men competing for her attention.

Then there was Gwendelyn, also from out of town, at least a year older, a little more sophisticated. It was from her brother that I learned to love the Red Sox. She loved to play kissing games and she had real breasts, which pressed provocatively against the dresses and blouses she wore. She attracted men three or four years my senior. Still I dreamed of her and she lived in my fantasies, at least for two summers. More important was Beverly who had flashing brown eyes, a cute smile and wonderful breasts, at least I imagined she had wonderful breasts underneath the sweaters and blouses, slips and bras that all girls seemed to wear to hide their bodies. I was in the seventh grade and she was in the eighth (a huge divide when we were twelve or thirteen.) She lived in my part of town and I tried to time my walk to school to meet her accidentally, as she came out of her street. I tried to meet her between classes at school. I was too shy to ask for a date. Once I did meet her truly by accident inside the theater and sat beside her during a movie. I even held her hand, but I did not have the courage to put my arm around her. At a corn roast I managed to kiss her very tentatively. I was too young and too inexperienced to seize the opportunity, or even to recognize the glance, the brief kiss as an opportunity. Soon she was noticed by the high school boys and she passed out of my orbit. At a high school reunion a few years ago I confessed to her that I tried to time my walk to school to meet her, and that I was madly in love with her when I was in the seventh grade. "Now you tell me," she said.

Trying to appeal to girls, meant that I spent more time in front of the mirror in the bathroom, to the great dismay of my sisters who claimed they needed to use the bathroom as well. I combed my hair, washed my face over and over again to try to ward off those pimples that somehow had appeared. I started to shave the few dark hairs on my chin. My father all his life used a straight razor, but I experimented with a Gillette safety razor in part because my father's razor scared me, and also, I suspect, I was influenced by the magazine and radio ads: "Look sharp, feel sharp, use Gillette blue blades." But it was my hair that gave me the greatest concern. It was very fine and refused to stay in place when I tried to approximate the swept-back style made popular by Gary Cooper, Van Johnson, and Ronald Reagan in the 1940s. In order to keep my hair from falling in my face I tried Kremel (advertised on the Gabriel Heater program), Vitalis, and other concoctions, but I finally settled on Wild Root Cream Oil. "Use Wild Root Cream Oil, Charlie," went the slogan, "it keeps your hair in trim." Alas, it didn't work for me. My hair just looked slicked down. One of the problems may have been Art Bacon's barbershop where electric trimmers got more use than scissors, and little attention was given to styling my difficult hair.

Art Bacon's barbershop was a male haven where men of all ages gathered to gossip, to tell off-color jokes, to discuss the latest ball game, and incidentally, to get a hair cut. When I was in high school and we had lost a basketball game I hated to go there because I knew all the men would have an opinion of the foul shot I didn't make, the pass I threw away, or the rebound I failed to get. The barbershop was also a place to read *Esquire*, *Argosy* and other men's magazines. The air-brushed pin ups and the photographs, regretfully, did not help much in my quest to study the undraped female form. I thought Rita Hayworth was more beautiful than Betty Grable, although my favorite move star was Veronica Lake who looked sexy as her blond hair fell over her face.

As part of the pre-*Playboy* generation I was handicapped. My friends and I even resorted to examining the *Sears Roebuck Catalogue* and the *Ladies Home Journal* looking for the lingerie ads. The occasional topless native girl in the *National Geographic* magazine didn't inspire us, but we kept up our search. We tried to devise ways to peak into the girl's locker room at the high school gym, however those who designed the gym must have understood the adolescent male mind because the two locker rooms were carefully separated. Summer was wonderful because the girls wore fewer clothes and they went swimming. World War II-era bathing suits were not very revealing, still the girls had to take off their clothes and then take off their bathing suits. When families or groups of young people gathered at our camp in Greensboro or at one of the other camps, the walls were thin and there were many knot holes. I still have clearly in my mind the image of two girls undressing as I spied on them in a neighbor's camp. They were a year or two older, and I can still see them unhook their bras, step out of their panties and stand there naked before they put on their bathing suits. I can still see their incredible white, almost translucent skin, the erect nipples, the pubic hair. My spying taught me that not all breasts are created equal, and that the real thing had little relationship to the pointed concoctions created by stiff bras to form the "sweater girl" look of the war years.

I fantasized about those luminous, innocent girls, yet about the sex act itself, I was woefully ignorant. I discovered a home medical encyclopedia in the hall closet, but the elaborate drawings depicting the male and female anatomy were not very helpful and about as romantic as the girls in the strip show at the Barton Fair, or the pornographic playing cards I glimpsed at Charlie Morris' pool room. I never became much of a pool player, still I liked to hang out there, in part I suppose, because my mother told me not to go there. Older boys gathered there and often bragged about their exploits with women. Charlie Morris seemed to be the authority on all things forbidden, and he sold condoms, except we didn't call them condoms. They were "rubbers," or "Trojans," using a familiar brand name. We would never have had the courage to buy such devices in one of the drugstores, but Charlie sold them, no questions asked. For years the condom I carried in my wallet was more a symbol of hope, than a need to be prepared.

The strange and sometimes terrifying longings of adolescence were for me closely associated with the romance of the war years. My older sister listened to "Your Hit Parade," and "Make Believe Ballroom." The popular songs of loss and separation are very much part of my memory of the war years: "I'll walk alone, but to tell you the truth I'll be lonely;" "You'd be so nice to come home to;" "Full moon and empty arms," "Sentimental Journey," and "That's My Desire" reverberated in the memory of my generation for a lifetime.

I loved the big band sound of Glenn Miller, Tommy Dorsey, and Harry James, and I learned to dance. I couldn't sing or even whistle a tune on key, but I could feel the beat and the rhythm when I was lured onto the dance floor. I seem to remember a dancing class where we learned the waltz and the foxtrot, but that is not where I really learned. There were dances after basketball games, where often the girls danced with each other and the boys hung around the edges. A couple of the older girls, however, would not let me sit on the sidelines. I have always been grateful to those girls. They even taught me the jitterbug.

After my sister went to college in the fall of 1944, I became master of the radio, and I continued to listen to the sentimental wartime songs. I also went to the movies. I fell in love with Elizabeth Taylor in *National Velvet*, and later with Theresa Wright in *The Best Years of Our Lives*. I longed to be old enough to join the Army. I especially wanted to be a pilot in part because in all the movies I saw there was a girl waiting at home for the hero to return. I tried to act nonchalant and disinterested around women, the way Humphrey Bogart did with great success, yet I remained shy and his technique didn't work for me. I discovered, however, that when you danced you didn't need to talk and that was especially true of square dancing, which was very popular in northern Vermont during the war and the years after the war.

I was in the eighth grade on May 8, 1945 when we heard that the war was over in Europe. In the morning of what would be known as VE Day, we were all ushered into the assembly hall at school. Along with the high school students we listened through the static on the radio to President Harry S. Truman announce the victory. He had only been president for a few weeks, and he did not sound very presidential. I had grown up in a family which, if they didn't quite hate FDR, they certainly didn't trust him. Yet he was the only president I had known, and Truman's flat Missouri accent was certainly no match for Roosevelt's sonorous voice. Truman announced that morning that we all had to get back to work to defeat the Japanese. Then, to boos and hisses, high school principal Leon Wagner told the assembled students that we had to get back to work as well; there would be no holiday. We trudged back to our classes, but even the teachers had a hard time that morning keeping their minds on the lesson of the day. Within an hour Wagner changed his mind and an announcement came over the public address system that we could take the rest of the day off. I went fishing with a few friends to celebrate.

A few months later the war was over in the Pacific. There was dancing in the streets in Hardwick, still the thing I remember best about VJ Day was that our family joined a couple of other families and celebrated by going on a picnic. "The War," as we always called it, proved to be a defining experience for our generation. When it was finally over in the summer of 1945, I was fourteen and a half. I could hardly wait to start high school.

World War II was a crucial event for members of the Lucky Generation. It dominated our childhood and adolescence. A few lost fathers or brothers, and others were forced to move with their families to be near military bases or centers of industry. Yet most of us who lived in small towns like Hardwick, faced no real tragedy. We were not old enough to join the armed forces. All we experienced was patriotism and romantic adventure. Shielded from the worst aspects of the war by censorship and propaganda, we saw the war as a struggle between good and evil. It was only much later that we understood the moral ambiguity of the war. Partly because we experienced the war as youngsters far from the battlefields, it was truly a "good war" for us. Interpreting the war as a clear-cut battle between the forces of light against the forces of darkness did not prepare us well for the complexities and contradictions of the post-war world.

Chapter 9

BREAKING AWAY

Some years ago, Lacy Baldwin Smith, distinguished British historian and fellow Greensboro summer resident whom I have known for forty years, asked me with a tone that suggested the incredulous: "Is it true that you grew up in Hardwick?" The question and his tone revealed the disdain often felt by summer residents in Greensboro toward the hardscrabble former granite town. I replied that it was indeed true, that I had not only grown up in Hardwick, I had also graduated from Hardwick Academy. Then he asked: "How did you get out?" "I went to Dartmouth," I said, giving the easy answer. In reality the explanation is much more complex and complicated. It wasn't easy to break away from a stable family and a comfortable hometown.

There was no large industry that young men and women in Hardwick could look forward to entering. The granite industry had declined in the 1920s and almost collapsed during the Depression. Teachers, parents, even ministers urged young people to "make something of yourself," but that implied that to accomplish something worthwhile you had to get out of town. In the generation before I came along, a large number of men worked in the granite industry, in the sheds or in the quarries, or they were employed by the stores and businesses that were supported by the major industry in town. There were few role models in town for me to emulate. The two doctors, the two or three lawyers, and the few bankers, didn't seem to represent ideal careers. I knew I didn't want to follow my grandfather and father in the store, and it never occurred to me to want to run a car dealership or to be an insurance agent like my Uncle Herman. Nor did I ever consider being a farmer like my Uncle Lovell Allen. The life of the farmer, tied down to his farm 365 days a year, did not seem attractive. Even my friends who grew up on farms rejected farming as a career.

There was a chapter of Future Farmers of America at the high school, but even those who joined said that FFA stood for "There is no future in farming in America," and that was especially true in northern Vermont. Some of my classmates joined the Armed Forces, always one way to escape the farm or the small town. And joining the Army or the Marines seemed like a safe career choice in the spring of 1949. A few of the girls in my class got married within a few weeks of our graduation, but eleven of twenty-three seniors went on to college, or to some form of post-secondary education. For the women, attending a teacher's college and preparing to be an elementary school teacher, or going into nurses training, were ways to escape. One of my best friends, Bob LeCours, was one of thirteen children in a French-Canadian farm family, and the first in his family to go to high school. His older brother and sister had stayed home to work on the farm and to help care for the younger children. Bob not only resisted his father's efforts to persuade him to quit school and stay on the farm, but he also became the first in his family to attend college. Following in his footsteps, all his younger brothers and sisters graduated from both high school and college. It took courage and stubbornness for him to break away. In my family, it was just assumed that my sisters and I would go to college; the only question was where.

In retrospect, I now realize that my ability to get out of town and aspire to achieve something more than working in my father's store, was influenced by many people. Most important was my mother, a university graduate herself, who encouraged me at every step, not only to read, to study, to learn, but also to take part in sports; to become independent and self reliant. She supported my projects. When I decided that I wanted to be an artist, she went to her trunk in the attic and found paint brushes and oil paints for me. I showed little talent, so that experiment did not last long. Neither did playing the piano. I took lessons for three months when I was about nine, losing interest when the baseball season began. When I became a Red Sox fan my mother started to follow the Boston team. When in high school I played football and basketball, she came to my games. When I discovered a new book, my mother read it so we could talk about it. She did not always approve of the books I chose to read, too much Horatio Alger, too much Tom Swift, she thought, but she never discouraged my eclectic reading habits. By the time I was eleven or twelve, we often read the same books. I remember discussing Richard Wright's *Black Boy* with her after we both read it when it was published in 1945. Then we read *Native Son*. We both were shocked by the racism and violence in Chicago, but we sympathized with the plight of Bigger Thomas.

I escaped my hometown through reading, and in other ways, I expanded my experiences. Looking back, I marvel at the freedom I was granted to roam around town and beyond; a freedom not given to my two sisters. With my playmates and friends, I would take off on Saturday morning, and not return until time for supper. I am sure that my mother was reassured by the protective nature of the small town, and the fact that everyone knew who I was, and they subtly monitored my actions. Yet no one could watch over us in our adventures on Buffalo Mountain—climbing trees, balancing on cliffs, and diving naked into water-filled, abandoned quarries. Sometimes we took foolish chances. We dug a tunnel into a sand bank and it collapsed on one of my playmates, Milton Gravel. Only the quick intervention of several men saved Milton from suffocating.

My mother warned me about some things. I was forbidden to go to the pool room, but that did not stop me from frequenting the place, and my mother must have suspected. She worried about the way I played with my friends in a local dump with abandoned cars and toxic waste everywhere. She told me not to go swimming in Cooper Brook because it was polluted with sewage. She warned me about dangers, yet she was the one who encouraged me to explore and take chances. Years later, she told me that her greatest worry was polio, and that was justified because several young people in town did get the dreaded disease at the end of World War II, including a man in his twenties, a former football player, who helped coach the high school team. One week he was a talented athlete, and the next he was in the hospital, and finally confined to a wheelchair, for the rest of his life.

I bought a bicycle when I was about ten, and that expanded my range and increased my independence. It was an awkward, heavy bike with balloon tires and no gears, but I paid for it with my own money. It was my prize possession. Going fishing alone in the streams, often miles from Hardwick, gave me opportunities for adventures. One of my favorite spots in the spring was the Corkscrew Brook, which tumbled down a hillside about three miles south of Hardwick, and eventually joined the Woodbury Gulf Brook. I always fished by myself—I would hide my bike in the bushes and walk up Corkscrew Road, so named because the road turned back on itself in order to negotiate the steep grade. The road eventually crossed an old railroad bed that had once been the Hardwick and Woodbury Railroad, a short line that connected the granite quarries with the cutting and polishing sheds in Hardwick. This road had been abandoned in 1934, and the rails torn up and sold for scrap in 1940. The Corkscrew Road continued for about a mile beyond the railbed, past an old, abandoned farm until it crossed a little bridge. I usually fished up from the bridge and I gloried in being without companions in the wilderness. It was my secret spot. I often caught a dozen or more brook trout, some of them almost black, because they lived in pools shaded from the sun. I sometimes spent an entire Saturday alone on my special hidden brook. A few years ago, I hiked up that road. The brook was still there, but I could not find the old farmhouse. The bridge was flooded by a beaver pond, and I found little that I remembered. Still that secret brook lives on in my memory.

Reading quietly and fishing alone may not have been the best training for dealing with people, and I am sure my mother worried about my solitary tendencies. She constantly urged me to play with other boys, even as she encouraged my reading. Ironically, the arrival of a new minister at the United Church in 1938, helped my socialization, and expanded my horizons. John Chester Smith was a graduate of Colgate University and Union Theological Seminary, and his wife, Betty, had grown up in Brooklyn. More importantly, they had two sons, Norman, a few months older than I, and Neil, a few months younger. We became good friends, and I was a frequent visitor in their house, the parsonage, on West Church Street. The Smith, Davis, and Cobb families became close companions. Leone Cobb was my mother's best friend. Like my mother, she was a college graduate who had taught in high school before she was married. She returned to teaching French and Latin when I was in high school. Those three strong-minded, intellectual women, who found themselves in a small town in northern Vermont, had a large influence on me. They read books, and they even organized their own book club at one point. I liked to eavesdrop on their conversations—to hear them discuss everything from the books they were reading, to their views on politics, religion, and the latest movie at the Idle Hour Theater.

In August 1943, when I was twelve, I went with the Smith brothers and their father John Chester Smith for a two-week adventure at Royal Ambassador Boys' Camp in Ocean Park, Maine. It was a Baptist camp and Jack (as he was called) had volunteered as a counselor and Neil, Norman, and I went along as campers. My mother probably suggested I be included. It was my first experience being away from home for an extended time, and my first encounter with a large group of new people. I was painfully shy, and I can still recall the terror I felt as I entered my cabin for the first time and had to confront seven boys my age and a counselor, but I quickly learned I had something in common with these boys. I went back alone the next summer, so my memories of the two summers fade together. Somewhere, I have a ribbon for winning first place in the 100-yard dash and a certificate for achieving honors in a course called "Missionary Heroes," and another for being an "Honor Camper," whatever that meant. The second summer, I earned a Junior Life Saving Certificate after many hours of instruction in the saltwater pool. I don't recall any heavy-handed religious instruction, though we did take classes, like the one on missionaries. I got my first experience taking notes during a lecture in one of those classes. The Christianity preached and practiced at the camp was of the liberal and muscular variety. We learned about Native American lore, sang songs, and worshiped nature around the campfire. We were encouraged (I suspect required), to take part in athletic events, to play baseball, run track, and to swim. It was here that I discovered that I had little future as a baseball pitcher. I also learned that it was unwise to keep my mouth open when diving into the saltwater swimming pool.

Among my cabin mates the first year, were a Black, a Jewish, and an Asian boy. I had never met a Negro, a term everyone used in the 1940s, yet I had been taught to treat everyone equally. He came from the Roxbury section of Boston, and had been sent to camp on a scholarship. I have long since forgotten his name, especially sad, because he became my best friend in the cabin. Royal Ambassador provided my first experience with eating in a common dining hall, and at being herded around by a camp director, and various counselors, most of whom were ministers. I loved the camp, and now realize that it was the first step in preparing for college and the Army, for the experience of living together with groups of men.

My weeks in Maine in the summers of 1943 and 1944, also introduced me to a different landscape. Ocean Park, just south of Old Orchard Beach, and fifteen miles from Portland, was established in the late nineteenth century as a Baptist, seaside resort. Ocean Grove in New Jersey, Wesleyan Grove on Martha's Vineyard, Silver Bay on Lake George, and Chautauqua in Western New York, are other examples of religious summer communities established in self defense by the Methodists and the Baptists, to provide some of the joys of vacation spots while eliminating, or at least controlling, the temptations of the more traditional resorts. Ocean Park is dominated by a large, octagon-shaped temple. The campers marched to that impressive structure for religious services, lectures, and even movies. It wasn't the religious nature of Royal Ambassador and Ocean Park that impressed me in 1943, but the fact that it was on the ocean. The area was flat and sandy and filled with scrubby pine trees. My family had spent a weekend at Old Orchard Beach the summer when I was six, but except for that brief stay, Royal Ambassador was my first introduction to the ocean—the smell of the salt air, the taste of the saltwater, and the ever-present sand in clothes and shoes. Before this trip, and the brief sojourn in 1937, I had not been away from the rolling hills, the swift flowing streams, and the mountains of northern New England. I liked the ocean—the rhythmic sound of the surf, the exposed expanse of sand at low tide, and the strange back flow of the tidal rivers. Still, I was homesick for the freshwater lakes of Vermont. I have spent many days on ocean beaches—from France, North Africa, Brazil, and the Netherlands, to California, and the New Jersey shore. Yet, I still prefer mountains and lakes to all the pleasures of the sea. I am so influenced by the landscape of my childhood and by summers on Caspian Lake, that I have never been completely happy near the sea, the desert, or the plains. Yet, it was my adventure in Maine during two summers during World War II, that gave me my first basis for comparison and helped me break away from home.

The war years were a time of gasoline rationing, but I was able to travel, not only to Maine, but also to New York City. Sometime in 1944, Jack Smith took a position as executive director of the Greater Hartford Council of Churches. That provided a perfect excuse for me to visit the Smith family in Hartford, Connecticut, and then to travel with Neil and Norman, to New York City. I am sure it was arranged by my mother and Betty Smith, but in any case, during spring break when I was fourteen and in the eighth grade, my parents drove one morning to Montpelier Junction, where I boarded the train for Hartford. My only other train ride had been very short and illegal. With two friends, I had hopped a freight car one day, and ridden the four miles from Hardwick to East Hardwick; but this was my first, real train trip.

I had a little suitcase and a lunch that my mother had packed for me. Why spend the money to go to the dining car? The train moved south to White River Junction, down the Connecticut River valley through Bellows Falls and Brattleboro, to Springfield, Massachusetts. I sat next to a young, attractive girl, perhaps fifteen or sixteen. A perfect chance for a romance, or at least to talk, but I was too shy to carry on a real conversation. I kept my head pressed against the glass watching the factories, the backyards of houses, the sidings with boxcars, and the towns and cities as we entered the stations. I was enthralled by the life on the train, the conductors, the passengers getting on and off, even the dining car with the Black waiters. The train seemed like a moving city traveling through the countryside. That first train ride during wartime, began my lifelong romance with the railroad.

The Smiths met me at the train station in Hartford, and I stayed for a couple of days at their suburban home in West

Hartford. I recall visiting the Mark Twain House, and some other sights, but Hartford paled in comparison to New York City. We were three adolescent boys, one thirteen, two fourteen, traveling alone to New York. What parents in their right minds would send three youngsters off to New York City by themselves? The times were different and more innocent, and Betty Smith and Bernice Davis were intent on providing new experiences for their sons. Those of us from the Lucky Generation who grew up in small towns, were able to take advantage of that innocence to expand our horizons. I had been traveling vicariously through books, the radio, and the movies, and now I had a chance to experience a part of the world I had imagined.

We were met at Grand Central Station by the Smith boys' aunt who lived in an apartment in a brownstone in the Bay Ridge section of Brooklyn. I was overwhelmed by the size of the station, the high ceilings, and the crowds of people all rushing about. We traveled to Brooklyn by subway and each day, she would give us directions to a destination or two: the Bronx Zoo, Rockefeller Center, the Statue of Liberty. After a day or two, we became confident as we switched from the local to the express, from the IRT, to the BMT, to the crosstown shuttle. The subway at five cents a ride, with free transfers, was the best bargain in town. We got lost, but never for long, and once in the Museum of Natural History, we became separated—but I don't remember being worried and we were reunited at the exit. We tramped around town, went to see the Rockettes, and a movie at Radio City Music Hall, but I have long forgotten the name of the movie. I marveled at Times Square, though I suppose with the war still on, it was not lit up with its usual splendor, but it seemed bright enough to me. The Bond Clothes Waterfall and the Camel ad, with the real smoke rings, made me stare like the tourist I was.

We went to the top of the Empire State Building, taking the express elevator to the eightieth floor, and then the slower elevator to the observation deck. A few months later, in the summer of 1945, a B-25 bomber flying from Massachusetts to Newark got lost in the fog and slammed into the Empire State Building. I read the news accounts of the disaster with special interest because I had been there. After V-J Day when I saw a newsreel showing the crowds of people celebrating the end of the war in Times Square, I remembered walking through those same streets. In the fall of 1945, I saw the MGM movie, *The Clock,* with Judy Garland and Robert Walker. I was fascinated by their tour down Fifth Avenue because I recognized all the landmarks. Like learning earlier at Fort Ticonderoga, that the events in books had actually happened, I was now learning to associate places in the news with sites I had experienced. There was a world beyond Hardwick, and not just in my imagination.

We toured the RCA building in Rockefeller Center, and watched television for the first time. We saw the experimental display that had been featured at the 1939 World's Fair, and was a forecast of what was to come. The television flickered, and was difficult to watch, but it seemed exciting at the time. We were all stamp collectors, so we spent several hours in the stamp department at Gimbels Department Store, enthralled by the displays of stamps from all over the world. I watched with amazement, as a well-dressed man bought a single stamp and paid for it with a fifty-dollar bill (was it a 1893 Columbus $5?). We browsed a huge bookstore, the first real bookstore I had ever seen. It made the small selection of paperbacks in the news stores in Hardwick and St. Johnsbury seem pathetic. The new books, in their pristine jackets, were stacked on tables and filled the shelves that went all the way around the store. On the mezzanine, there were sets of books—rare, old volumes and leather-bound classics. Years later, I identified the bookstore as Scribner's, at 48th Street and Fifth Avenue, now, unfortunately, converted into a store that sells perfume and cosmetics. One day, we took the subway to Long Island, to inspect the site of the 1939 World's Fair. Not much remained of the famous fairgrounds, but nearby was LaGuardia Field where we watched airliners (probably DC-3's) take off and land. I was fascinated by airplanes, but my first flight would have to wait until I was finally drafted into the Army. In March of 1955, I flew on a commercial airliner from New York to Chicago, then to Los Angeles, and finally to Seattle, on my way to Alaska. It took over eighteen hours on the prop planes of the day, but I was thrilled, and I kept thinking of the first airliners I had seen that day at LaGuardia Field.

Much of the time the Smith boys and I spent in New York, we just walked around looking in amazement at the people, and at the displays in the store windows. It was still wartime, and there were many soldiers and sailors on the streets. We ate several times at Horn and Hardart Automats. I can still see the woman with white gloves turned gray who changed paper money into nickels. We placed them in slots, three nickels for a sandwich, two for a piece of pie. The glass door opened magically and we removed our prize. We had lunch in a delicatessen, where I had a hot-pastrami sandwich on rye and a piece of cheesecake for the first time. Neither of these delicacies was available in Hardwick, Vermont. Each night we returned to the Brooklyn apartment, where there were many books and magazines. I remember discovering and reading a book about the Flying Tigers, the group of American airmen based in the wartime capital of Chongqing, who painted their P-40s to look like tigers, and fought the Japanese before the United States entered the war. Many years later, while lecturing in China I visited the Stilwell Museum in Chongqing that honored the Flying Tigers, and suddenly my mind flashed back to the time in 1945, when I stayed in a brownstone in Brooklyn.

The Smith boys and I saw a great deal of New York in a week, but there was a lot we did not experience. We did not go to the Museum of Modern Art or the Metropolitan Museum, and we had no clue that the New York School of Abstract Expressionism was just emerging in the city. We did not venture into Chinatown or Greenwich Village or see a Broadway play. We didn't visit Yankee Stadium or Madison Square Garden. We did not enter the great ballrooms and nightclubs that I had been admiring in the movies, the magic rooms where orchestras played, and sophisticated men and women sipped their cocktails and danced. That would have to wait for another day. We didn't go to the Hotel Pennsylvania, although we all knew the Glenn Miller song that had made the telephone number of the hotel famous: Pennsylvania 6-5000. Since that first trip to New York, I have been there hundreds, even thousands of times. I have lectured and done research there, gone to conventions and had lunch and dinner with editors, stayed with friends, even slept in the Rockefeller Fifth Avenue apartment. Each time I am in New York, my mind flashes back to that first visit in 1945. That trip introduced me to an urban world filled with technological marvels that I had only imagined before. I rode a city bus, a subway, a passenger train, an escalator, an elevator, and a taxi for the first time. I used a dial telephone and saw television (even though it was just an experimental model). More importantly, I fell in love with the city, and since then a balance between urban and rural, between the city and the small town, has been a part of my life.

New York was a revelation and opened up a fascinating new world, but I had to return to Hardwick and complete the eighth grade. The spring and summer of 1945, were exciting because on May 8, the war in Europe ended and by mid-August, the war was over in the Pacific. For four years, we had heard promises and predictions about the exciting things that would happen "after the war," but in Hardwick the new utopia didn't emerge. The soldiers returned, but many went off to college using the G. I. Bill, or they drifted away to find better employment opportunities elsewhere. Many of those who had obtained jobs in the war-related industry in Hartford, or Springfield, Vermont, remained in their new homes, or at least they didn't return to Hardwick. My grandfather had a difficult time adjusting to the inflation of the war and post-war period. My grandmother had to drag him to a store to buy a new suit, because he insisted that if you couldn't buy a good suit for twenty dollars, he would get along with his old, and worn clothes. New cars began to come off the line in 1946. I recall the excitement we all felt when the father of one of my friends bought a new Kaiser. My father nursed his 1940 Packard for several years after the war because his business did not improve much in the post-war years. In fact, it may have declined because he faced more competition from the chain stores—but he did purchase a Jeep truck to replace the horse and wagon for grocery deliveries.

As I got older, I felt more and more pressure to work in the store. My Saturday duty of restocking shelves was extended occasionally to waiting on customers. During the summers of 1945 and 1946, I worked for two weeks while one of the regular clerks was on vacation. My father knew I disliked working in the store, and he never tried to convince me to follow in his footsteps. My mother, who often quietly mediated between me and my father, insisted that I had an obligation to work in the store, but she also helped me escape. Several years later after I had graduated from college, I did work in the store for an entire summer after one of my father's clerks died. I came to appreciate my father's work life that summer, and to understand how much he was respected in town for being friendly, cooperative, and impeccably honest. That was easier to comprehend at the age of twenty-two than at fifteen.

Sometime during the winter of 1947, when I turned sixteen, it occurred to me that unless I came up with a plan, I would find myself working in the store all summer. I never felt comfortable making small talk with the customers, and I saw nothing rewarding or intellectually stimulating about restocking the displays of Campbell Soup, and making sure there was enough Shredded Wheat on the shelves. The long hours—from seven in the morning to six at night—left little time for reading or baseball, and perhaps I saw a trap; that if I started working in the store on a regular basis, I would eventually follow in the footsteps of my father and grandfather.

With my mother's help I wrote about twenty letters to summer camps, mostly in Vermont, New Hampshire, and Maine, offering my services for the summer as a counselor. In truth, I had little to offer except some experience as a camper and a Junior Life Savings Certificate earned at Royal Ambassador, but that was not much. Most of the camps didn't even bother to respond to my letters, but Camp Abnaki on Lake Champlain, offered me board and room and thirty-five dollars for the summer. I accepted the offer immediately. In retrospect in was an important decision for it continued the process of breaking away from family and hometown.

Camp Abnaki, according to a current brochure, "is located on the southern tip of North Hero Island along the shores of Lake Champlain." The camp, founded in 1901 by the YMCA, was named after the Native American tribe, part of the Algonquin nation (now the tribe, but not the camp, is usually spelled "Abenaki"). It was one of many boys' camps founded at the turn of the century, designed to teach self-reliance, Christian virtues, and to train boys to become men by exposing them to a semi-military discipline and to the outdoor life. A few years ago, I drove into Camp Abnaki, which still welcomes boys each summer. In my memory the road went straight from Route 2 into the camp, but I discovered that there were several turns and a couple places where I had to make a decision about which way to proceed. I finally found the camp. It was late spring, and the campers had not yet arrived. As I wandered around the deserted grounds, I saw little that looked familiar except the shoreline, and the dining hall. Finally, a middle-aged man came out of one of the buildings and asked if I needed help. It turned out he was the director. I explained that I had been a counselor there in 1947. He took me into the library where, after going through the photo albums, we finally found a photograph from my year. There I was with the other counselors, the director, the camp nurse, and various staff people. Only one other counselor that summer was still in high school. All the others were college students and almost all of them were veterans of World War II. While I was seeking a new experience, they had lived. They helped me grow up.

Studying the 1947 photograph, I found many faces that looked familiar, but I could find a name for only one, the director, Clyde Hess. There he was in the front row, perhaps in his late forties, with glasses and close-cropped hair, and a self-satisfied look on his face. A career-YMCA-man, he ran a tight ship. In fact, my experience as a camp counselor at the age of sixteen, was the closest thing to the military that I experienced until I went into the Army seven years later. The public address system blared reveille in the morning, and campers and counselors alike had to fall out and line up at attention, while a group of senior campers raised the flag. At noon, there was chow call and we all marched to the dining hall. At night, the public-address system played taps, and all the cabins had to be dark. In my memory, each cabin had four-double-bunks to house one counselor and seven campers. During the first half of the summer, my campers were seven and eight years old, and I was called into Hess's office a couple of times to hear him complain that my cabin was messy and that my charges did badly at inspections. One of my campers was homesick, and cried for forty-eight hours until his parents came to rescue him. Hess blamed me for this failure, and implied that I had told the parents that the child's unhappiness was partly the fault of the camp. I learned that in a structured environment one did not blame the system, at least not publicly.

I discovered something about military order and the chain of command that summer; I also learned something about protest and disobedience. With about two weeks left in the season, the counselors all went on strike and threatened to quit unless Hess eased some of the rules that kept the staff on a short leash. Hess had to capitulate because he could not replace the whole group that late in the season. The result was, that for the last part of the season, we could stay out later, meet together after our cabins were quiet, and get a little more time off. Although I was a follower in the strike, I learned a lesson about the power of solidarity.

I had no particular skills at age sixteen, yet I coached baseball and track, refereed basketball, and took my turn every few days on the waterfront. We had a crisis one day on my watch. At the end of the swim period, all of the campers had left the water, and we discovered a tag that had not been turned over. We used the buddy system and each camper was supposed to turn over his tag when he left the water and make sure that his buddy did the same. For a desperate fifteen minutes we assumed that the camper had drowned, especially when his buddy could not remember when he had last seen him. After searching the bottom and preparing to get out the grappling hooks, we were relieved to learn that the missing camper had been found hidden away in the woods, reading a comic book.

I participated in all the camp traditions, including camp fires and games of capture-the-flag, and I tried to keep my little campers under control. I often think of those campers, especially a little boy (I think his name was Waldo) who wore glasses, had no athletic ability, and was picked on by the other youngsters. I liked him because he didn't give in, and had a stubborn sense of survival. I wonder what happened to Waldo. Even though there was a well-stocked library at the camp, I had little time to read that summer. It was the year Jackie Robinson broke the color barrier in baseball, but I had little time to follow baseball in any detail. The facilities were rather primitive and the food poor, justified by the philosophy of the camp, which was to expose boys to hardships, and make them into men. I was trying to pretend that I was a man myself. Following the lead of some of the older counselors, I experimented that summer with drinking beer and smoking cigarettes. That is all it was, an experiment, for I hated the taste of the beer, and I was not tempted by tobacco because I thought of myself as an athlete, since I was getting ready for football season in the fall. I did not become a beer drinker until I was in college, and it was not until the government gave me free cigarettes when I was in the Army that I became briefly addicted to tobacco, or to the ritual of smoking.

All counselors had an occasional day off from our duties at the camp. We usually went into Burlington, Vermont's largest city, but still a small town by national standards. Camp Abnaki had its own railroad stop so we took the Rutland Railroad into Burlington, but there were no return trains at night. Unless we met someone returning to the camp by car, we were forced to hitchhike along the dreary and nearly deserted Route 2, across the sandbar bridge to South Hero and Grand Isle, before we arrived sometimes early in the morning at North Hero and Camp Abnaki. Knowing we would get into trouble if detected, we tried to sneak onto the grounds and into our cabins, but we usually failed. On one trip to Burlington, I watched a Northern League game in which Robin Roberts, a college player who would later become a star with the Philadelphia Phillies, pitch a shutout. On another occasion, a group of us went to a dance pavilion at Mallet's Bay, where we listened and danced to Harry James and his orchestra. The big bands were beginning to fade in popularity in the post-war years, and were forced to play in the small towns across the nation. We had no dates for the dance, but a group of single women were willing to dance with lonely counselors. My Hardwick experience gave me confidence and I danced with several attractive women. For a brief moment, we felt transported back to the romance of the war years.

The great adventure from the summer of 1947 that remains fixed in my memory, is an expedition with two of the older counselors to the North End in Burlington, in search of a brothel, which they called a whorehouse, or at least what they thought was a whorehouse. When we finally found the right address, I lost any sense of adventure and decided to wait outside. When my friends emerged from the house a short time later, they were filled with tales of sexual adventure. I always suspected that they made up most of their exploits, but more assuring, I suppose, they never laughed at my hesitation or lack of courage.

My summer as a counselor when I was sixteen, was in some ways the worst summer of my life, mostly because of the semi-military discipline and the tough director. But in other ways, it was the most important, for it forced me to become independent, and it established a pattern of leaving home in the summer. Going to college seemed like an extension of my summer adventures. Yet no matter how many times I packed up and left, I still thought of Hardwick as my hometown, and the landscape of northern Vermont as ideal. As I grew older, life became a matter of constant leavings, but Vermont remained my home and anchor. I was able to break away because I knew where I came from. Yet there were many times that summer at Camp Abnaki, when I longed to be back with my friends in Hardwick and Greensboro.

The next year, the summer of 1948, I got a job as a bellhop at a summer hotel in Bethlehem, New Hampshire. I don't remember how I got the position, but it may have been a traveling salesman who alerted my father to the opening. In any case, neither my father nor my mother suggested that I should stay in Hardwick and work in the store. By 1948, they had accepted my need to get out of town. For the next five years, I worked in summer hotels, two years in Bethlehem, in the White Mountains, two years in the Adirondacks, and one year on the shore south of Boston, in a section known locally as the "Irish Riviera." I made good money, mostly in tips, which helped with college expenses. One year, I saved almost six hundred, the cost of one year's tuition at Dartmouth in the 1950s. Some of my Dartmouth friends spent their summer drifting around Europe. I needed to earn some money, and in the process, I continued to gain confidence, to expand my social skills, and to learn more about the ways of the world.

Bethlehem, New Hampshire is a resort town, sometimes called "The Gateway to the White Mountains." At 1,600 feet above sea level, it gained a reputation in the nineteenth century for having a healthy climate, and for being free of hay fever. At the peak of its popularity in the 1890s, it had more than thirty hotels, the largest being the Maplewood and the Sinclair. By the time I worked there in the summers of 1948 and 1949, the numbers of hotels had been reduced to about twenty, and the resort was in decline, although I did not realize it at the time. Bethlehem had prospered in the age of the railroad. Guests came by rail to Littleton, and then were transported up the hill five miles to Bethlehem. Subsequently, in the age of the auto, Bethlehem and other older resorts could not compete with the new hotels, and the resorts that provided much more than clean air and broad porches. The Reynolds Hotel, where I worked, could accommodate about a hundred guests in the main hotel and the annex next door. It was owned by William Aiken, a jovial sixty-year-old businessman. Aiken and his wife were devout Catholics, and they gave free vacations to young priests. The priests, who usually arrived in pairs, would quickly shed their clerical clothes, and spend their week in Bethlehem drinking and dancing at the Maplewood Casino.

Despite the priests who stayed at the Reynolds, Bethlehem by the late forties was primarily a Jewish summer resort. Many of the hotels were exclusively Jewish and Kosher, but the Reynolds had what was called a "mixed clientele." I was completely naïve. The only Jewish people I had known in Hardwick were the junk dealer and his wife, and a couple of women, married to Christians, who attended the Protestant Church. I quickly learned about Rosh Hashanah and Yom Kippur. I sampled potato pancakes, or *latkes*, lox with bagels, *gefilte* fish, chopped liver, and other delicacies. Most of the guests came from New York and they talked about New York politics, the new state of Israel, and the Holocaust. I heard Yiddish phrases for the first time. I learned the meaning of *mensch* and *chutzpah* that summer. Because the vacationing New Yorkers read *The New York Times*, I also started a lifetime habit of reading the *Times* every day.

In recent years, I have sometimes driven through Bethlehem on my way to Maine on Route 302. I park my car, and walk around to recapture the Bethlehem of the summers of 1948 and '49, but little remains. All of the big hotels—The Sinclair, the Alpine and the Maplewood—have burned or been torn down, but the Maplewood Casino still survives, although it is now the clubhouse for the golf course. The Reynolds has been replaced by a bank. The library, where I checked out books, is still there, and so is the post office building where I gathered with bellhops from the other hotels to collect the mail in the early evening; but it has been converted into a commercial block. Many of the elaborate summer houses remain; still, I always leave town a little disappointed that I haven't found more to trigger my memories of the two summers I worked there at the end of the 1940s.

The two summers I worked at the Reynolds, I was the only bellhop. In addition to helping the guests with their suitcases, and occasionally their trunks, I mowed the lawn, ran errands, made small repairs, and occasionally drove the hotel station wagon to Littleton to pick up guests who had arrived by train. The Reynolds, a three-story wooden building that faced Main Street, had no bar or nightclub—no entertainment, except a wide porch with chairs for rocking. A few rooms had private baths, but most of the guests had to use a bathroom down the hall. The bedrooms were spartan at best, and had probably been last remodeled in the 1920s. There were three meals a day, though many guests were on "the modified American plan" that included a room and two meals a day. There were two or three waitresses who worked in the dining room and two chambermaids. Sometimes I was pressed into action to help them out. Now and then, I was asked to deliver a breakfast tray to one of the rooms. On one occasion, I knocked on the door and was told to come in by a woman who was perhaps in her thirties. To my embarrassment, all she had on were a bra and panties. She asked me to place the tray on the stand next to the bed, and told me I could stay. Sometime later, I realized that she was conniving to seduce me, but at the time I was too naïve and scared, so I did not linger to find out. I backed my way out of the room as quickly as possible.

The second summer at the Reynolds, the woman who had worked in the office for many years became ill and couldn't continue. Mr. Aiken asked if I would run the office in addition to being the bellhop. I rather enjoyed taking reservations and managing the chart, so that all the rooms were filled and none were over booked. It was much like a jigsaw puzzle. Later in another hotel, I learned that the manager routinely over booked so he would always be assured of having a full house. Trying to make a living managing a hotel for three months in the summer was difficult. I handled a lot of money that summer. I cashed checks, made bank deposits, billed guests, and otherwise acted like I knew what I was doing.

One of my duties the second year, was to inform the head waitresses whether the guests were Jewish or gentiles, so they could be placed on the proper side of the dining room that had an invisible line down the center. The gentiles sat on one side and had somewhat better china and glassware. The Jewish guests sat on the other side. Everyone laughed at the invisible line, but no one challenged the custom. I could identify the obvious Jewish-sounding names, but I had difficulty with Miller, Benson, and others, and I had no experience identifying Jewish faces. Within two weeks, I placed Jewish guests on the wrong side of the dining room and, because of my naïveté, the whole segregated system collapsed.

Antisemitism was not only present in Bethlehem. It was so rampant in summer resorts that special Jewish summer hotels were established in the Catskills, and in other places.

In 1950 and 1951, I worked at Rocky Point Inn, a much larger hotel in the Adirondacks. I think it was in 1950 that Margo, a Skidmore College student who worked in the office, wrote and published a newsletter each week which included a list of newly arrived guests. One week some personal friends of the owner, with a Jewish sounding name, stayed at the hotel at the owner's invitation. But when Margo published their names in her newsletter the owner was furious. He did not want it known that Jewish guests were staying at his hotel even if they were his friends.

A 1948 brochure called "Where to Stay in Stowe," the Vermont ski resort, listed eighteen of twenty-six hotels, inns, and ski lodges as "restricted." Many of the farm homes and guest houses also refused to take Jewish people. There was antisemitism even in bucolic Greensboro. A development called "The Vermont Summer Estates, Inc.," laid out by three local businessmen in the late 1920s, had a clause in the deed that read, "No part of the herein conveyed property shall be leased or sold to any member of the Hebrew race." I knew nothing of such restrictions when I was growing up and spending summers in Greensboro. The development did not live up to the optimistic projections and the clause was more or less ignored.

Later, in the early 1970s, Supreme Court Justice William Rehnquist brought vacation property in the former "Estates" development. When he was nominated to become Chief Justice in 1986, Senator Patrick Leahy of Vermont revealed the restrictive clause in his deed. For a day or two the Greensboro Town Clerk's office was crowded with national television, radio, and newspaper reporters intent on covering the scandal. The offensive clause had been made mute by federal legislation, but ethnic prejudice left over from the 1920s embarrassed a Supreme Court justice. I first talked to large numbers of Jewish people and New Yorkers (and to me they were the same) at the Reynolds in Bethlehem. When I was not running errands, I sat in the office. I chatted to all of those who stopped by. I was fascinated with the conversation of many of the guests. They spoke about books and about politics. The summer of 1948 was the beginning of the Truman-Dewey Presidential campaign with Henry Wallace running on the Progressive Party ticket. Many of the guests were supporting Truman and a few argued for Wallace. My family, staunchly Republican, was supporting Thomas Dewey. In fact, I heard Truman praised for the first time that summer and I began to question my Republican heritage. Four years later in 1952, when I cast my first ballot, it was for Adlai Stevenson. Both the Republican and the Democratic conventions were televised from Philadelphia that summer, but there was no television reception in northern Vermont and New Hampshire in 1948. We listened to the conventions on the radio.

Of all the people who stopped to chat in the hotel office, I was most intrigued by Ginny from Brooklyn, who came with her grandmother and stayed for several weeks. She was a beautiful and sophisticated redhead, at least I thought she was beautiful and sophisticated. She was two or three years older than I, and had completed a couple of years of college. Because I worked at the hotel desk from 7:00 A.M. until about 9 P.M. there was not time to "date," but another complicating factor was that Ginny was going out with a couple of older men including a twenty-eight-year-old garage mechanic. This didn't please her grandmother. Except for one brief necking session in the laundry room, our relationship was platonic and intellectual. We talked about books. She introduced me to some of the literature she had been reading in college. When she mentioned a book, I rushed to the local library and checked it out. We talked about Hemingway, not only *A Farewell to Arms,* but *The Sun Also Rises*, and some of his early Nick Adams short stories. We read Fitzgerald, not just *Gatsby*, but also *Tender is the Night*. She talked about Kafka and Camus, T. S. Eliot, and James Joyce. I first heard the word "existentialism" from her lips.

We were intense and naïve, and I longed to have more than an intellectual relationship with her. But with her encouragement, I began to write during those summers at the Reynolds, not just short stories, but also novels or what I hoped would become novels. Ginny claimed to be writing a novel, but she never let me read it. One of my "novels" was strongly influenced by John P. Marquand. I had been reading *Point of No Return* and *B. F.'s Daughter.* Marquand wrote about the upper class, about Harvard and Princeton, apartments on Central Park South, large estates in suburban Boston, and summer homes in Maine. He also described talented athletes who accidentally ran into old girlfriends at elegant parties. In my attempt at fiction, I invented a world something like his (a world I knew nothing about), and my narrator managed to start a new affair with an elegant young woman closely modeled after my high school girlfriend. It was sentimental stuff. My other attempt at fiction was an historical novel set at the time of the Revolution. I had been reading the historical novels of Kenneth Roberts and Van Wyck Mason, but my characters were stiff and my attempt at love scenes, where the hero finds a way to go to bed with the beautiful maid, were laughable. When I cleaned out my father's house after he died, I came across my yellowing manuscripts written in long hand. I could barely stand to read the awkward dialogue and the sentimental scenes. I threw the whole stack of papers away, but I did save a short story about a bellhop at a summer hotel who falls in love with a beautiful and sophisticated redhead.

I started my freshman year in high school about three weeks after VJ Day. The euphoria of the end of the war gradually turned to the new, emerging reality of the cold war. During my high school years, the nation was faced with the irony and contradiction of trying to rebuild and reconstruct former enemies, Japan and Germany, in order to oppose a former friend, the Soviet Union. The transition was difficult for me especially because I had become a great admirer of the Russian people. Influenced, I am sure, by wartime propaganda and totally ignorant of Stalin's ruthless tactics, I read about the defense of Stalingrad, and eagerly followed the exploits of the Russian ski troopers. I also collected Russian and Soviet stamps and found it difficult to think of the Soviet Union as the new enemy.

Churchill delivered his "Iron Curtain" speech in Fulton, Missouri, in the spring of my freshman year. Truman decided to send aid to Turkey and Greece to prevent them from falling to the threat of communism in the spring of my sophomore year. Just as I was finishing my junior year, the Berlin airlift kept that city from falling completely under Soviet dominance. About the same time, Congress passed a new selective service act to replace the earlier act that had expired in March 1947. Eventually, that act would affect my life, but I barely noticed it at the time, because I was having too much fun in high school.

Entering high school in the fall of 1945, did not mean going to a different school building; we simply went upstairs in the old Academy building, which had been built in the 1890s. The wooden stairways were worn from the footsteps of many generations of students. The building smelled of a combination of the linseed oil used on the floors, the reek of Chemistry lab on the third floor, and the damp woolen coats and jackets that were hung outside the classrooms. There were only twenty-three students in my graduating class and just a few over a hundred students in the entire high school. A small school meant a rather unimaginative curriculum, many young and inexperienced teachers, and limited extra-curricular activities. Yet there were many advantages—I took part in almost everything that came along. I acted in plays, sang in the glee club (even though I couldn't sing), wrote for the newspaper and yearbook, participated in a mock United Nations (where I think I represented Belgium), was a delegate to Boys' State where I learned about state government (I ran for Attorney General—or was it Secretary of State—and lost). I also played varsity basketball, baseball, and football.

Some of the instruction was inadequate. If I had wanted to major in science or math in college, I would have been at a big disadvantage. In the years after the war, we had many young teachers just out of the Armed Forces, or a teacher's college, and they usually lasted only a year. One history teacher required us to copy large chunks out of the textbook to keep us busy. But Leone Cobb, my mother's friend, who had gone back to teaching during the war, and Chandler Mosher, the principal, taught English and forced us to write essays, short stories, and book reviews. When I got to college and had to write long essays and stories for freshman English; I felt as well prepared as those who had gone to Exeter and Andover. Aspiring to become a writer even in high school, I took a semester of typing my senior year. Surrounded by girls training to be secretaries, I learned to type fast, if not very accurately, and to use all my fingers.

The most influential teacher I had was Zeke Robinson, who taught history, English, and civics, and perhaps some other subjects, in junior high school. He was also a good athlete, who coached basketball. He was my first male teacher after a succession of women teachers in the lower grades. In class he would often ignore the lesson of the day and tell us stories, or quote from a book that he was reading, but he was too imaginative to make us memorize dates or copy from the textbook. One day he reached into his bookbag and pulled out a copy of Francis Parkman's *The Oregon Trail.* He spent the whole period telling us what a wonderful writer Parkman was and how the book described his adventures as a young man traveling west in 1846. I knew a little about Parkman because at the age of about twelve I had been given a complete set of Parkman (eighteen volumes I think) by my great aunt Jennie Randall. They had belonged to her son who had died young. It was the Frontenac Edition with uncut pages which I promptly cut so I could read the exciting stories in Mountcalm and Wolfe, *Count Frontenac and New France*, *The Conspiracy of Pontiac*, and the other volumes. Many of the tales of the struggle between France and England for North America complimented the stories I had been reading by Kenneth Roberts. Here was a teacher who knew about Parkman, and he encouraged me to read more of those volumes. Much later I learned that Parkman was a racist who hated the Native Americans and the French, an elitist who despised the lower classes and all Catholics, but he could write and he inspired me at the time.

I suspect that Robinson was lazy and the reason he told stories was that he had not prepared the lesson of the day. I admired him greatly and as an eighth grader he allowed me to practice with the high school basketball team. I now realize that he was an important role model for me. He was both a reader and an athlete and he somehow indicated to me that I could do both as well.

Zeke Robinson only stayed in Hardwick two years. At the end of the second year he was fired by the superintendent for being a homosexual, and for possibly molesting young boys. It was a big scandal in town. I had some inside information because my mother was on the school board. When certain people came to visit her, I would retire to my room above the kitchen and listen to conversations through the register in the floor. At the time, I had only vague concepts of what being homosexual meant. My mother even questioned me about my relationship with Zeke Robinson. It is true that he had a couple of special friends among the male students. Was he gay? Probably. Did he molest young boys? I have always doubted it, but I will probably never know. I defended him at the time. But George Jenkins, the superintendent, was convinced that he was a threat, and had to go. Yet, I have always been thankful to Zeke Robinson, whatever his flaws, for he let me know that it was all right to be both a reader and a ball player.

Basketball was an important part of my life in high school, more important than studying Latin, French, or History. Basketball, more than baseball or football, is an intimate game, requiring teamwork and instinct. More like jazz than a symphony, it is based on one impromptu move after another. Intellectual analysis doesn't count for much in a game of instinct and invention. Hitting the open man, making the right pass on a fast break, blocking out, setting a pick, having the courage to take the last shot, those are the things that won respect from your teammates. I can shut my eyes today and see Wendell Powers, John Hall, Rodney Storey, Bill Robb, and the moves they made on the court. I was a bookish boy who got all A's and being accepted on the court and in the locker room was an important rite of passage.

The game we played in the 1940s was a different game in many ways from the game that is played today. We played below the rim, and we used push shots and running one-handers rather than jump shots. A few players still used the two-handed set shot and more than a few shot their free throws underhand. During time-outs, the players were not allowed to talk to the coach. We gathered at one end of the court and sat on the floor while our opponents sat at the other end. Sometimes the coach would send a message through the water boy, who brought water and sliced oranges to the players; we didn't get the detailed and intense instructions at crucial moments that today's coaches think important. Often, we called a timeout, so that one of the players could finish a story started at a previous timeout. Sometimes, we called a timeout to watch the cheerleaders perform. Orleans had an especially attractive and sexy cheerleader. We called many timeouts when we played Orleans. At high school reunions, when the men gather in the kitchen, and the women in the living room, the former athletes replay some of those ball games. I am always startled by the details that some of my teammates recall. Perhaps, these were the best years of our lives.

I played in every game for Hardwick Academy during my sophomore, junior, and senior year. During that time, we had one very good team, one average team, and one bad team. High school basketball was an important social event in town. Hundreds of local fans flocked to watch the high school basketball team play, and many drove many miles to out-of-town games. They were upset when the team lost. Near the end of a close game during my sophomore year, I stole a pass and drove the length of the court for a layup and missed. The next Sunday before church the organist and choir director confronted me and said, "Why did you miss that shot?" I wanted to make that shot in the worst way, and I was humiliated by the choir director's question. Yet, as I recall the exchange many years later, it indicates how intensely involved the residents of Hardwick were with the fate of the high school basketball team. Because I played on that team I was very much a part of the community.

I also played football in high school, which seems strange because the high school never had more than fifty or sixty boys. A new coach, Ki Beardly, convinced the school board that Hardwick should have a football team. Teaching football to a group of young men, most of whom had never seen a game, was a challenge. The cheerleaders were even more ignorant and had to be told when to urge the team to "hold that line." But field a team we did, for in four years Hardwick played five games a year, often against much bigger schools. I played three of those four years, and because I could run fast, I managed to score seven touchdowns in each of the last two years I played. That is a record that will stand, because in 1950, the school decided to switch from football to soccer.

We used the T-formation with a limited playbook, and occasionally we switched to the old-fashioned single wing. After a brief stint at quarterback I settled on fullback. I rarely plunged into the line for a short gain (the usual role of the fullback), but I ran the ends. My favorite plays were 38 and 31 (back number three into the one or eight holes). The quarterback faked to the halfback, and I counted one thousand *one*, one thousand *two*, one thousand *three*, and then took a lateral pass from the quarterback. If the defensive end took one step toward the fake, I could get the around the end for six or eight or more yards. With a small squad, everyone also had to play defense. I was a cornerback (which we called defensive halfback). In one game in the fall of 1948 against St. Johnsbury Trade School, I scored four touchdowns including an 80-yard punt return. I was prepared to become a football star in college, but I quickly learned that in football, as in other areas, there were those with more speed and more skill. Still football and other sports were important to my development. I learned how to win and how to lose. I also overcame my shyness, learned how to get along with other young men on the field, and in the locker room.

The places my friends and I "hung out" after school or after games were the pool hall, the bowling alley, two drugstores, and a couple of restaurants. The pool room and the bowling alley were mostly male places, but girls were constantly on our minds. We tried to meet a girl accidentally for an ice-cream soda after school. Then there were real dates when we would actually call a girl and go with her to a movie at the Idle Hour Theater. And there were big dates when we took a girl to a dance, and really big dates when we arranged well in advance to take a girl to the junior prom. I dated one girl off and on through much of high school, but she was beautiful and popular, so I had rivals for her affection. When she consented, we went to many dances together. I couldn't sing but I could dance, or at least I felt confident dancing. There were dances after most basketball games, dances in the warm weather at pavilions at Joe's Pond, Cole's Pond, and in remodeled barns. Local orchestras provided the music, and we slow danced to songs like: "I'll be loving you, always," and we imitated the jitterbug to Glenn Miller's "String of Pearls." The big band sound of the war years still remained popular in northern Vermont for many years after World War II.

We also learned to square dance. At the Wolcott Town Hall on Friday nights, the fiddler and square dance caller was "Crazy Chase." His real name was Alfred Chase, but everyone called him Crazy Chase, in part because he dressed in women's clothes. Today he would be called a cross-dresser, an expression we never heard in the 1940s. He could fiddle expertly and with great enthusiasm, and he was an excellent caller. At some dances, the square dance calls were in French, and I often found myself swinging an eight-year-old girl, and, then, seventy-year-old grandmother, in the same set.

Finding a way to the dances out of town was a problem, unless someone could borrow a car. We usually found a way, and one didn't need a date to have fun because there were always single women who danced with each other or hung around the side waiting to be asked. One of my friends once remarked, "I am not very good on the dance floor, but I'm great at intermission." Intermission meant trying to get your date to "make out" in the back seat. Those sessions were made difficult in part by the incredible number of slips, blouses, sweaters, skirts, girdles, and garter belts that girls wore in the 1940s, and used as defenses in the sexual games we played. Only later at a summer hotel in the Adirondacks, did I discover that straps came unhooked and panties came off.

Fear of pregnancy was the main reason men and women of my generation did not "go all the way" in high school. In the days before the pill, when few had even heard of a diaphragm, and condoms were unreliable and difficult to obtain, our girlfriends used that fear to keep us under control. Yet, I knew girls in high school who did get pregnant. There were quickly arranged marriages, or, in one case, an extended visit to relatives in another town. The day of my high school graduation, when I was to give the valedictory address, and then the whole gang was to have an all-night party, my mother took me aside and gave me a lecture about being careful because a pregnant girlfriend would mean no college, no career. She implied that I would have to stay in Hardwick and work in my father's store. I listened, but secretly. I thought, "I wish that were an option." For my girlfriend was successfully fending off my persistent advances. There was a line from a popular song that went, "The only time she holds me is when we are dancing." That did not quite describe the extent of my relationship at the party after graduation, but almost. The party broke up about 2:00 A.M., in any case. My high school romances were filled with anxiety and were decidedly unconsummated.

In the late summer of 1948, I increased my political and religious education and enhanced my rather idealistic and romantic view of the world by going to a Christian Youth Conference in Grand Rapids, Michigan. I was active in the local young people's group at the United Church in Hardwick, and somehow got appointed during my junior year in high school to serve on the council of the state non-denominational Christian Youth Organization. It was at one of these meetings in Burlington, that I learned of the meeting in Grand Rapids to be held August 31 to September 5, 1948. Somehow a brochure for the conference has survived. It was called the Christian Youth Conference of North America, and the slogan was: "United! Committed! In Christ: For the Facing of These Days." The last phrase implied the threat of Communism in an Atomic Age.

I joined the Vermont delegation, a group of about thirty-five, who chartered a bus for the long trip west. Most of the delegates were college students, but there were a few high school students including Betty, a smart, attractive young woman from a neighboring town. I had seen a lot of her at various meeting, and looked forward to getting better acquainted. In addition to a possible romance, I was attracted by the travel and adventure. I had been stuck all summer in a hotel in Bethlehem, New Hampshire, so even a trip to Michigan seemed exciting. Our bus left from Burlington, picked up a few delegates in Rutland, and then made it to Glen Falls, New York, where we stayed overnight in tourist homes. The next day we traveled to London, Ontario, with a stop at Niagara Falls, my first look at this tourist attraction and American icon. I still have a few snapshots of the gang taken on the Canadian side of the falls.

Grand Rapids was the biggest city I had visited since my trip to Hartford and New York. We were all placed in private homes scattered around in different neighborhoods. I had to learn to negotiate the city bus system, and I remember once, late at night, getting off at the wrong intersection leaving me with a two mile hike. Yet I survived, and the conference was fun. There were 5,000 delegates from all over the country, with guests from Europe, Asia, and Africa. The youth conference, I now realize, was made up of mainstream Protestant denominations. There were no Southern Baptists, or Pentecostals, no one from the Jehovah's Witness Church, or The Seventh Day Adventist. The Conference was laced with an overwhelming faith in the goodness of human nature (despite World War II and the Holocaust). There was a strong dose of the social gospel and a missionary zeal to transform the world through good works. I can't recall much of the religious aspects of the conference, though I suppose there were prayers and hymns and a church service. I now realize, the conference was part of a postwar ecumenical movement to downplay denominations and to promote world peace. It was an election year so the Young Republicans and the Young Democrats were there alongside a small group who were supporting Henry Wallace and the Progressives party. There was an even smaller group of Socialists, but they had the advantage of having their candidate as one of the speakers. Norman Thomas, the perennial socialist candidate for president, gave an eloquent speech and a plea for world peace. The United World Federalists predicted a United States of the World by 1955. Civil Rights was also on the agenda. I heard speeches given by Cleo Blackburn, an African American settlement worker from Indianapolis, and by Thurgood Marshall, in 1948 the Director-Counsel of the NAACP, who would play a major role in the Brown-v. Board of Education ruling in 1954. It was all very exhilarating, though my expected romance with my friend Betty failed to materialize. She apparently met other people more interesting than those on the Vermont bus, and so did I. I stayed up late at night discussing religion and politics with young people from different parts of the country. One evening I went with a group to an amusement park outside of town. I remember a college girl from Ohio. She didn't treat me like a high school student, and there were kisses and hugs on the Ferris wheel. But what I remember most of all, was the idealism (or was it sentimental optimism?) of a group of young people meeting in 1948, who thought they could promote social justice, equality, and world peace.

A few weeks after I returned from Grand Rapids, I joined a number of other high school students from Hardwick to visit the Freedom Train, one of the government's attempts during the early days of the Cold War to increase patriotism and love of country. The Freedom Train started out from Philadelphia on September 17, 1947, taking one-hundred twenty-eight historic documents including the Declaration of Independence, the Constitution, and Lincoln's Gettysburg Address, around the country. In small towns and cities across the nation, American citizens stood in line to view these sacred documents, but the train did not get to Vermont until the fall of 1948. The Freedom Train was parked on a siding at Montpelier Junction, when we walked through the specially designed railroad cars to look at the documents. The experience didn't increase my love of country, nor my patriotism as I recall, but I did welcome the chance to get the afternoon off from school, and an opportunity to sit next to the girl I was dating that fall.

A few months later, in January 1949, when I turned eighteen, I went with a classmate to St. Johnsbury to register for the draft required of all males by the Selective Service Act of 1947. That also did not seem like a patriotic act, more like a rite of passage, but within two years that classmate and several of my other high school friends would be fighting in Korea.

While they were in the Army or the Marines, I was in college. In an odd way, it was football that led me to Dartmouth. Chandler Mosher, the high school principal, who had a son a year younger than I, invited me to join them on an annual pilgrimage to watch Dartmouth play either Columbia or Cornell in the November homecoming game. I was impressed by the crowd of 12,000 that jammed Memorial Field (small, I later learned, by collegiate football standards, but impressive to me.) I was excited by Hanover on a football Saturday, the huge library defining one side of the green, the old college buildings, and the festive nature of the crowds on Main Street before the game. I came to imagine that Dartmouth was the way a college should look. During one of those football weekends, I wandered into the stacks of Baker Library. I had never seen so many books, and I imagined having a chance to read them all. I also fancied myself a football player. I had a local reputation and managed to score fourteen touchdowns in my junior and senior years. Each time I watched a college game, I imagined myself scoring touchdowns for Dartmouth. During my senior year when it came time to apply to college, I only filled out the forms for Middlebury College and Dartmouth. I didn't apply to the University of Vermont, in part, because it didn't have a very good football team, and, in part, because my sister, my mother, and many others I knew, had gone there. Compared to Dartmouth, the Vermont campus didn't seem like a real college to me. In retrospect, I wonder why I didn't apply to Harvard or Yale, but in 1949, I couldn't stretch my imagination quite that far.

I was admitted to both Middlebury and Dartmouth, but in the same mail as my acceptance letter from Hanover came a letter from Tuss McLaughry, the Dartmouth football coach inviting me to come out for the team, and explaining how I could apply for financial aid. When Dartmouth offered me a larger scholarship than Middlebury, that clinched it. My football career at Dartmouth was brief, but my college experience led to graduate school, and a career in researching, writing, and teaching history at the university level.

In September 1949, after I had worked all summer at the Reynolds Hotel in Bethlehem, New Hampshire, my parents drove me the eighty-five miles from Hardwick to Hanover in my father's Jeep truck, the same truck he used to deliver groceries at the store. In the back of the truck was a mattress, a desk, a bureau, a lamp, and a couple of chairs. In 1949, Dartmouth dormitories were not furnished except for an iron bed without a mattress. When we arrived at New Hampshire Hall, I went inside the dormitory and met my two roommates—one from Long Island and the other from Kansas City. We knew we were privileged. We didn't know that we were part of the Lucky Generation.

My father helped me move the furniture and my other possessions into the room. I carried a Royal portable typewriter, that I had bought with some of my summer earnings. After all my things were arranged, my parents and I stood awkwardly by the truck. Then we shook hands, and I went back into the dorm. My parents drove away. I could say that the trip to college was the crucial event in breaking away, and that when I went alone into the dorm on that September day I never looked back. Yet I did look back and I went back, but only after I had broken the ties to my hometown. From Hardwick I went on journeys to many parts of the world, but it was Hardwick that made those journeys possible, and it is to Hardwick that I often return in my memory.

ROOSEVELT AND GARNER
TOWNSEND PLAN
LANDON KNOX

ACKNOWLEDGMENTS

THIS IS A BOOK about history and memory. Over many years various people have helped me define the place where the two meet. Alice Kessler-Harris, Ivan Dee, Elizabeth Dow, Charlene Mires, and Charlie Morrissey have read the entire manuscript. Some of the stories and descriptions related here were originally published in a very different format in *The Hazen Road Dispatch*, the journal of the Greensboro Historical Society.

Many people have shared their memories with me, beginning with my family. My father, Harold F. Davis (1894-1977), and my mother, Bernice Allen Davis (1896-1954), told me stories. My grandparents helped me understand their generation. My sister, Marjorie (1934-1965), who died much too young, helped to put our family in a wider context. My sister, Florence (1926-2021), checked my memories and often disagreed with my interpretation.

Many people helped me recall and make sense of the events of my childhood and youth. These include: Sarah and Paul Philbrook, Tootie and Wendell Powers, Ann and Tony Trujillo, Neil and Norman Smith, Leone and Roscoe Cobb,

Jack and Betty Smith, Pam Crandall, Lorraine Hussey, Joyce Slayton Mitchell, and Patty Thomas Shea. Helen Dimick invited me to talk on several occasions to the residents of the Greensboro Nursing Home. We talked about the old ways, and they helped me understand both history and memory.

A special thanks to Elizabeth Dow who had faith in this project when others did not.

ABOUT THE AUTHOR

ALLEN F. DAVIS was born and grew up in Hardwick, Vermont. His parents owned the general store his grandfather built. He graduated from Hardwick Academy in 1949, and from Dartmouth College in 1953. He earned an MA from the University of Rochester and a Ph.D. in American Intellectual History from the University of Wisconsin in 1959. He is the author or editor of a dozen books including *American Heroine: The Life and Legend of Jane Addams*, *Still Philadelphia: A Photographic History*, *Generations: Your Family in Modern America History*, and *Postcards From Vermont*. He taught American History at the University of Missouri and Temple University in Philadelphia. He was visiting professor at the University of Texas, and he held the John Adams Chair in American Civilization at the University of Amsterdam. He has lectured widely in the United States, Europe, and Asia. He is an elected member of the Society of American Historians, and the former president of the American Studies Association. He lives in Philadelphia, but he spends summers at the Davis family camp on Caspian Lake in Greensboro, Vermont, only seven miles from where he was born.